THE RELIGIOUS EXPERIENCE: CLASSICAL PHILOSOPHICAL AND SOCIAL THEORIES

Irving M. Zeitlin

PEARSON

Prentice
Hall

Upper Saddle River, NJ 07458

Library of Congress Cataloging-in-Publication Data

Zeitlin, Irving M.
  The religious experience : classical philosophical and social theories /
Irving M. Zeitlin.— 1st ed.
     p. cm.
Includes bibliographical references and index.
     ISBN 0-13-098239-3 (pbk.)
  1. Religion—Philosophy—History. I. Title.
  BL51 .Z45 2003
  200—dc22

                                                                           2003015096

AVP/Publisher: Nancy Roberts
Executive Editor: Chris DeJohn
Editorial Assistant: Veronica D'Amico
Prepress and Manufacturing Buyer: Mary Ann Gloriande
Marketing Manager: Marissa Feliberty
Marketing Assistant: Adam Laitman
Cover Art Director: Jayne Conte
Cover Design: Lisa Boylan
Full-Service Project Management: Carmen Corral-Reid, nSight, Inc.

This book was set in 10/12 New Century Schoolbook by Laserwords Ltd. and was
printed and bound by Courier Companies, Inc. The cover was printed by Coral
Graphics.

Pearson Education LTD.
Pearson Education Australia PTY, Limited
Pearson Education Singapore, Pte. Ltd
Pearson Education North Asia Ltd
Pearson Education, Canada, Ltd
Pearson Educación de Mexico, S.A. de C.V.
Pearson Education—Japan
Pearson Education Malaysia, Pte. Ltd
Pearson Education, Upper Saddle River, New Jersey

10 9 8 7 6 5 4 3 2 1

ISBN 0-13-098239-3

For my beloved grandchildren, Rebekka, Jacob, Kayla, Isaiah, Albert,
Caleb, Ethan, and Daniel

CONTENTS

thinkers conceded that there were sacred areas into which they must not venture, spheres in which revelation, faith, and ecclesiastical authority offered the answers and gave the orders. Scientific curiosity as applied to those spheres was an unwelcome intrusion into holy ground. It was this inviolable domain of the *sacred* that distinguished the Middle Ages at their most scientific and skeptical moments from the later ages of criticism. The medieval mind was dominated by the church, literally, intellectually, and emotionally. In contrast to the medieval era, the thinkers of the Enlightenment regarded all aspects of human life and works as subject to critical examination.

In their attitude toward religion as toward other institutions, there was diversity among these thinkers. One must not think of the Enlightenment as a monolith. Some of these thinkers were, ostensibly, agnostic. Montesquieu, for example, argued that if there is a God, he must necessarily be just. For Montesquieu, a "law," whether in nature or in society, referred to "the necessary relations deriving from the nature of things." It followed, for Montesquieu, that "justice is a true relation between two things: the relation is always the same, no matter who examines it, whether it be God, or an angel, or lastly man himself."[1] Aiming thus to secularize ethics and morality, Montesquieu continues: "Thus if there were no God, we would still be obliged to venerate justice, that is, we should do everything possible to resemble that being of whom we have such an exalted notion and who, if he exists, would necessarily be just. Free though we might be from the yoke of religion, we should never be free from the bonds of equity" (106).

Others among the Enlightenment thinkers were thoroughgoing materialists and atheists. Baron d'Holbach, for instance, contended that the unavoidable verdict of common sense upon religious views is that they have no foundation; "that all religion is an edifice in the air; that theology is only the ignorance of natural causes reduced to system; that it is a long tissue of chimeras and contradictions" (141). For Holbach, there is only one criterion by which to assess a system of morals, and that is whether it conforms to human nature and needs. If it conforms, it is good; if it fails to conform, it should be rejected as contrary to the well-being of our species. Hence, for Holbach, there is no reason to suppose that an atheist cannot have a moral conscience.

La Mettrie was another materialist and atheist who published a book entitled *Man a Machine.* "The human body," he proposed, "is a machine which winds itself up" (205). Employing this mechanistic metaphor, La Mettrie held that all talk about a soul separate from the body is nonsense. Without food the soul pines away and dies together with the body.

But there were also prominent Enlightenment thinkers who retained a religious outlook. In a letter to Ezra Stiles, a fellow member of the American Philosophical Society and president of Yale College, Benjamin Franklin stated his own personal creed: "I believe in one God, Creator of the universe. That he governs it by his Providence. That he ought to be worshipped. That the most acceptable service we render to him is doing good to his other children. That the soul of man is immortal, and will be treated with justice in another life respecting its conduct in this" (166).

Thomas Paine also retained a personal religious creed, the essentials of which he stated in *The Age of Reason*:

> I believe in one God, and no more; and I hope for happiness beyond this life.
>
> I believe in the equality of man, and I believe that religious duties consist in doing justice, loving mercy, and endeavoring to make our fellow-creatures happy . . . .
>
> I do not believe in the creed professed by the Jewish church, by the Roman church, by the Greek church, by the Turkish church, by the Protestant church, nor by any church that I know of. My own mind is my own church. (175)

If we compare the forms the Enlightenment assumed in Britain, America, Germany, and France, there can be no doubt that it was in France that the conflict of the Enlightenment with the Establishment became the most intense and dramatic. Typically, it was the French philosophe who was most uncompromising in his opposition to the old regime—the monarchy, the nobility, and the church. The philosophes tore down the old regime intellectually, thus paving the way for its actual destruction by the revolution of 1789.

In France more than elsewhere the struggle between the philosophes and the old regime became especially harsh. The issues were not only social and political but also religious. Indeed, often the religious issues were the most salient. In mid-eighteenth-century France two bitterly opposed camps confronted one another. On the one side stood the authoritarian and intolerant Catholic Church, and on the other stood the predominantly irreligious philosophes.

It is in this context that the writings of Rousseau on religion stand out as distinctive and extraordinarily significant. Most of Rousseau's friends among the philosophes were anti-Christian deists or even atheists. The atheists, as we have seen, proposed that one can reject the belief in God and yet possess a conscience and conduct oneself in accordance with the basic ethical and moral principles. The materialists and atheists denied the existence of an ethical Deity and Teacher but nevertheless accepted the moral principles that originated in the belief in such a Deity. Rousseau, however, discerned certain disturbing implications in the more extreme materialist views: Do not such views carry with them the danger of leading to a moral vacuum or to moral relativism? If we may state what disturbed Rousseau in the words of a later thinker, it would be: "If God is dead, is everything permitted?" This is, of course, the question Dostoyevsky addressed in criticism of the proto-Nietzschean characters he had created in his great philosophical novels. So it was in opposition to the extreme materialist views of his time that Rousseau sought to clarify and formulate his own religious outlook.

Rousseau's writings on religion deserve special attention for another reason. Although he shared certain Enlightenment principles, he also anticipated several key ideas of the so-called Romantic-Conservative Reaction. This was an early nineteenth-century intellectual movement that emerged as a critical response to the Enlightenment and the French Revolution. The Romantic thinkers turned away from what they considered the naive optimism and rationalism of the eighteenth century. They did so not only by recognizing the irrational factors in human conduct but also by assigning them positive value. Tradition, imagination, feeling, and religion were now regarded as natural and positive. Deploring the disorganizing consequences of the French Revolution, the Romantic and Conservative thinkers attributed those consequences to the folly of the revolutionaries who had uncritically accepted Enlightenment assumptions and had attempted to reorder society according to rational principles alone.

In reaction to the eighteenth-century exaltation of reason, the nineteenth century therefore extolled emotion and imagination, leading in that way to a great revival of religion, poetry, and art. Moreover, in opposition to the Enlightenment's elevation of the individual, the Romantics elevated the *group*, the *community*, and the *nation* as the most highly valued concepts. Historic memories and loyalties were viewed as binding the individual to a *nation*, a category now raised to a position of supreme importance. Gone was the cosmopolitanism of the Enlightenment. Increasingly, the nineteenth century turned to the investigation of the *origins* of existing institutions rather than to their transformation according to rational principles. A *historical* outlook emerged in which more than ever before institutions were regarded as the product of slow, organic development, and not of deliberate, rational, calculated construction.

Although the Romantic movement was evident throughout Europe, its form varied from one country to another. In England and especially in Germany, the movement reflected a strong national reaction to the radicalism of the Enlightenment as it manifested itself in the Revolution and Napoleonic expansionism. In general, the Enlightenment conception of a rational, *mechanistic* universe was now rejected. In every area of culture— literature, art, music, philosophy, and religion—an effort was made to free the emotions and the imagination from the austere rules and conventions imposed during the eighteenth century. In religion, the importance of inner experience was restored; in philosophy, the mind was assigned a creative role in shaping the world.

This movement, beginning with the writings of Rousseau and Hume and developing further with the philosophy of Immanuel Kant, expressed a shift in emphasis from the mechanistic universe of Newton to the creative character of the personality. The aim of this movement was to liberate the mind from the purely rationalist mode of thinking. Rousseau was a pioneer in that regard. He was less inclined than most of his colleagues among the philosophes to counsel the reconstruction of society in accordance with abstract, rational principles alone. Inner moral will, conscience, and conviction were for him also important for human liberation.

The foregoing historical background will prove to be useful in our later discussion of Hegel and his critics. Indeed, because Hegel, the Left-Hegelians, Marx, Nietzsche, and Max Weber were German intellectuals, we shall need to provide more background, showing how the Enlightenment and the Romantic Reaction expressed themselves in the German context. First, however, we need a full exposition of Rousseau's religious philosophy, which is important not only in its own right but also because it profoundly influenced Hegel and other thinkers considered in later chapters.

NOTES

[1]Isaac Kramnick, ed., *The Portable Enlightenment Reader* (New York: Penguin Books, 1995), p. 106. Hereafter, all references to this work will be cited in parentheses immediately following the quoted passage.

CHAPTER 1

ROUSSEAU

Rousseau is justly famous not only for his political theory but also for his ideas on education, found primarily in *Émile* (1762), probably the most important text the Enlightenment had produced on the education of children. Rousseau called this text "*mon traité d'education,*" and it is a treatise on education where its content is concerned. As many commentators have observed, however, the most striking feature of the work is its form, half essay and half novel. It is an imaginative work in which Rousseau plays the role of tutor, bringing up Émile from infancy to manhood, and counseling parents at each stage how to care for and educate their children.

At the age of sixteen, under the guidance of his tutor and with the expansion of his sympathetic imagination, Émile begins to see himself in his fellow creatures and to be touched by their signs of pain. Émile is now beginning to put himself in the place of those who can claim his pity. It dawns on him that the fate of miserable and wretched individuals may one day be his own. He recognizes that he stands on the edge of an abyss into which he may be plunged at any moment by innumerable, unexpected, and unavoidable misfortunes. Émile is learning to put no lasting trust in his good health and fortune because it may be entirely temporary. He is also gaining a sensitive conscience and trying to relate to others as he would have them relate to him. He does so thanks to his own reflections on the human condition and despite the fact that his tutor has until now spoken not a word to him of religion as such. But now that Émile is learning to think for himself, the time has come, his tutor believes, to help him understand what it really means to be a truly religious human being. Hence, in book 4 of *Émile* we encounter a section called "The Creed of a Savoyard Priest" (Profession de foi du vicaire Savoyard). Although this section is supposed to be an essential element of Émile's education, it is clear from the text alone that the "profession of faith" is more than just that. As P. D. Jimack has observed, it is more, too, than the advice

Rousseau had received some thirty years earlier, as he claims in his introductory remarks to this section of the book. Rousseau himself acknowledged in a letter to a friend and in his *Reveries du promeneur solitaire* that the "profession of faith" was his own, and that it was his aim to set down the basic religious-moral principles with which he would guide his conduct for the rest of his life. In these terms, although the creed is an integral part of *Émile*, it can be read as an independent essay conveying the essentials of Rousseau's religious outlook.

THE CREED OF A SAVOYARD PRIEST

In the unfolding of his creed Rousseau is guided by common sense and a devotion to truth. He was brought up in a church that permitted no doubt but failed to convince him of its doctrine's validity. When he turned to the philosophers, he found them to be proud, assertive, and no less dogmatic than the church. So now Rousseau begins to think for himself and compose his creed on the basis of his experience. The first truth he is forced to accept is that he exists and that he possesses senses through which he receives impressions. His sensations take place in himself, but their cause is outside of him.

Next, Rousseau decides that everything outside himself that acts upon his senses, he will call "matter." In that way he becomes as convinced of the existence of the universe as of his own existence. The "mind," for Rousseau, is not a passive entity, a mere receptacle as it was for John Locke and other Empiricists. The mind, for Rousseau, is an active, creative power. With his powers of reflection Rousseau reasons that everything he perceives through his senses is matter, sometimes in motion and sometimes at rest. When it comes to animals and humans, Rousseau posits spontaneous or voluntary motion. If you ask him how he knows there are spontaneous movements, he will reply, I know it because I feel them. I want to move my arm, and I succeed without any other immediate cause of the movement but my own will.

Rousseau is thus leading up to a polemic against the extreme, mechanistic form of materialism. He is thoroughly convinced that the natural state of matter is a state of rest, and that it has no power of action in itself. Rousseau's mind refuses to accept the notion of inorganic matter moving of its own accord. The world's movements are due to some external cause, a cause he cannot perceive, but which nevertheless exists, an inner voice assures him. Rousseau invokes Newton, who had discovered the law of gravitation. Rousseau observes, however, that gravity alone would soon reduce the universe to a motionless condition. Newton was therefore compelled to add a projectile force to account for the elliptical course of celestial bodies. It followed for Rousseau that the first causes of motion are not to be found in matter itself. The more he reflected on the action and reaction of natural forces playing on one another, the more he saw that one must always go back from one effect to another until one arrives at a first cause in some *will*.

Rousseau then proceeds by distinguishing "motion" from "action." Inanimate bodies, from this standpoint, are capable of motion, not action, for there is no real action without *will*. This was Rousseau's first principle, which meant for him that it is a will that sets the universe in motion and gives life to nature. Rousseau acknowledges, however, that his first principle is an article of a creed, and therefore something of a dogma.

Rousseau's method, by which he arrives at a supreme will, is to reason about his own experience. He asks how a will can produce a physical action and answers that it does so in himself. Whenever he wills to move a limb of his, it moves. Incomprehensible to him, however, is the notion that an inanimate body, when at rest, can move itself. Will, then, is the cause of motion, and Rousseau cannot conceive of matter alone producing motion.

Rousseau recognizes that the doctrine he has laid down is obscure, but at least there is nothing in it that is foreign to reason and experience. Can we say as much of the materialist doctrine? he asks. And his answer is in the negative. If philosophers believe differently, it is owing to the chief source of human error, abstract ideas. Rousseau is contemptuous of the jargon of metaphysics, which, he says, has never led to the discovery of a single truth but has filled philosophy with absurdities. For example, when metaphysical philosophers speak of a "blind force" diffused throughout nature, are they presenting a real idea to our mind? They claim they are saying something significant when they speak of a "universal force" or "essential motion," but actually they are saying nothing at all. Those who say that matter *sets itself* in motion are uttering words without meaning.

Rousseau also refuses to entertain the notion of the universe being in a state of chaos. He cannot picture the absence of order in the universe. So Rousseau is ready to take a further step in his argument: If matter in motion points to a will, matter in motion in accordance with fixed laws points to an *intelligence*. This is the second article of his creed—a supreme, conscious, creative, active Being exists. And if one challengingly asks Rousseau where that Being exists, he replies as others have for thousands of years: The Supreme Being manifests himself in the phenomena of nature.

To appreciate fully what Rousseau is trying to accomplish, we have to recognize that he is striving to make his case not by means of reason alone. He is urging his readers to go beyond cold reasoning and to listen to the *inner voice of feeling*. Indeed, that is precisely where he differs from his fellow *philosophes* and where he adumbrates a key feature of the Romantic movement. For Rousseau, if one listens to the "inner voice" and is free of blinding prejudices, one cannot fail to see that the visible order of the universe proclaims a Supreme Intelligence. The opposite view, which attempts to deduce the manifold, complex phenomena of nature from the blind mechanism of matter set in motion by chance, requires all sorts of absurd assumptions.

Rousseau is of course writing in a pre-Darwinian era and against the background of the physical discoveries of Galileo, Kepler, and Newton, all of which pointed to universal order based on fixed laws. Newton himself posited a Being who had set the universal clock in motion. It is not surprising, therefore, that Rousseau's creed rests on the belief that the world is governed by a wise and powerful will. He says explicitly, "I see it or rather I *feel* it, and it is a great thing to know this."[1]

To the question, however, of whether the universe has always existed or was created, Rousseau knows not the answer and is even unconcerned with the question. For regardless of whether the universe is eternal or created, it is a certainty for Rousseau that the totality is one integral whole, proclaiming a single Intelligence. It is this Supreme Intelligence, willing and acting through his own power, whom Rousseau calls God. To the intelligence of this Being Rousseau adds power, will, and kindness. Although this Being hides himself from our senses, Rousseau nevertheless believes not only that he exists but that human existence depends on his existence. Rousseau thus sees God everywhere in his works. But again, Rousseau arrives at this understanding not by means of reason alone. He says, "I feel him within myself" (417).

Now that Rousseau has considered the conditions that enable him to feel and conceive the existence of God, he next wishes to discover his own place in the order of things. At once he sees his membership in a species and recognizes that by his own will and the instruments he controls, he can carry out his will. Recognizing the distinctive capacities of his species, Rousseau sees that human beings have become the lords of the earth. But he is not puffed up by the fact. On the contrary, as he strives to discover his own place within the species, he notes different ranks and the men who fill them. What a sight now meets his eyes! Whereas nature showed him harmony and order, the human race displays nothing but confusion and disorder. Humans are in a state of chaos. And Rousseau asks rhetorically, "O Wisdom, where are thy laws? O Providence, is this thy rule over the world? Merciful God, where is thy Power? I behold the earth, and there is evil upon it" (419).

As Rousseau now centers attention on the human condition, he begins to offer us valuable insight into the contradictions of human existence. On the one hand, human nature prompts us to concern ourselves with the grasping of eternal truths and the pursuit of justice and true morality; on the other hand, human nature also allows us to enslave ourselves to our senses and passions. As Rousseau reflected on these conflicting tendencies, he recognized that he, too, as an individual, feels himself to be at once a slave and a free man. He perceives what is right and loves it, and yet he does what is wrong. He tries to listen to the voice of reason but is carried away by his passions and suffers most in the knowledge that he might have resisted them, but failed.

Rousseau thus achieves a level of self-understanding. He always has the power to will, but not the strength to do what he wills. When he yields to temptation, he surrenders himself, in effect, to the influence of external objects. So Rousseau is aware of will through the consciousness of his own will, which sometimes succeeds and at other times fails. His own will is also self-evident in his ability to make judgments—to judge and choose between good and evil, between truth and falsehood. Freedom, therefore, is a reality for Rousseau: the principle or motive power of all human action is in the will of a free being. "It is not the word freedom that is meaningless, but the word necessity" (422). Human beings are free to act and are animated by an immaterial substance. That is the third article of Rousseau's creed.

Rousseau now explores the implications of freedom for humanity's relationship to the Divine. If humans are at once active and free, that means they act of their own accord. Hence, what humans do freely is no part of the system determined by Providence, and it cannot be imputed to Providence. What Rousseau intends to underscore here is that God is not a puppeteer and we are not marionettes. Providence does not will the evil that humans perpetrate when they ignore or disobey the ethical teachings of God and abuse the freedom granted them. Nor does Providence intervene in human affairs to prevent evil. For what would be the point of granting humans freedom if Providence were to intervene everywhere and every time evil is done? Providence has made humans free so that they might choose the good and refuse the evil. The misuse of human freedom cannot undermine the general cosmic order, but the evil humans do reacts upon themselves. To complain that God does not prevent evil is to complain that he has given us freedom together with the understanding of what is right and what is wrong. Rousseau therefore declares: "Man! Seek no farther for the author of evil; the author is you yourself. There is no evil other than the evil you do or the evil you suffer and both come from you" (424).

Rousseau's creed thus rests upon the foundational premise of a God who is supremely powerful, supremely good, and supremely just. This conception of an all-powerful ethical deity raises the question for Rousseau, whether God owes something to his creatures.

Rousseau believes that God owes humans all that he promised when he gave them their being. Implicit in Rousseau's view is the biblical conception of a covenantal relationship between God and humanity.

God gave us the idea of the good and made us feel the need for it. That is tantamount to promising humanity the good if people obey his ethical commandments.

In his education of the young Émile, Rousseau will not teach the materialist doctrine, that after death there is nothing. For Rousseau, the existence of a soul, which the materialists dismiss as nonsense, is a reality that he *feels* and is aware of. That which his feelings and fancy picture is enough to console him in this life and to provide hope for a life to come.

As for the fate of the wicked in the life to come, Rousseau says he takes little interest in it, but he finds it hard to believe that Providence would have condemned them to everlasting torment. If the supreme justice calls for vengeance, it will take place in this life. It is the nations of this world and their errors that are the ministers of punishment. It is in the insatiable hearts of the wicked, consumed by envy, avarice, and ambition, it is in their own false prosperity that the avenging passions punish. "What need is there to seek a hell in the future life? It is here in the breast of the wicked" (428).

The more Rousseau strives to comprehend the so-called infinite essence of God, the more he recognizes the limitations of reason itself. What he knows, however, with certainty about God is that he demands a certain conduct from humans. He demands justice and mercy. Rousseau finds these truths not in higher philosophy but in the depth of his heart. What he feels to be right or wrong he finds in his conscience, the voice of the soul, the repository of God's ethical teachings. Reason often deceives us; we have a good right to doubt it. But conscience never deceives us.

Rousseau avers that despite the extraordinary variety of manners and customs among the many nations of the world, one will find everywhere the same ideas of right and justice. He insists that there exists at the bottom of the human heart an innate principle of justice and virtue by which we judge our own actions and those of others to be good or evil. It is that principle which Rousseau calls conscience and which he regards as universal. He challenges the philosophers to point to a single country on earth where to be honest, helpful, and generous is scorned, and where the traitor is held in honor.

To defend his point of view Rousseau urges us to distinguish between our acquired ideas and our natural feelings. Feelings precede knowledge. Seeking what is good for us and avoiding what is bad for us is a desire we get from nature; it is not something we learn. The love of good and the hatred of evil are as natural to us as self-love. Here, again, we see how Rousseau departs from his fellow philosophes. The decrees of our conscience are not rational judgments; they are feelings. We had feelings before we had ideas, feelings of self-love, fear, pain, the desire for well-being, the dread of death. Moreover, humans are by nature sociable, or at least fitted to become sociable, and this again is due to innate feelings.

But when Rousseau uses the word *innate* with reference to conscience, he fully recognizes the social source of it. He writes: "Now the motive power of conscience is derived from the moral system formed through the two-fold relation to himself and to his fellow human beings. To know good is not [necessarily] to love it; this knowledge is not innate in man; but as soon as his reason leads him to perceive it, his conscience impels him to love it; it is this feeling which is innate" (436).

It is natural for all human beings to love themselves and to seek their own well-being. It is therefore a crucial question for Rousseau whether and in what circumstances our concern for others can prevail over our love for ourselves and our own well-being. There is nothing wrong with loving oneself, but there is something wrong with loving oneself at the expense of others. Hence, for Rousseau, good individuals order their lives with regard for others, while the wicked order their lives for themselves alone. But on what ground can one say that Rousseau's understanding of the "good" is based on a valid moral principle? Certainly not on the ground of reason alone. What is essential, Rousseau insists, is a transcendental principle that enables us to say this is good and that is evil. For Rousseau, the transcendental principle is God. "For if there is no God," he writes, "the wicked is right and the good man is nothing but a fool" (438).

If, for Rousseau, the chief moral virtues are not arrived at by means of reason, how are they arrived at? They are ultimately derived from the divine teachings or commandments, but they are naturally innate, engraved in our hearts, so to speak. In his *Discourse on Inequality*, where he presents his conception of the "state of nature," Rousseau proposes two principles that govern human conduct in the natural state. The first provides us with an ardent interest in our own preservation and well-being, while the second evokes in us a natural aversion to witnessing the destruction or suffering of another sentient creature, especially if it is one of our own kind. Our desire for self-preservation and our ardor for our own well-being are moderated by an innate repugnance against seeing a fellow creature suffer. Our moral duties are therefore derived from both divine law and natural law. For Rousseau, then, humans *feel* compassion for their fellow human beings, and they also *feel* themselves to be the instrument of the Omnipotent who wills eternal justice and who will bring about our good through the cooperation of our wills with his.

We see, then, that in Rousseau's Deistic view our first natural impulses are good; we pity our fellow creatures when they suffer, and our moral duties to others are of the essence of Rousseau's "natural religion." Finally, we see that Rousseau denies that the Creator interferes either in the laws of the universe or in human affairs. If our first natural impulses are good, and our vices are of our own making, we have no right to blame the Creator for the ills we ourselves have created and for the fact that we are divided against ourselves in so many ways.

All this implies, for Rousseau, that the wicked who assert they were driven by "circumstances" to crime are liars as well as evildoers, for they refuse to perceive that their crimes and injustices are of their own making, the result of their own will. Rousseau thus advances an ethic of individual responsibility: Providence has granted humanity the knowledge of right and wrong and the power to do right. Providence has given us a *conscience*, that we may love the right; *reason*, that we may perceive it; and *freedom*, that we may choose it. Hence, when we do wrong, we have no excuse. We do it of our own free will (441).

Rousseau's creed is, therefore, a form of *natural religion*, which is not to be confounded with atheism or irreligion, which are its exact opposite. Natural religion, says Rousseau, is the knowledge God has given to his mind, and the feelings he has put into his heart. And Rousseau believes that true religious-moral conduct requires nothing more than that knowledge and those feelings. Indeed, Rousseau further believes that the "more"—in the form of special doctrines—that has been added to natural religion, far from ennobling the conception of the Supreme Being, tends to confuse, mystify, and even degrade the conception of the Almighty. Rousseau therefore urges us not to confuse the doctrines and rituals of religion with religion itself: "It is a vain sort of conceit which fancies that God concerns himself with the shape of the priest's vestments, the order of the words he pronounces, the gestures he makes before the altar and all of his genuflections" (444).

Humanity's disunity is no less evident in matters of religion than in other social spheres. Rousseau decries the fact that there exists a multitude of diverse sects holding sway on earth, each accusing the other of falsehood and error, each believing that only its own doctrines are correct. In contrast, natural religion contains all of the true "theology" that one can obtain for oneself by the use of one's own faculties. To pretend to know more, as in the innumerable official theologies, is pretentious and fraudulent. Rousseau thus rejects any form of human authority that contradicts the simple but essential elements of natural religion: "He who in preaching religion hides it beneath mysteries and contradictions, teaches me at the same time to distrust that religion. The God whom I adore is not the God of darkness, he has not given me understanding in order to forbid me to use it; to tell me to submit my reason is to insult the author of reason" (450).

In the concluding pages of his creed Rousseau also calls into question the reliability of the so-called sacred texts and books and offers in their place the one book that is open to everyone—the book of nature. He avers that a righteous heart is the true temple of the Godhead, and he reminds us again that no true religion can absolve us of our moral responsibility. At the same time, however, Rousseau does, in the end, draw from the sacred texts of Judaism and Christianity a paramount principle: "To love God above all things and to love our neighbor as oneself is the whole law" (468). This, of course, comes from the New Testament, Mark 28–33, where in response to a scribe's question, "Which is the first commandment of all?" Jesus replies that to love God with all of one's heart, soul, mind, and might is the first commandment; the second is to love one's neighbor as oneself. And the learned Rousseau knew that the Hebrew Bible is the source of these utterances attributed to Jesus. That one should love God with all of one's heart, soul, and might is found in Deuteronomy 6:4, and that one should love one's neighbor as oneself is found in Leviticus 19:18. And this is the spirit of Rousseau's final words to Émile: "My child, self-interest misleads us; the hope of the just is the only sure guide" (471).

ROUSSEAU ON CIVIL RELIGION

Rousseau makes another highly significant contribution to our understanding of religion in his *Social Contract*. Centering attention on Christian commonwealths, in his chapter "Civil Religion," Rousseau addresses two fundamental questions: Is religion useful to the body politic? Does Christianity provide the best ideological support of a commonwealth? Responding to the first question in the affirmative, Rousseau points to the fact that no state has ever been founded without religion as its base; and responding to the second question in the negative, he asserts that Christian doctrine is at bottom more injurious than serviceable for the strong constitution of the state. To defend his response to the second question, Rousseau begins by dividing religion into two categories, religion of the individual and religion of the citizen. The first, devoid of temples, altars, and ritual, is expressed in the inward devotion to God and the eternal moral obligations. This is the pure and simple religion of the gospel that enjoins obedience to the divine, natural law. The religion of the citizen, in contrast, is the official, organized religion established in a single country. This category consists of tutelary deities, dogmas, and rituals that are laid down by law in a given state. To a nation practicing such religion, its own ways are sacred, whereas all outside ways are infidel and barbarous.

It is to the religion of the citizen that Rousseau gives the name "civil religion." Civil religion is good, says Rousseau, in that it unites divine worship with a love of the civil laws and homeland, teaching citizens that service to the state is at the same time service to the tutelary deity. But this kind of religion is also bad, based as it is on error and lies. It makes people superstitious, replacing the true worship of the divine with empty ceremonials. It is bad, too, insofar as it becomes tyrannical, making the people intolerant and bloodthirsty.

In sharp contrast, there is the Christianity of the gospel in which individuals look upon themselves and all others as children of the same God and, therefore, as brothers and sisters. From a political standpoint, however, the Christianity of the gospel is defective in that it contributes nothing to the strengthening of the civil laws, the chief social bonds of a good society. Far from attaching the citizens to the state, the gospel detaches them from it and, indeed, from all worldly matters, since the Christian homeland is not of this world. In order for a true Christian society to prevail in peace, every citizen without exception would have to be an equally good Christian, since all it would take is one ambitious hypocrite to establish a tyranny over his pious compatriots. A Christian republic is a contradiction in terms, for in preaching submission and servitude, Christianity is too favorable to tyranny for tyranny not to take advantage of it. True Christians, Rousseau observes, are servile because this short life has so little value in their eyes.

Given, then, the shortcomings of the two categories of religion he has reviewed, Rousseau proposes a form of civil religion wholly positive in its effects. In Rousseau's social contract citizens have no obligation to account to the sovereign for their beliefs, except when those beliefs, when put into practice, are injurious to the community. Since the civil sovereign has no competence in the "other world" with which religion is concerned, the sovereign has no business even taking notice of individuals' religious opinions, so long as they are good citizens. For Rousseau, there is a purely civil profession of faith, and it is the sovereign's responsibility to determine the articles of that faith not as religious dogmas but as moral principles of civic duty without which it is impossible to be either a good citizen or a loyal subject. The positive dogmas of this civil religion are simple and few in number: "The existence of an omnipotent, intelligent, benevolent divinity who foresees and provides; the life to come; the happiness of the just; the punishment of the sinners; the sanctity of the social contract and the laws.... As for the negative dogmas, I would limit them to a single one; it is intolerance. Intolerance belongs to the cults we have rejected."[2]

Theological intolerance, Rousseau avers, inevitably threatens the sovereignty of the sovereign even in the temporal sphere. For in conditions of religious intolerance the priests become the real masters. Under the laws of good civil religion there can, therefore, be no exclusive national religion. In a good polity, all religions that themselves tolerate others must be tolerated, so long as their dogmas prompt no actions contrary to the laws of the state and the duties of the citizen.

Rousseau thus provides the guidelines for the kind of civil religion that is characteristic of open, democratic, and decent societies. Good civil religion provides the citizenry with the moral ideals and principles with which to assess the justice or injustice of the government's conduct.

Rousseau's original ideas on civil religion profoundly influenced later thinkers, notably Hegel, whose early theological writings, as we shall see, were primarily concerned with the question of how to create a civil religion based on reason and on fundamental moral principles.

NOTES

[1]Jean-Jacques Rousseau, *Émile, ou De l'education*, (Émile, or On Education), text established by Charles Wirz, presented and annotated by Pierre Burgelin (Paris: Gallimard, 1969), p. 416. Translations are mine. Hereafter, all references to this work will be cited in parentheses immediately following the quoted passage.

[2]Jean-Jacques Rousseau, *Ouevres complètes*, III, (Complete Works, Vol. 3) Library of the Pléade, under the direction of Bernard Gagnebin et Marcel (Paris: Pléade, 1964), pp. 468–69.

CHAPTER 2

HEGEL

The Enlightenment, as we have seen, posited the eventual triumph of reason over unreason. In eighteenth-century Germany, however, although the leading philosophical idealists were somewhat influenced by the secular orientation of the French Enlightenment, the main trend was to return to the earlier spiritualist tradition. The source of that tradition was ancient Gnosticism, a mystical doctrine according to which matter is evil, and emancipation comes from the contemplation and knowledge of the Divine Spirit in the universe. Such knowledge was an illumination of the mind whereby one ascends the hierarchical ladder of being to the contemplation of the pure, Divine Spirit. Prophets, philosophers, and sages were the chief transmitters of this tradition.

In eighteenth-century Germany, *Geist* (spirit) was the key concept of this Gnostic tradition, the aim of which was the "revelation" of the inner, creative forces of originality and spontaneity. The inner, creative spirit was to express itself in the production of higher forms of literature, religion, and art. At the same time, German philosophers were advancing a conception of society as an *organism* built up from below by associations based on a community of interest. Influenced by Edmund Burke, German philosophers venerated ancient institutions, arguing that the organic quality of such institutions revealed a higher fitness to human needs and would serve as the strongest cement to bind the people together in communities against the atomization of mechanistic rationalism.

A renewed attention was now paid to the organic and the "natural" as the source of creative spontaneity, but rooted in the national, cultural soil. These ideas were dramatically expressed in a new movement known as *Sturm und Drang* (storm and stress). As the term suggests, this was an exciting movement of short duration, reaching its apex in the 1770s and 1780s and then burning out. It was chiefly a literary movement of young authors, its best-known representatives being Herder, Schiller, and Goethe. The movement was a highly emotional revolt against what was perceived as the cold rationalism of the dominant French culture. The primary inspiration came from Rousseau, who was the chief critic of what was coming to be called "civilization," signifying high achievements in the sciences and the arts. For Rousseau, "civilization" was unnatural, since science, art, and especially social conventions created artificial constraints that prevented human beings from acting naturally and spontaneously and from expressing their true selves. Everything in civilization spoke to the intellect, nothing to the feelings and the convictions based on them.

Rousseau, as we have seen in *Émile*, sought a way of freeing the "natural man." In *The Social Contract* he posited an original state of nature in which human beings lived a life of spontaneous, free impulse. With civilization, however, there was no return to that springtime of simple, naive, and impulsive human existence. Nevertheless, humans could rise to a higher level where they used reason to recognize the limits of reason. In *The Social Contract* Rousseau proposed that human beings might, under the right circumstances, achieve a higher form of freedom by democratically imposing upon themselves laws of their own choosing. As the historian William Bossenbrook has observed,

> Nowhere was the influence of this frame of thought greater than in Germany. In France Rousseau became the prophet of popular sovereignty, but in the Germanies he became the symbol of inner freedom from the artificial molds of civilization, and he pointed the way to organic growth and development leading to the consciousness of dynamic inward form.[1]

Under the influence of Rousseau, key German figures wrote in opposition to certain elements of French rationalism: Herder opposed the notion of civilization as a progressive advance from savagery to enlightenment; Kant opposed the rationalist assumption that science provided the universal key to knowledge and morality; and Goethe opposed the view of the cosmos as a merely mathematical-mechanistic order.

ROMANTICISM AND NATIONALISM

Some of the characteristics of the German Idealist movement were accentuated in reaction to the French Revolution and to Napoleonic imperialism. But those events also turned the movement in new directions. At first, German intellectuals greeted the events of 1789 as opening a new era in human development. The Declaration of the Rights of Man was hailed as a new stage in humanity's ascent to liberty, equality, and fraternity. The young Hegel, studying theology at Tübingen at the time, was among those caught up in the general enthusiasm. But as the Revolution entered its more violent phase beginning with the massacres of 1792 and culminating in the reign of the guillotine terror of 1793–94, enthusiasm waned and attitudes changed.

Like Edmund Burke and under his influence, certain German thinkers constituted themselves as a liberal opposition to the radicalism of the Revolution and the imperialism of Napoleon. Burke's *Reflections on the Revolution in France* was published in 1790 and translated into German by 1793. The impact of Burke's work, perhaps greater in Germany than in Britain, initiated a second phase in the Idealist and Romantic movement. The first phase, as we have seen, was an effort to free the artistic personality and creative spirit. In its second phase, however, Romanticism turned to the concept of "nation" or "national community" as a means of restoring the organic continuity with the historic past after the Revolution and Napoleon had appeared to be severing the German people from their ancient roots. A return to the medieval sources of German culture therefore became a major tenet of the Romantic movement's conservative phase.

It was in the course of the second phase that *Geist* and *Staat* (spirit and state) became embodied in the concept of *Volk* (people or nation). And it was Hegel who contributed much toward bringing *Volk* and *Staat* together in a new synthesis of historical development that was to have a decisive influence on German thinking during the remaining sixty-six years of the nineteenth century. For Hegel, Reason or Spirit was immanent in history. He therefore sought to convey how the universal Reason unfolded and manifested itself in history. "Reason" or "Spirit" was a synonym for the immanent, divine Providence, guiding history in its progressive development from lower to higher stages of rational self-consciousness and freedom, and achieving its highest stage in the Prussian state. Hegel regarded the Western peoples as the most advanced in embodying reason and freedom, and he proposed that the state is the framework in which a people strives to realize its destiny. As the Greeks, Romans, and Germans, for example, appeared on the world stage, each group made its contribution to the progressive advancement of universal reason by means of its distinctive political and cultural achievements.

The process by which Reason manifests itself in history is through the struggle of opposites, which operates in historical development as it does in a dialogue or in individual reasoning. Hegel's dialectical philosophy proposes that any position taken with regard to any issue has only a partial and not an absolute character, and therefore evokes a negative response. The unification of opposites takes place in a dialectical fashion, as each thesis engenders its own antithesis, thus forming a new synthesis, which becomes a new thesis engendering, in turn, an antithesis, and so on. This dialectical process is continuous in history, progressively unfolding the potentialities inherent in each national culture.

Hegel tried to encapsulate the dialectical character of his philosophy in his celebrated aphorism that "what is real is rational and what is rational is real." But this aphorism contains a fundamental ambiguity, which Hegel's conservative and radical followers interpreted to suit their respective ideological purposes. Emphasizing the real—the historically existing state—pleased the conservatives interested in justifying the status quo. The radicals, in contrast, stressed the other half of the aphorism, that the "rational is the real"—that the rational is a revolutionary process, that history is moving toward higher and higher forms of human association. In Germany, the Prussian conservatives stressed the first part of Hegel's formula, while the most radical thinker who appropriated and reinterpreted the second part was Karl Marx.

We can see, then, that Hegel's Idealism is a translation of his religious-moral outlook into philosophical terms. He transformed reason into a supreme cosmic force, which he variously calls the Idea, the Spirit, Reason, the Absolute, or, finally, God. As we shall see, however, the Romantic movement also left its mark on his philosophy.

Hegel was born in 1770, when the age of Reason and Enlightenment was closing and the Romantic movement was emerging. In his youth he had studied theology at Tübingen. Already in his youth and under the profound influence of both the Enlightenment and the Romantic movement, he proposed that religion should be not a matter of dogma but rather a living power in the real life of a nation. Religion should be popular, the concern of the nation as a whole; religion should speak to the concerns of human beings in *this* world. A key element of Enlightenment thought repudiated the asceticism of certain Christian doctrines. In opposition to such doctrines, the philosophes had brought to the fore the vital importance of joy and happiness. Hegel, following the philosophes in that regard, also stressed that in contrast to the gloominess of the cross, religion should exalt not suffering and martyrdom but joy in earthly life. In this respect he was inspired, like many of his generation, by the Greek culture of classical antiquity, its political freedom, philosophical wisdom, sense of beauty and artistic perfection, and, not least, sensual enjoyment of life.

One of Hegel's momentous insights is his conception of the cosmos as an integral totality. Life on earth is a unity. All attempts to separate spheres or zones of the living unity are artificial and mechanical. Together with the pioneers of the Romantic movement, Hegel conceived of the cosmos and especially life as an organic unity. Much of his philosophy, as we have seen, may be understood as a struggle to reconcile opposites through their transcendence. The Romantics had rejected sharp boundary lines between, for example, poetry and philosophy, imagination and reality, the divine and the human, the ideal and the real, and so on. In the early phases of his philosophical career Hegel enthusiastically embraced these tenets of the Romantic movement. Eventually, however, he diverged from the Romantics in one notable respect, insisting that ultimate unification can be brought about only by a rational rather than a Romantic method. The original unity of all things, Hegel increasingly came to believe, is not merely a truth resulting from a mystical or poetic intuition but also a truth discoverable by means of *logic*. The role of logic he developed in his dialectical method. But he also parted from the Romantics in arguing that religion, not poetry, yields insight into the deepest things. A spiritual, not an aesthetic, "intuition" must underlie reflection on ultimate reality and truth.

HEGEL'S EARLY ESSAYS ON RELIGION

In the years between 1793 and 1795, the young Hegel wrote three essays on religion. The first is called the Tübingen Essay; the second, Berne Fragments; and the third, The Life of Jesus. Let us have a brief look at each in turn.[2]

In the Tübingen Essay Hegel makes the following points. Religion is essential to and pervasive in human experience, but the predominant form of organized religion is inadequate in its response to the deeper human needs. While Christianity in its purest form teaches a few basic, universal moral principles that most people can grasp and agree to, much of official, Christian theological doctrine, ritual, and ceremony is irrational and even degrading. Hence, the typical Protestant Christian experience is a vacillation between sensuous self-indulgence and then self-hatred owing to an abstract and unattainable ideal of perfection or piety. So Hegel at the age of twenty-three is already proposing that *reason* must prove its value by realizing itself in the world of humanity. To restore religion's higher aims, it must be humanized.

Hegel was, however, skeptical that any enhancement in the rational understanding of theological issues would accomplish the aim of making religion more relevant to human needs. For even if the basic moral truths could be properly formulated, only a few individuals could put them into practice successfully, while the vast majority in times of distress would resort to superstitions and fetishistic rituals. What is really needed, then, is not enlightenment and science but a practical wisdom that would speak to the multitude in such a manner as to enhance their sense of autonomy, dignity, and self-worth.

With that aim in mind, Hegel believed he could respond effectively to a major objection that had been raised against Kant's theory of moral perfection. Critics of Kant had argued that unless we can identify empirically some sort of moral impulse in human nature, we have no right to assume the existence of such an impulse. Hegel, however, influenced in this regard by Rousseau, proposed that quasi-moral sentiments do in fact exist in human nature—compassion, amicability, goodwill. Hegel went even farther, insisting that humans possess a capacity for love. But he also recognized that the right conditions are required for that capacity to be realized. Humans are such many-sided creatures that almost anything can be made of them. A religious power is therefore necessary to bring out and sustain the higher ideals of moral and political virtue.

Hegel thus aimed toward a more humanized religion that would have its source in reason—not in the Enlightenment's extreme form but rather the reason of the Romantic movement. What Hegel sought here is the kind of reason espoused by Rousseau—the kind of reason to which the heart and the conscience can relate and give assent. The Romantic movement had emphasized the distinctiveness of each nation's history and culture. The Romantic influence is therefore again evident in Hegel's proposition that the doctrines of a rational, moral religion must be adapted to the moral level of consciousness of the people for whom the doctrines are designed. The new form of religion must meet the needs and interests of everyday life while at the same time reinforcing the higher moral impulses and motives. In that way it might be possible to create a nonalienating civil religion based on the political virtues. What is unmistakable here is the profound influence of Rousseau.

In the fragments of the Berne period (1793–94), the young Hegel is critical of both Judaism and Christianity, of the former for its purportedly nationalistic narrowness, and of the latter for its sectarian and authoritarian character. In these fragments Hegel repeats some of his earlier observations: that the modern-day, enlightened, and sophisticated Christian is skeptical of and embarrassed by his own faith. He is torn between his rational intellect, on the one hand, and his need for faith and meaning, which reason alone cannot provide. So the Rousseauian influence is again quite evident in Hegel's main objective—to revitalize the people's morale and morality by creating a good civil religion in Rousseau's sense. In creating such a civil religion, Hegel expresses the optimism of his era. Contrary to some of the critics of the moral condition of Europe at the time, Hegel sees sound moral elements on which to build. He accuses such critics of confusing the decline of ancient ethical simplicity with the decline of morality as such. What seems to have eluded the critics, Hegel observes, is that for all the corruption and decadence of the modern age, modern society tends to survive its recurrent crises, whereas the older societies, which we tend to idealize, had succumbed to their crises.

Hegel reiterates his conviction that the universally valid core of the religious experience, which must become an essential element of a good civil religion, consists of the heart and the conscience. Good civil religion will impel citizens to live in accordance with the moral virtues and will prompt them, when they err, to repent and atone.

But Hegel acknowledges his perplexity as he faces the question of how a civil religion embodying the chief moral virtues might be instituted. Morality cannot, after all, be instituted in the way that law can. After reflection, he rejects conventional Christianity as a candidate for his ideal of a viable civil religion. He rejects it because, in his view, it radically alienates its adherents from the life process itself. For, on the one hand, the Christian's faith in an afterlife of eternal salvation is supposed to make him indifferent to the trials and sufferings of this world; but, on the other hand, because he is uncertain of the form the afterlife might take, he lives in fear of lengthy purgation or even eternal damnation.

In the eighth and ninth fragments Hegel avers that a genuine religious experience consists of a strong disposition to moral virtue, animated by the belief in a transcendent telos. The "idea of God" is to be understood as expressing humanity's moral purpose as a species—a purpose transcending all ephemeral preoccupations. And as Hegel continues in these fragments to assess conventional Christianity as a candidate for a good civil religion, he again rejects it for its "arcane, incomprehensible dogmas," which he regards as an affront to universal reason. Peter Fuss and John Dobbins, the editors and translators of these fragments, remark that Hegel's diatribe against Christianity might well have been penned by a Voltaire. And yet, Hegel preferred Jesus to Socrates as humanity's ideal, spiritual prototype because of his human-transcending character. Hegel quickly adds, however, that it is only a minuscule portion of humanity that is capable of truly imitating Jesus.

Hegel's most salient criticism of Christian doctrine is the contradiction between reason's teaching that a life of virtue and justice is its own reward, and Christianity's freedom-denying doctrine that original sin precludes our being really good. The other objectionable element of the doctrine is that happiness, if it is to be found at all, is to be found only in an afterlife, where it is dispensed by the grace of the Deity in what appears to be an arbitrary fashion. Even the doctrine of the historical actuality of Christ, made into an article of faith and a condition of salvation, offends reason and common sense because, in the editors' words, of its "esoteric, authoritarian and exclusionary character."

In the light of these shortcomings of conventional Christianity, Hegel asks how it might come to pass that in a new Christianity virtue would be loved for its own sake. Although Hegel in these fragments never succeeded even to his own satisfaction in outlining a good civil religion for his time, he did hold out some prospect for realizing it in the future. For the elements of such a religion were quite similar to Rousseau's: that it be based on the chief moral principles and virtues, and that their practical application promote a social and political atmosphere in which citizens are conscious of their liberty, dignity, and mutual responsibility.

The young Hegel considered it a "world-historical outrage" that Christianity had failed to develop a socially and politically more effective and dignified form of religion. However, in spite of its failure in that regard, Hegel believed that Christianity had in fact contributed to the idea of a moral person, which made Hegel hopeful that in the right circumstances individuals would become less inclined to create dehumanizing institutions and less susceptible to the mental desperation implicit in all forms of otherworldliness.

We see that if for Hegel Christianity in its prevalent form showed no real promise of soon becoming a rationally and morally centered civil religion, deeply rooted in the populace as a whole, it did at least offer the prospect of coming closer to a religion of reason and virtue. It is evident throughout these essays that although the young Hegel stated that he prefers Jesus to Socrates as the prototype to be imitated, Socrates, as the chief symbol of Greek rationality, figures prominently in Hegel's intellectual consciousness. Indeed, Hegel attributes to Jesus Socratic qualities. In his essay The Life of Jesus, he portrays him as an apostle of reason and virtue, and of little else. Accordingly, Hegel makes light of Jesus' role as prophet and miracle worker and depicts Jesus as steadfastly refusing to claim any divine authority or status for himself. Moreover, Hegel has Jesus censure his coreligionists for their sensuality and other failings, which Hegel believes are no less characteristic of the modern Christian's outlook. "Thus," as the editors of these essays remark, "Hegel's Jesus not only feels alienated from his own people, but would feel equally if not more so in Christian Europe" (14).

It appears, then, that Hegel's admiration of ancient Greek culture was such that he made Jesus a Socrates of sorts. And given the profound Hellenistic influence on early Christianity, one can understand Hegel's inclination in that regard. For in John's Gospel (1:14), he says, "And the Word [*logos*] was made flesh, and dwelt among us." Thus, for Hegel, Reason (*logos*) as Divinity enters the world to impart to humanity its rational capacity; and Jesus' exhortations are intended to awaken the rational faculty and to move humanity toward moral and spiritual perfection. The editors of these fragments therefore argue convincingly that for Hegel it is the moral substance of the Gospel story that is of paramount significance; and that of lasting value even in his time was Jesus' rational personhood, an attribute he shared, in Hegel's view, with other non-Christian paragons.

HEGEL'S LATER PHILOSOPHY OF RELIGION

In the years between 1821 and 1831, the last decade of Hegel's life, he gave a series of lectures on the philosophy of religion. These lectures, like the early fragments, remained unpublished in his lifetime but were eventually reconstructed and published on the basis of his own manuscripts and several student notebooks.

As might be expected, "spirit" is the most salient concept in the mature Hegel's lectures. Spirit, for Hegel, is the word that best describes the innermost principle animating both individuals and communities. Spirit accounts for the active and creative side of human beings and inspires us to strive to realize our potential. It is spirit, therefore, that gives purpose and meaning to our lives. The danger to which Hegel calls attention in these lectures is that the advance of science, and the materialistic inferences modern man draws from the advance, will increasingly weaken and undermine the creative impulses of European citizens and cultures.

What we need to remember, however, is that "spirit" for Hegel is no merely secular concept. On the contrary, it is a synonym for the Divine. Hence his concern that the more the physical sciences expand, the more the sphere of the knowledge of God narrows. This is a dangerous tendency for several reasons, not the least being Hegel's conviction that science is not and cannot be a substitute for religion. Science cannot give human life meaning; it cannot tell us how to live or what we *ought* to do.

Hegel conceives of religion as consciousness of our connectedness with God. Hegel's intention here is to employ his distinctive dialectical method to grasp God as Spirit. The dialectical method, as we have seen, views history developmentally, owing to the immanence of Spirit or Reason in history. Because it is the essence of Spirit to concretize itself in history, Hegel believes that in the study of religion one must give careful attention to the diverse manifestations of the religious spirit in the *subjective consciousness* of successive generations. Hegel's point here is an anticipation of the view of Wilhelm Dilthey and the other proponents of the *Geisteswissenschaften*, the spiritual or cultural sciences. Hegel therefore also anticipates a key element of Max Weber's *Verstehenssoziologie*—that an authentic understanding of human beings requires an adequate grasp of the subjective meanings and motives of their actions.

Hegel, as a philosophical Idealist, has no patience for the materialistic doctrine that religion is an invention of the imagination. For Hegel, any religion worthy of the name is a product of the Divine Spirit, and since the Divine is both Spirit and Reason, religion consists of both faith and reason, two essential elements that cannot really be separated. Hence, for Hegel as for Socrates, philosophy, in its higher, purer forms, can be a way of worshiping, celebrating or serving God (19).

Hegel was, of course, an erudite student of the world religions, East and West. In his *Philosophy of History*, he discusses the cultures and religions of China, India, Persia, the Assyrians, Babylonians, and Medes, as well as Syria, Semitic western Asia, Judea, Egypt, and, finally, the Greek, Roman, and Germanic worlds. As he examines the world religions in his lectures, he avers that they have been too sense-bound; they represented themselves in a primitively sensual fashion and therefore have inadequately fulfilled the needs of the human spirit. The major religions had failed to ripen and mature so as to include what Hegel regards as essential, namely, rational thought.

Thinking, for Hegel, is both analytical and synthetic. Thinking explores the inner qualities of a given phenomenon that distinguish it from everything else, while discerning its interconnections with everything else. That is one aspect of what Hegel meant by thinking dialectically. But his complex conception of thinking requires more than that. It requires the attitude of trying to grasp a phenomenon in not only its current but also its potential form. This is done by discerning the internal, latent tendencies of a phenomenon that often conflict and promise to change the existing form. Dialectical thinking can be fruitfully applied to all aspects of the cosmos, but especially to all aspects of the human condition. There are no exceptions to that rule. "The most foolish delusion of our time," Hegel insisted, "is the opinion that thinking is disadvantageous to religion, that religion's survival is the more secure the more it abandons thinking" (20).

From the standpoint of Hegel's insistence on rational criteria for the evaluation of religion, Christianity was the highest form of religious consciousness, but that was true for him only potentially, not actually. For he believed that Christianity's actual beliefs and practices were at odds with its inner moral meaning. So, for example, Hegel could not embrace Christendom's doctrine of the Incarnation as signifying that God became man in order to die for our sins, thereby presumably absolving us of responsibility for them. For Hegel, such a doctrine was unacceptable because human beings, endowed as they are with the ability to distinguish right from wrong and endowed, too, with enough freedom to choose between them, always remain responsible for their actions. In this respect Hegel is again in full agreement with the basic articles of Rousseau's creed. Since for Hegel as for Rousseau, the character of a people's religion is reflected in its morality and its political constitution, the highest form of civil religion must embody a morality of freedom and an ethic of responsibility.

Hegel appears to have challenged Kant's view that we can know reality only as it appears to us but not as it actually is in itself. Shortly before his death in 1831, Hegel wrote that "when people assert that man cannot know the truth, they are uttering the worst form of blasphemy.... The modern despair of truth being knowable is alien to all speculative philosophy as it is to all genuine religiosity" (24). It is clear that Hegel the man and philosopher believed in divine power and eternal truth, certainly in the moral realm.

Hegel's religious philosophy therefore requires the understanding that for him "divine universal reason," entailing the principles of morality, is no mere abstraction. On the contrary, it refers to the transcendent ethical injunctions that ought to guide responsible action. Failure to act in accordance with the transcendent moral principles leads individuals and societies to self-alienating and self-destructive consequences.

NOTES

[1]William J. Bossenbrook, *The German Mind* (Detroit: Wayne State University Press, 1961), p. 224. Hereafter, all page references to this work will be cited in parentheses immediately following the quoted passage.

[2]G. W. F. Hegel, *Three Essays, 1793–1795*, edited and translated with an introduction and notes by Peter Fuss and John Dobbins, (Notre Dame, Ind.: University of Notre Dame Press, 1984). I have studied these fragments, but as I prepared an exposition of their contents, I found I was largely repeating what the editors have said better in their superb introduction. My discussion of these fragments is therefore a summary of the editors' commentary. All page references to this work are cited in parentheses immediately following the quoted passage. See also G. W. F. Hegel, *Early Theological Writings*, translated by T. M. Knox, with an introduction and fragments translated by Richard Kroner (Chicago: University of Chicago Press, 1948).

CHAPTER 3

THE YOUNG OR LEFT HEGELIANS

T he twenty years between 1830 and 1850 in Europe and especially in France began and ended with revolution. In Germany the chief impulse to political and social agitation came from France. Stimulated by the revolutionary events in France, associations and clubs of young students emerged in Germany during the 1830s and 1840s in opposition to the monarchy, nobility, and church. Among these clubs was a group of young intellectuals who earlier had been profoundly influenced by Hegel's philosophy but who now found Hegel too conservative. The group came to be called Left Hegelians because they retained certain ideas of Hegel's dialectical philosophy but rejected his philosophical Idealism and the political conservatism of his mature writings.

As we look back on those writings, it would be hard to deny that Hegel's outlook took a conservative turn. In 1806, Hegel left Jena after Napoleon's victory over the Prussians. Most Hegel scholars would agree that thereafter Hegel's attitude toward life was shaped by the events that followed the defeat of Prussia, and that his thinking increasingly reflected the transition from the revolutionary to the reactionary era in the political history of Europe.

With regard to Hegel's view of the state and, in particular, the Prussian state as the manifestation of the highest form of Reason, Richard Kroner has observed: "Hegel was admittedly a defender of the sovereignty of the state. His belief in civil liberty was limited by his belief in the superior prerogative of the nation at large. He therefore defines the state as the perfect totality of the nation." From Hegel's conception of history shaped by Providence, Kroner continues, "a certain quietism resulted, satisfaction with actual conditions. It cannot be denied that in this acquiescent attitude a danger is involved. What we call "historicism"—a belief in the absolute determination of the historical process against which the will of man is powerless—is certainly a symptom of weariness and pessimism. Though Hegel was not a historicist in that sense, he opened the door to this unbalanced philosophy."[1] Moreover, like many other close students of Hegel, Kroner observes that "a presentiment of weariness and decay does seem to have haunted Hegel at the height of his maturity, as it haunted Goethe and other contemporaries." Kroner then cites a famous passage from Hegel's preface to his *Philosophy of Right*: "When philosophy paints gray in gray, a form of life has become old, and this gray in gray cannot rejuvenate it, only understand it. The owl of Minerva begins its flight [or spreads its wings] only with the falling of dusk." And Kroner comments: "This is a melancholy consideration, after a life devoted to the discovery of truth and the advocacy of freedom and right. We may lament this resignation. But the author of these words may well have had a foreboding of what was in store for Germany and the whole Continent."[2]

The Left Hegelians, then, were reacting against the conservative side of Hegel's thought and also against his philosophical Idealism, as we have said. The most prominent members of the group were Ludwig Feuerbach, Bruno Bauer, Max Stirner, David Friedrich Strauss, Karl Marx, and Søren Kierkegaard. Their attack upon the religious premises of the existing order had far-reaching effects in the development of a radical secularism and existentialism. All of these men with the exception of Kierkegaard were thoroughgoing materialists who paid a personal price for their radicalism. Feuerbach, Bauer, and Stirner were dismissed from their teaching positions, and Marx and Kierkegaard were reduced to the direst of circumstances. Marx was driven into exile, living often in jeopardy of the police. Probably the most lonely figure among them was Kierkegaard, a Dane, who first had been an admirer of Hegel's and who then turned against him, seeking God in the isolation of human solitude.

The significant writings of this group were concentrated in the 1840s. Their general point of departure was the second half of Hegel's formula, namely, that the "rational is the real." What that meant for them from a dialectical standpoint was that all institutions, religions, and philosophies, as the expression of the onward march of reason, have no special sanctity in themselves; they are transitory, marking only the transition to reason's next creations. Like all social forms, Christianity, capitalism, and the state will be transcended by superior forms. For every positive historical form, its negation can be projected. The assault on existing values and institutions was directed first against religion as the source of the sanctity of existing political and social forms. In Germany from the time of the Reformation, religion had provided legitimation formulae for the state, and now Hegel—quite disappointingly in the eyes of the Left Hegelians—had sought to cement the union of religion with the state by making universal reason culminate in Protestant Christianity and the Prussian state. In response to this conclusion of Hegel's, the Left Hegelians employed Hegel's own dialectical logic to repudiate the identity of reason and actuality, and in so doing contributed substantially to the undermining of faith in traditional Christianity. They went even farther, contributing greatly to the exposure of religious and philosophical illusions in general.

There is a sense in which Hegel himself had provided these opponents with the ammunition with which to combat him. As we have seen, he made reason the paramount means by which to come to know the divine spirit and its manifestations in history. It seems that with this fundamental premise Hegel had inadvertently opened the door to the Left Hegelians, champions of anti-Christian materialism. For although Hegel believed that revelation is the ultimate source of our knowledge of right and wrong, he tends in the end, in such works as his *Phenomenology of Mind*, to subordinate revelation to reason. Hence, as Richard Kroner has convincingly remarked, "Divine inspiration seems no longer necessary when reason can provide what, in the biblical view, can be taught only by the prophet" (54). Kroner suggests that at the end of the *Phenomenology* the supplanting of revelation by reason seems to imply a shift of the center of gravity from God to man. Kroner acknowledges, however, that "this danger only looms behind the façade of Hegel's system. Hegel himself did not succumb to it. He would have solemnly protested against such a conclusion. But the fact that soon after his death some of his disciples drew this conclusion may serve as a warning" (54). In any event, Hegel's disciples did in fact shift the center of gravity from God to humanity.

David Friedrich Strauss, in his *Life of Jesus*, published in 1835, proposed that what we have before us in the Gospel portrayal is a mythical conception of Jesus originally derived from Jewish messianism but fused with elements from Hellenistic mystery cults. The historical Jesus, Strauss argued, and the Christ of faith are not to be confused. The latter is a product of a later culture, having a history of its own, independent of the actual historical personage it purports to describe.

Ludwig Feuerbach, in *The Essence of Christianity* (1841), his most influential book, proposed from his materialistic standpoint that religion, and the Christian religion in particular, does in fact reveal the essential qualities of the human being. Insofar, however, as those qualities are mistakenly attributed to God, the human being is deprived of them. Humanity is thus separated from itself—alienated from itself—for it has failed to recognize itself in the Otherness it calls "God." Feuerbach argues that the qualities attributed to the Divinity, such as goodness, justice, love, mercy, and foresight, are in fact objectified qualities of what human beings are capable of in the right circumstances. Human beings, in their desire for perfection, project their wishes onto a hypothetical, supernatural being that exists only in their imagination. Thus Feuerbach reduces the otherworldly, supernatural essence of God to its worldly and actual basis in the essence of humanity.

Max Stirner, in *The Ego and His Own* (1844), goes farther, laying the foundations of anarchism and moral nihilism. Feuerbach had argued that only the general idea of humanity has any reality where ethical consequences are concerned, providing hope for higher forms of human brotherhood. Stirner, however, insists that *all* ideals are illusory. There is no reality but the ego and the objectives it sets itself.

Karl Marx agreed with Feuerbach that criticism of religion was necessary before one could proceed to a criticism of society; for religion had throughout history served dominant groups as a primary means of turning the oppressed and exploited away from remedying their circumstances in the present by offering them the illusory prospect of a heavenly paradise. Religion had thus served as an "opium for the people." Marx, however, also diverged from Feuerbach, arguing that with his notion of the brotherhood of humanity, he had merely set up another religion. Historically, "humanity," so called, or the human race has always been divided against itself in antagonistic classes, the latest forms of which are capitalists and wage-earning proletarians. Marx eventually broke with the other Left Hegelians, as we shall see, leveling against them telling criticisms and developing a social theory of his own.

Let us, then, consider fuller expositions of the Left Hegelians' ideas and then see how Marx and his collaborator, Friedrich Engels, responded to them.

FEUERBACH ON THE ESSENCE OF RELIGION

Feuerbach is intent upon repudiating Hegel's philosophical Idealism from a materialist standpoint. In opening his series of lectures on what he calls the essence of religion, Feuerbach states rather dramatically that he is as sick of political idealism as he is of philosophical idealism, and that he and his circle are determined to become political materialists. Feuerbach thus maintains that those who wish to understand the human condition realistically must stand physically on its foundation, namely, nature. For it is only in direct communion with nature that humanity can become whole again and cast aside all supernatural fantasies.[3]

For Feuerbach, what appeared to be missing from Idealist philosophy were real, *sensuous* human beings, and what appeared as the primary defect of religion was its entirely illusory character. Feuerbach's philosophical aim, therefore, was to replace the fictitious cosmic being known as God with the real world and nature; and replace the abstract unreal man of Idealist philosophy with real, sensuous human beings endowed with reason (14).

Feuerbach proposes that in order to understand the religious experience realistically, we have to recognize that the basis of the experience is a feeling of *dependency*. The first object on which humans had felt dependent was nature, and nature, therefore, was the first object of religion. As dependent, vulnerable creatures, humans were in awe of the diverse natural phenomena on which their survival depended. Some of those phenomena actually threatened human survival. Hence, dependence and vulnerability gave rise to *fear*, so early human groups made the frightening aspects of nature the principal objects of their religious veneration. The explanation of religion by fear further commends itself to Feuerbach in light of the fact that even among the culturally more advanced peoples the supreme Godhead is a personification of such natural phenomena as arouse the greatest fear in humans—the god of storms, thunder, and lightning.

Yet fear, Feuerbach recognizes, is not the complete and sufficient explanation of religion. For once a particular danger has passed, fear gives way to an opposite emotion, which attaches itself to the same object as did the fear. It is the feeling of release from danger—a feeling of delight, joy, love, and gratitude. Indeed, natural phenomena that arouse fear and dread are the same that have the most beneficial consequences for human beings. The god who destroys trees, animals, and humans with his thunderbolt is the same god who fructifies the fields with his rain. Thus it is neither fear nor joy alone that constitutes the ground of the religious experience. What is needed, Feuerbach maintained, is a concept that embraces both emotions—*dependency*. Fear relates to death, joy to life. Fear is the feeling of dependency on an object that has the power to destroy; joy and love are emotions of dependency on an object to which humans are grateful for life and well-being. Hence, for Feuerbach, the feeling of dependency is the only general term by which to designate and explain the psychological ground of religion. And what he perceives in early "nature religion," he attributes to all religions.

Feuerbach's conception of human dependency implies that given the vulnerable nature of human beings, their egoistic or subjective needs are such as to constitute religion as a cry for help. What do humans most desire, if not the good, the useful, the beneficent? What humans desire and yearn for, they worship, Feuerbach asserts. He cites the ancient Greeks, who regarded helpfulness, kindness, *philanthropeia*, as the essential attributes of divinity. Feuerbach cites more evidence from classical antiquity: "No god," says Socrates in Plato's *Theaetetus*, "is hostile to man." "What," says Seneca in his letters, "is the ground of the gods' beneficence? Their nature. It is absurd to suppose that they wish to do harm; they are not even capable of doing so." "It is no more absurd," says Plutarch in an essay against the Stoics, "to deny the immortality of the gods than to deny their providence and love of mankind." So Feuerbach observes that "among the Greeks, the gods, or at least the best of them, were therefore termed 'givers of the good,' and *soteres*, saviors" (58).

When Feuerbach asserts that *egoism* is the fundamental principle of religion, he therefore means that a being's worthiness to be worshiped depends solely on its relation to human welfare. If humans seek only the beneficial and useful in the divine, then the subjective or psychological ground of divinity is to be found in egoism, which relates everything to itself, evaluating it accordingly. "Egoism" refers not only to the individual and his or her loved ones but also to the individual's community. Thus, even if, say, one asks something for one's country, one asks also for oneself, for generally, one's own welfare is inseparable from that of one's compatriots.

To convey the twofold character of dependency, Feuerbach cites religions in which humans worship animals and plants that they nevertheless eat. "The need that impels me to eat an object is twofold in character: it subjects me to the object and at the same time subjects the object to me" (81). And lest one suppose that this phenomenon is peculiar to so-called primitives, Feuerbach adds, "And yet, even Christians eat their God." The fact that humans worship as religious objects things that they also eat provides Feuerbach with the opportunity to compare the pagan with the Christian view. The object of the pagan feeling of dependency is a real, sensuous object:

> whereas the object of the Christian feeling—apart from the God made flesh and therefore edible—is an infinite, universal, merely cogitated or represented object and therefore not physically enjoyable or useful. But an object of enjoyment it remains, precisely because it is an object of need, of the feeling of dependency, except that for a Christian it is the object of a different kind of enjoyment, because it is also the object of a different kind of need; for what a Christian wants of his God is not so-called temporal life, but eternal life; in his God he satisfies not an immediately sensuous or physical need, but a spiritual need, a need of the soul. (82)

But, of course, for Feuerbach the materialist, the Christian view of thus fulfilling a spiritual need is false and illusory.

Feuerbach agrees with Spinoza in defining nature not as a being acting with will and reason but as a being that acts in accordance with its inner necessity. But Feuerbach rejects both Spinoza's and Hegel's view of a divine principle immanent in nature. For Feuerbach, it is turning things upside down to say that God manifests himself in nature. The simple, palpable truth is quite the opposite, that originally, at least, nature manifests itself to humans as divine: the phenomena of nature made on humans the impression that they are governed by spirits or deities. How, Feuerbach polemically asks, can a being who is not material or corporeal be the cause of events that are exclusively the consequence of material, corporeal processes? A god, therefore, is merely the hypostatized and objectified essence of the human imagination. This is equally true of Christianity, says Feuerbach, where the God, as a product of fantasy, becomes an all-powerful, supernatural being. Feuerbach cites the words of Luther and Calvin. Not bread, says Luther, "but the word of God feeds the body naturally." Calvin states explicitly that God of the Old Testament created light before the sun, so that humans might see that the beneficent effects of light were not necessarily connected with the sun.

Feuerbach also cites certain dominant theological doctrines that deprive humans of any freedom of action or choice. The same Calvin, he observes, who regards men who do good as mere instruments of God calls it godless and absurd to infer that all crimes are therefore committed by God's decree or will. How malicious it is, Feuerbach remarks, to deny human autonomy in one case and to recognize it in another—to dispose of the good humans do as by the grace of God, but to hold humans guilty of the evil they do.

Feuerbach is unrelenting in ridiculing the doctrine of *creatio ex nihilo*. When someone asserts that the world was created from nothing, he is, in effect, saying nothing at all. This *nihil* is an evasion, a sidestepping of the obvious question: Where did the Spirit get the nonspiritual, material substances of which the world consists? We are, moreover, merely begging the question if instead of saying God created the world from nothing, one says, as did Hegel, God created it out of himself, out of spirit. How, Feuerbach asks, does real, physical matter issue from spirit?

As Feuerbach centers attention on the Christian religion and the role of faith or belief, he offers the view that the word *faith* in the Christian context means nothing other than *imagination*. "Faith," says Luther, "is in truth all powerful.... For faith brings into being what is not, and makes possible things that are impossible." But this omnipotence of faith, Feuerbach comments, is simply the omnipotence of the imagination. The symbols of Christian faith, according to Luther, are baptism and communion. The substance of baptism is water, the matter of communion is bread and wine. For faith, however, the natural water of baptism is spiritual water, as Luther called it, and the bread and wine of communion are the Lord's flesh and blood. What is this, asks Feuerbach, if not the work of the imagination? He quotes a sermon of Luther's in which he states: "I have often said that the way in which God appears to a man depends on that man's frame of mind; as you think and believe, so you have Him." And in Luther's commentary on the Second Epistle of Peter, "If you regard Him as a God, He will behave as a God toward you." What is this conception of things, asks Feuerbach, if not the product of fantasy?

The Christian faith, Feuerbach observes, is based only on the sense of hearing. "Take away the word," says Calvin in his *Institutes of the Christian Religion*, "and no faith is left." And "although man should earnestly turn his eyes to the contemplation of God's works [i.e., nature], he must above all direct his ears toward the Word, for the image of God impressed on the glorious form of the world is not effective enough." For Feuerbach, however, the word, too, is an image, from which it followed that the Christian God is a product of the imagination; and if image worship is idolatry, then Christian worship of the spiritual God is also idolatry.

Feuerbach observes that the Christians accused the pagans, the Protestants accused the Catholics, and the rationalists accuse the Protestants of idolatry "in each case for the same reason, for worshipping a man, an image of God (for man is made in God's image)...instead of worshipping the original God himself. But I go still further and say:...all worship of images is idolatry. For God did not make man in His image; on the contrary, man...made God in his image" (187). This idea was, of course, anticipated by Voltaire, who once quipped that God created man in his image, and then man returned the compliment. Indeed, Feuerbach is, in effect repeating the Enlightenment's critique of religion in general and of Christianity in particular. He does not deny that Jesus was a historical person, but he does deny that "Jesus was a Christ, a God or son of God, a miracle worker, born of a virgin, that he healed the sick by a mere word, quelled storms by a mere command, awakened dead men who had begun to rot, and that he himself was raised from the dead" (190).

Returning to his central thesis, that the religious imagination is rooted in the feeling of dependency, Feuerbach observes that this feeling never ceases in an individual, "for at every step he takes, some harm may befall him.... This feeling of anxiety, of uncertainty, this fear of harm that always accompanies man, is the root of the religious imagination" (196). For Feuerbach, then, the essence of the religious experience is a cry for help and protection from the evils that can befall innocent individuals and their loved ones. Humans believe in gods because they yearn for happiness. Humans believe in perfect beings because they themselves wish to be perfect. They believe in immortal beings because they themselves do not wish to perish. But insofar as humans attribute such superhuman qualities to imaginary beings, they diminish themselves. In the presence of the deities humans have invented, they feel themselves to be insignificant—nullities.

Although Feuerbach does not explicitly employ the concept of *alienation* in analyzing this phenomenon, it is evident that what he has described is alienation in Hegel's sense: *a condition in which humans fail to recognize themselves in the Othernesses they have created or acted upon.* Hence, for Feuerbach, insofar as humans fail to recognize themselves in the deities they themselves have created, they suffer from a definite form of self-alienation. So estranged are they from themselves that they fail to recognize the so-called gods as nothing more than their own desires for perfection projected upon hypothetical, imaginary beings. For Feuerbach, it is not only the so-called elementary or "primitive" religions but also the world religions that are the products of alienation.

When Luther, again, assures his followers that God, as their beloved Father, will grant whatever they ask, Feuerbach, the materialist, replies that such utterances and beliefs are shameful and silly sophisms. If humans would only open their eyes and use their reason courageously, they would cease to be beclouded by such notions and see reality for what it is. Indeed, they would rebel against a purportedly caring Providence that allows millions of innocent human beings to suffer the most terrible torments and unconscionable injustices. Feuerbach shared the optimistic mood of the nineteenth century together with its notions of social evolution and progress. He therefore proposed that humans would someday master the art of leading moral and happy lives without a god. When humans will conduct themselves properly of their own accord, as their own nature, reason and inclination tell them to, the need for religion will cease (212–213).

Feuerbach's critique of religion carried with it certain social and political implications. The paramount task of his time, as he saw it, was to disseminate scientific and rational education in all classes and in all walks of life. Only in that way would humans reach that higher stage of social development in which they might rid themselves of their illusions and strive to fulfill themselves in this world.

MARX'S CRITIQUE

Already in his youth, Marx had recognized in his well-known "Theses on Feuerbach" that Feuerbach's materialism and, indeed, all previous forms of materialism suffered from a major defect. For when Feuerbach speaks of the human, *sensuous* nature, he tends to reduce it to what he calls the "common 'bestial' urge to eat and drink, the common 'bestial' instincts of sexuality and love of young" (260). Feuerbach's emphasis throughout appears to be on what humans have in common with other members of the animal kingdom, but not on what is uniquely human. This one-sided emphasis was for Marx misleading because it ignored the active, creative side of the human being; it ignored the human being as an active, creative subject. And Marx acknowledged in his theses that the active, creative side of our nature was first discovered and illuminated by the philosophical Idealists.

In fairness to Feuerbach, he does say that the "negation of the next world has as its consequence the affirmation of this world; the denial of a better life in heaven implies the demand of a better life on Earth; it transforms the hope of a better future from a concern of idle, inactive faith into a duty, a matter of independent human activity. ... The necessary conclusion to be drawn from the existing injustices and evils of human life is the determination, the active striving to remedy them" (283–284). But as

Feuerbach never went beyond the expression of such general sentiments, to address what Marx came to regard as the most glaring injustice of his time, namely, wage slavery, Marx believed that his criticism of Feuerbach's materialism was a fair one. Moreover, Feuerbach proposed that "we must replace the love of God by the love of man as the only true religion" (285). This prompted another materialist in the circle of the Left Hegelians, notably Max Stirner, to argue that the notion of the "love of humanity" is just as abstract, metaphysical, unnatural, and existentially inauthentic as the notion of the love of God. And as we shall see, Marx and his colleague Engels will make a considerable effort to repudiate Stirner's view.

MAX STIRNER

It is Stirner more than any other thinker of the early nineteenth century who deserves the epithet "proto-Nietzschean," and it is likely that Nietzsche had read Stirner's book and been profoundly influenced by it. The degree to which Nietzsche is anticipated by Stirner both in ideas and in prose style can hardly be a coincidence. Their central concerns are too similar, as are their key concepts: anti-Christ, immoralism, priest-morality, and egoist-superhuman or higher-type individuals. Stirner also wrote of the "death of God" and the so-called decadent nature of democracy.

The book for which Stirner is best known is titled *Der Einzige und sein Eigenthum*, which has been translated as *The Ego and His Own*.[4] Stirner's egoistic motto is "Realize yourself!" which is in sharp contrast to Socrates' "Become just!" Stirner likens himself to a singer in the heights of his song, who sings for his own sake, not for anyone else, and not for the sake of truth. Like Nietzsche after him, Stirner employs an aphoristic style and founds his project on the rejection of traditional concerns, which for him amount to *nothing*—the Good, the Divine, so-called humankind, Truth, Freedom, Justice, the People, the Fatherland, and so on. He himself is his only concern, and in that concern there is neither good nor evil, for neither of these has any real meaning for him.

What Thomas Hobbes attributed to the state of nature as a war of each against all, Stirner attributes to the social world. Because everyone cares only for himself, he comes into conflict with others, and the battle of selves becomes inevitable. Hence, victory or defeat, that is the question for everyone. The victor becomes the lord or master, the vanquished the subject, the victor exercising supremacy as a right, the vanquished the duties of a subject. They become and remain enemies, each looking out for the other's weaknesses.

When we are children, our instincts are vital, and the feeling of self strives to defer to nothing and no one. Soon, however, our natural impulses meet with the objections of the mind, the objections of one's own conscience. Why? Because the notion has been instilled that certain thoughts and actions are bad, unreasonable, unchristian. But the *real* man, for Stirner, has only bodily, personal, and egoistic interests. Only when a man has fallen in love with his corporeal self and has derived pleasure in himself as a living, flesh-and-blood individual has he acquired a *selfish* interest so necessary for self-realization.

Stirner wants to reject all metaphysics, not only notions of God but notions of "man" as well, which have been mistakenly rendered sacred by the materialists. For the actual reality of the human condition is the individual striving to extend and expand his own individuality. The individual exists only in raising himself and not remaining as he is. "Man," for Stirner, with an uppercase *M*, is an ideal, which is the same as saying it is nothing. There is no difference, for Stirner, between looking to "humanity" as an ideal and looking to God or Christ.

Nietzsche's superman-ascetic priest dichotomy, as we shall see in a forthcoming chapter, parallels Stirner's egoist-cleric contrast, and they also share an underlying assumption that the modern individual's malaise stems from moral rather than from economic or political repression. Each individual, says Stirner, carries stern moral injunctions in his breast—hence, he cannot *will* to gain freedom, he can only wish or petition for it. What would happen if the "slave" really willed with the full energy of his will? But no! Instead he renounces will for the love of Morality, which is why he is condemned to remain a slave. Even where Enlightenment and Rationalism have challenged and weakened conventional morality, courage is lacking to devote oneself wholly to egoism.

Stirner also anticipates Nietzsche in denouncing self-renunciation and the repression of instincts. There sits youth, writes Stirner, with its deathly tired head and pale cheeks. Poor children, the passions beat at their hearts, and the rich powers of youth demand their right. Nature quivers in their limbs, the blood swells in their veins while fiery fancies excite the gleam in their eyes. But then the conscience sets in, and the young innocents turn their eyes upward, and they pray. The storms of nature are hushed, and the surging sea of their appetites is calmed, but only apparently so. For the imaginary "soul" is saved, but the body tends to languish.

Human beings, Stirner asserts, have continually sought a standpoint *outside* of the earth and have found it in the world of the mind—in ideas, concepts, essences, and "heaven." Indeed, heaven is the unreal standpoint from which the earthly doings of humans are looked down upon and despised. Christianity has thus succeeded in "delivering" us from a life determined by our nature, from the appetites impelling us. Humans, according to the ascetic doctrines of Christianity, should not allow themselves to be actuated by their appetites. So Stirner wants us to reject and repudiate all doctrines of asceticism. It is only through the "flesh" that one can break the tyranny of the mind, for it is only when an individual hears his flesh along with the rest of his physical self that he hears himself wholly.

The idea of the "sacred" renders people powerless and humble. And yet nothing is sacred in itself. It is one's declaring it sacred, one's bending of the knee that makes it so. "Sacred" is a phenomenon of consciousness and conscience; it is everything that stands before and "above" the egoist as an obstacle to his will to life. For little children as for animals, the sacred has no existence. Only later, as children learn the distinctions "good" and "bad," do reverence and "sacred dread" step into the place of natural fear. That, for Stirner, is the standpoint of religion and all metaphysics— holding something outside oneself as mightier, greater, and higher. It is the attitude in which one projects onto an alien, hypothetical something such supernatural powers that one yields and surrenders oneself to it in devotion, humility, and servility. Religion is the phenomenon that bars the way to an individual's self-will.

Instilling fear is an attempt to raise a barrier against the ego's self-will. But fear is not enough, since there is always the effort to overcome what is feared. But when something is regarded as sacred, it is not only feared but revered. With reverence, one has internalized a power from which one no longer strives to liberate oneself; one is subjected to it with all the strength of faith. One believes! Even for nonbelievers, however, morality itself has acquired a sacred status. Moral concepts in and of themselves are now revered. From infancy, one is indoctrinated with the notion that one must be moral. Whether morality itself is an illusion is a question no one dares to address. It remains exalted above all doubt. Spiritual men have taken it into their heads to realize the concepts of goodness, of love. They want somehow to establish the kingdom of love on earth, in which no one any longer acts from selfishness. This idée fixe will surely lead the human species to ruination.

Stirner now introduces the concept of "clericalism" to denote an ascetic outlook according to which one lives for a "lofty" idea, cause, doctrine, or system, which prevents all worldly desires and self-seeking interests from springing up in him. Stirner appears to be the first of modern thinkers to use "cleric" (*der Pfaff*) to symbolize the resentful, inhibited, devitalized perpetrator of morality, whose teachings paralyze the will and deprive it of any inner power. "Cleric," in these terms, does seem to anticipate Nietzsche's "ascetic priest" (*asketischer Priester*). "Clericalism" implies that one feels oneself called to live and work for an idea or a "good cause," and to renounce all pleasures and enjoyments that flow from sources other than the "sacred interests." Such "sacred interests," for Stirner, are not only the traditional religious-moral interests but also, for example, those of Fatherland, Science, and Revolution. Stirner thus assails the secular ideals as well, arguing that he who is infatuated with Man leaves real persons out of account insofar as the infatuation floats in the rarefied atmosphere of an ideal, sacred interest. "Man" in the abstract is not a person but a spook.

Stirner, like Nietzsche after him, envisioned a break with the past in which strong-willed individuals would arise and no longer allow debilitating doctrines to be inculcated by the "clerics." The new, higher types would have no sympathy for the follies that the "clerics" have been whining, raving, driveling, and chattering about since the beginning of history. The new, strong-willed individuals will destroy original sin and all other debilitating stupidities inherited from the past. "If you command them," writes Stirner, "'Bend before the Most High,' they will answer, 'If he wants to bend us, let him come himself and do it; we, at least will not bend of our own accord.' And if you threaten them with his wrath and his punishment, they will take it like being threatened by the bogeyman. If you are no longer successful in making them afraid of ghosts, then the dominion of ghosts is at an end, and fairytales find no faith" (84–85).

The new, strong-willed individuals will also see through the latest metamorphoses of the Christian religion, such as humanism, liberalism, democracy, and communism. All of these secular religions, Stirner argues, exalt "Man" to the same extent that any traditional religion exalts its idol or god, turning "Man" into something otherworldly and alien, and setting real human beings beneath it.

Nietzsche was not the first to cry out, "God is dead!" and "we have killed him" (*The Gay Science*, sec. 125). Much earlier Stirner had made the same proclamation, and he went on to say that the job was only half done:

> At the entrance to the modern time stands the "God-Man." At its exit will only the God in the God-Man evaporate? And can the God-Man really die if only the God in him dies? They did not think of this question, and thought they were through when in our time they brought to a victorious end the work of the Enlightenment, the vanquishing of God: they did not notice that Man has killed God in order to become now—"sole God on high." The other world outside us is indeed brushed away, and the great undertaking of the Enlighteners completed; but the other world in us has become a new heaven and calls us forth to renewed heaven-storming: God has had to give place, yet not to us, but to—Man. How can you believe that the God-Man is dead before the Man in him, besides the God, is dead? (109)

Stirner also seems to have anticipated Nietzsche's concern with the "bad conscience" and its repression of human drives. Viewing the human individual as a bundle of impulses, desires, and passions, Stirner observes that from the beginning of history the traditional question was:

How are these passions to be adequately and correctly regulated, if not in obedience to God's commandments? And if not in obedience to God, then at least in obedience to the moral principles and the voice of reason which in the course of the bitter experiences of history have been raised into law? Wouldn't the passions lead us to do destructive and senseless things without the light of a guiding star? Stirner's reply is much the same as that given later by Nietzsche. "If the individual only deemed himself a beast," writes Stirner, "he would easily find that the beast, which does follow only *its* impulse (its advice, as it were), does not advise and impel itself to do the "most senseless" things, but takes very correct steps. But the habit of the religious way of thinking has biased our mind so grievously that we are terrified at *ourselves* in our nakedness and naturalness; it has degraded us so that we deem ourselves depraved by nature, born devils" (116). Thousands of years of civilization have obscured from us what we actually are, deceiving us into thinking that we are good when we deny ourselves. Shake that off, Stirner urges, and become the open egoists that your nature intends you to be. Become an almighty ego!

Stirner proposes that "might is right." The ego secures its freedom insofar as it makes the world its own, takes possession of it for itself, "by whatever might"—persuasion, ultimatum, even by means of hypocrisy and deceit. The ego's freedom is diminished when it cannot realize its will on another object, whether it be an object without will, like a rock, or with will, like another individual or the state. One circumvents a rock obstructing one's way until one has power enough to blast it; one submits to the authority of the state until one has gathered enough strength to overthrow it. "Why," Stirner asks,

> is the freedom of the peoples a "hollow word"? Because the peoples have no might! With a breath of living ego I blow peoples over, be it the breath of a Nero, a Chinese emperor, or a poor writer. Why is it that the German legislatures pine in vain for freedom, and are lectured for it by the cabinet ministers? Because they are not the "mighty"! Might is a fine thing, and useful for many purposes; one goes farther with a handful of might than with a bagful of right. You long for freedom? You fools! If you took might, freedom would come of itself. See, he who has might "stands above the laws." (121–22)

Freedom, for Stirner, that is granted or given is no freedom at all. Only the freedom one *takes* for oneself is the real egoist's freedom, the product of will so gratifying to one's passions. Notice, says Stirner, that when the Greeks came of age they drove out their tyrants and did not wait for the tyrants to grant them their freedom.

My ego, says Stirner, is the only judge of whether I am in the right or not. Others can only decide whether to endorse my right. To the question, what or who gives me the right to do this or that, the traditional answer is God, love, reason, humanity, and so on. But in reality it is only my own might that gives me a right. There is no right outside of me. If it is right for me, it is right, and if that does not suffice to make it right for others, that is their problem, not mine. Let them defend themselves against my right. If something is right for me and I want it, though it is not right for the whole world, then I neither ask the world for its opinion nor care about it. That is the rule for every strong individual who knows how to value himself, "for might goes before right, and that—with perfect right" (127). Formerly, Stirner observes, divine reason was placed above and against human reason; now human reason, so called, is placed above and against egoistic reason, which is rejected as "unreason." Little do people realize that neither divine nor human reason is real, and that the only reason is that of the individual. The strong-willed individual is the irreconcilable enemy of every generality, every fetter.

Property, for Stirner, is essential for the self-realization of the individual. To what property is the individual entitled? Only to that which is in his power to obtain. One gives oneself the right to property by taking it to oneself. Might, again, is the key: Everything over which one has might, and which cannot be torn from him, remains his property. Egoism and selfishness decide the issue, not justice, not mercy, not goodness, not love, nor any other form of selflessness. Egoism never thinks of sacrificing or giving away anything it wants. It simply decides that what it wants it must have and will acquire. "Take hold," Stirner proclaims, "And take what you require! With this the war of all against all is declared. I alone decide what I will have" (167–68).

Stirner thus repeats the phrase Hobbes employed to describe the "state of nature" as a state of war. Whereas Hobbes, however, advanced the valid proposition that a strong common power is necessary to bring the "war of each against all" to an end, Stirner turns the exercise of unbridled power and coercion into a principle for individual action. From a theoretical standpoint, then, it appears that for Stirner human individuals always remain in a state of nature and war, as do states in the international arena. Stirner urges his readers not to dream of the most comprehensive commune, "human society," but rather to see in others only means to one's own egoistic ends. No one, he says, is his equal; everyone, without exception, is his property. Much of what Stirner has to say here is polemically directed against Bruno Bauer and some of the other Left Hegelians in his circle who had proposed that one should respect the "fellow-man" in all human beings. To this Stirner replies: "For me no one is a person to be respected, not even the fellow-man, but solely, like other beings, an *object* in which I take an interest or else do not, an interesting or uninteresting object, a usable or unusable person" (214). Stirner does not shy away from taking his doctrine to its logical conclusion: "*My* satisfaction decides about my relation to others, and . . . I do not renounce, from any excess of humility, even the power of life and death" (222).

We see, then, that in one's relation to the world Stirner holds that one should no longer do anything "for God's sake," or for so-called humanity's sake, but only for one's own sake. Stirner's philosophy therefore represents the most provocative pre-Nietzschean assault upon Western values in the modern era. It is an endorsement of egoism, hedonism, anarchism, and the doctrine that "might is right." Just as Marx had leveled significant criticisms against Feuerbach, he and Engels found it necessary to devote more than half of their early book, *The German Ideology*, to a systematic critique of Stirner's philosophy.

THE REBUTTAL OF STIRNER BY MARX AND ENGELS

With the exception of Stirner, all of the Young Hegelians believed that classical German philosophy had made an extraordinary contribution to knowledge by underscoring the *social* nature of consciousness. What Kant, Fichte, and Hegel had expressed in the language of philosophical idealism, the Young Hegelians formulated in more historical and sociological terms: The "individual" is an abstraction; there is no self without an other. There is no such thing as an individual living outside some sort of social context, which implies that whether one likes it or not, one always has definite social obligations and even rights, however limited they may be, in that context. But Stirner, who could find in his head only his own self and consciousness, and no other ego, somehow regarded the social nature of mind and self as a serious threat to individual freedom and the autonomy of the personality.

Marx and Engels begin by acknowledging some of the merits of Stirner's work, such as the honesty in his contention that one should consider oneself. This contrasted with the less-than-honest, sickly altruism of several contemporary writers who exhorted their readers to consider only others. Positive, too, was Stirner's insistence that freedom must mean freedom to act: Where one is nominally free but lacks the material means with which to realize oneself, one is actually unfree. As a materialist, Stirner claimed that he had rejected Idealist philosophy in its entirety. To this Marx and Engels replied that Stirner had merely rejected specific ideals such as God, humanity, and immortality. But he had unsuspectingly retained the Idealist *method*, which disregarded the historical and social context of ideals and which sought to discover an abstract ideal through abstract logical analysis. Stirner had, therefore, inadvertently replaced the abstractions of religion and speculative philosophy—God and Man—with an even more preposterous abstraction, the "Ego." What is the "self"? Marx and Engels ask. Is it not an abstraction from a whole complex of social relationships, of selves in relation to one another? In the words of Marx and Engels:

> Individuals have always and in all circumstances "started out from themselves," but since they were not unique in the sense of not needing any connection with another, and since their *needs*, [and] consequently their nature and the method of satisfying their needs, connected them with one another (relations between the sexes, exchange, division of labor), they *had* to enter into association with one another, not as pure egos, but as individuals at a definite stage of development of their productive forces and requirements, and since this association, in its turn, determined production and needs, it was, therefore, precisely the personal, individual behavior of individuals, their behavior to one another as individuals, that created the existing conditions and daily reproduces them anew.... Hence, it certainly follows that the development of an individual is determined by the development of all the others with whom he is directly or indirectly associated, and that the different generations of individuals entering into relation with one another are connected with one another, that the physical existence of later generations is determined by that of their predecessors, and that these later generations inherit the productive forces and forms of association accumulated by their predecessors, their own mutual relations being determined thereby. In short, it is clear that a development occurs and that the history of a single individual cannot possibly be separated from the history of preceding or contemporary individuals, but is determined by this history.[5]

The heart of the rebuttal, then, is the recognition of the fundamental interdependence of the self and the other, and the impossibility of separating them outside of one's imagination. Stirner's notion of "one's own" is therefore a highly artificial abstraction from the interdependent nature of all individual activities in any society. Every individual, without exception, is directly or indirectly dependent on others for his or her livelihood, not to mention love and affection; and every individual is dependent on the accumulated store of social knowledge and material. No individual can therefore justifiably make the claim that "his own" was acquired solely through his own efforts. This has definite implications for Stirner's notion of a "higher-type" or "egoist-superman" and for a similar notion we will later encounter in Nietzsche's theory. For even when a higher, creative individual works alone, it is undeniable that much more than his own unaided efforts have gone into the production of the specific goods he has created—the much more being other human beings from whom he has learned the techniques, traditions, language, and knowledge without which he could do nothing. This is true even of the genius, for no matter how gifted, creative, strong, or "superior" an individual might be, he owes his achievements, in large measure, to others.

So Marx, though he refers to his methodological outlook as a "materialist conception of history," nevertheless diverges significantly from Stirner as he did from Feuerbach. It remains for us to have a close look at Bruno Bauer's work, and to see how and why Marx also diverged from him.

BRUNO BAUER ON THE SO-CALLED JEWISH QUESTION

Bruno Bauer was perhaps the leading member of the Young Hegelian circle. His critical analyses of the New Testament and the first three Gospels are still treated with respect by scholars. To understand why the status of Jews in Germany was discussed by Bauer and other intellectuals, we have to recall that Germany of the 1840s should really be referred to as "the Germanies," for it consisted of over three hundred autonomous principalities. Germany became a unified nation-state only in the late nineteenth century, under Bismarck. Moreover, the Germanies of the 1840s were ruled by a regime consisting of the monarchy, the landed nobility, and the church. Under that regime the inhabitants of the German principalities were subjects, not citizens, and, of course, there was no equivalent in Germany to the American Constitution or the Code Napoleon, establishing the basic civil rights of citizens.

Indeed, one of the main preoccupations of the Young Hegelians and other liberal thinkers was how to bring about in Germany the level of political emancipation France had achieved. Hence, in the 1840s political emancipation and citizenship rights were focal points in the discussions among the Young Hegelians and, in particular, between Bauer and Marx. In a word, the question was what rules are to be followed in deciding whom to define as citizens in the German states, whom to include, and whom to exclude.

In *Die Judenfrage* (The Jewish Question), published in 1843, Bauer rejected the demand of both German Jews and liberal Germans to grant the Jews civil rights. Jews had been living in the German principalities at least since the thirteenth century, but because they were a non-Christian minority, they had been ghettoized and treated as a "guest people." As was the case in other European countries, the guest status was granted to the Jews when they were perceived as economically useful, and the status was often withdrawn when the rulers decided that the Jews were no longer needed because members of the "host" nation had acquired the desirable economic skills. In the early nineteenth century, Jews had no civil rights in the Germanies. They were, for example, excluded from the universities. The few Jews who had gained admission to the universities were, in effect, non-Jews, since their fathers had converted to Protestantism. In the Germanies of the time, then, being a Christian was a prerequisite for even the semblance of citizenship, and therefore for entry into the educational and governmental institutions and the liberal professions.

When Bauer rejected granting to the Jews equal civil rights, he grounded his objection in theological arguments, asserting that Judaism was an insurmountable obstacle to the participation of Jews in the development of modern life. Viewing Judaism as a relic of a bygone era, Bauer held that although Judaism had possessed some validity in the world of the ancient Hebrews, that validity was limited and historically relative. For with the appearance of Jesus of Nazareth and the early Christian community, Judaism had been superseded once and for all.

From Bauer's standpoint, contemporary Jews stubbornly clung to their superannuated religion because their "Oriental nature" dictated such an attitude. Following Hegel in that regard, Bauer maintained that the denizens of the Orient had yet to recognize that they were free, and gifted with reason. Given, therefore, the "Oriental nature" of the Jews, they were, presumably, incapable of effectively participating in the development of the modern epoch. They slavishly adhered to old casuistical doctrines, Bauer alleged, and to ritualistic practices. They consequently failed to keep apace of modern historical developments, and the chief reason for their failure was their religious tenacity, their steadfast refusal to abandon their faith.

As a materialist, atheist, and critic of religion in general, Bauer therefore proposed that in order for the Jews to become citizens, they would first have to become atheists. Bauer proposed this, he said, not out of any anti-Jewish animus but in the best interest of the Jews. Treating Judaism as an exception to the rule that all religions must be subjected to hardheaded, rational criticism would do the Jews more harm than good. Those who want to spare the Jews the pains of criticism are the worst enemies of the Jews. No one who has not gone through the fires of criticism will be able to enter the new world soon to come.[6]

Actually, Bauer's critique, far from being merely theological, aims to advance the claim that Judaism is at odds with modern historical reality. The Jewish Law, he alleged, having no relevance to the modern world, is a dead letter. In Bauer's critique of Judaism, he follows Hegel's theory of four stages of religious development: the Oriental, the Greek, the Roman, and the German-Christian. The criterion distinguishing the stages is the degree to which the people in question have overcome their separation from God. Bauer accepts the Hegelian proposition that he is living in the German-Christian stage of history; but Bauer also believed that this stage will soon be transcended by leaving religion behind altogether. Having, therefore, to address the question of Christianity's status in this developmental scheme, Bauer posits the appearance of Jesus as a turning point in the world history of religion.

In Bauer's view, Jesus had identified his consciousness with that of God, with God the Father. The early Christian community went one step farther by identifying itself as an entire united community with God. Theologically, Bauer interprets this as the beginning of the religious, historical process in which a general union of humanity and God would be achieved. Thus, for Bauer, the fundamental difference between Judaism and Christianity was that in Judaism the separation of humanity from God was still significant insofar as God is conceived as beyond humanity; whereas Christianity, in the concept of the Incarnation, had elevated humanity to the level of the Divine. Christianity therefore represents the highest stage in the development of the world religions.

Great as this achievement was in raising human consciousness and reducing the degree of separation of humanity from the Divine, it was nevertheless inadequate for Bauer, since it remained within the confined illusory framework of religion. The next and purportedly higher stage (the final and fully human stage) to which Bauer eagerly looked forward, was to be a totally secularized consciousness—atheism. As Bauer perceived his contemporary epoch, atheism was struggling for light and supremacy. Only an atheistic consciousness is a free consciousness for Bauer, and only a free consciousness could widen the boundaries of freedom. Europe, Bauer believed, had entered the highest stage of development in which Europeans would soon recognize the notion of the Divine for what it is—a manifestation of human self-alienation.

It followed, for Bauer, that Judaism stands in the way of this emancipatory process, theologically as well as politically. Since Judaism represents a throwback to the Oriental stage, Jews must make a dialectical leap into modernity. How? By abandoning their faith. Jews must, in a word, stop being Jews in order to achieve civil emancipation. Christians, on the other hand, possessing a less alienated consciousness, need take only a small step or two in order to enter the modern era.[7]

Bauer employed the Hegelian concept of self-alienation which, as we have seen, refers to the failure to recognize oneself in the otherness one has created or acted upon. Any and all religions are, for Bauer as for the other Young Hegelians, manifestations par excellence of human self-alienation. From Bauer's standpoint, however, Judaism was an exceptionally glaring manifestation, since it had allegedly remained fixed at its Oriental stage. Hence, to emancipate themselves and to attain the atheistic consciousness Bauer aspired to, Jews must take the necessary steps in abandoning their faith. But the German states at the time were Christian, not secular. The equality of opportunity implied by citizenship was not a *right* in Germany that had to be granted to non-Christians. Bauer therefore insisted that the gaining of political equality in citizenship was a project of enlightenment. Political equality may only be attained by those who, whether Christians or Jews, are prepared to struggle for a free (i.e., atheistic) consciousness. However, the followers of both faiths are subjects of a Christian state and therefore unfree.

So although Bauer writes as if the stubborn retention of Judaism is the sole obstacle to the political emancipation of the Jews, he also recognizes another equally formidable obstacle. As Marx, in his lucid interpretation of Bauer's position, observed: "The *Christian* state, *by its very nature*, is incapable of emancipating the Jews. But, adds Bauer, the Jew, by his very nature, cannot be emancipated. As long as the state remains Christian, and as long as the Jew remains a Jew, they are equally incapable, the one of conferring emancipation, the other of receiving it."[8]

For Bauer as for Feuerbach and the other members of the Young Hegelian circle, it is owing to the distorted mirror of religious belief that humans diminish their own powers by assigning them to a chimerical reality in the heavens. This sad reality is no less evident in Christian states where instead of serving humans by granting them true citizenship, the state subjugates them. This has been true in Germany since the time of Luther, who first inspired the desire for freedom in the people and then turned against them, siding with the princes when the people rose up against them in the peasant revolts of the sixteenth century. So Bauer recognizes that Christianity has been an ideology with definite political implications. Christianity, he observes, not only undermines self-confidence and discourages self-mastery but also has favored the interests of the privileged and powerful against those of the poor and weak. Originally, Christianity showed promise of becoming a great step forward in human self-understanding and the expansion of freedom, as in the early church's institution of social equality and communal property. This promise, however, was never fulfilled. Instead, from the time of Constantine to Bauer's own day, Christianity has developed as an ideology in which the quest for freedom was no longer to be an earthly endeavor. Christianity failed as an emancipatory project by transferring the hope for salvation to the world beyond. But though Christianity has failed in that respect, it is but a step away from an emancipatory, secular consciousness. That is true for Bauer not only because he agreed with Hegel that the highest form of religion requires reason, but also because it appeared to Bauer that reason and science were rapidly secularizing the minds of contemporary Christians. Bauer apparently believed that the rational and moral elements of Christianity would become more and more prominent until they have finally supplanted Christianity as a religion. Judaism, however, is so out of step with the march of history, Bauer concludes, that the Jews should never be granted equal citizenship in the German states unless they willingly make the conscious dialectical leap into atheism.

NOTES

[1] G. W. F. Hegel, *Early Theological Writings*, translated by T. M. Knox, with an introduction and fragments translated by Richard Kroner (Chicago: University of Chicago Press, 1948), p. 65. Hereafter, page references to this work will be cited in parentheses immediately following the quoted passage.

[2] Ibid., pp. 65–66.

[3] The present exposition is based on Ludwig Feuerbach, *The Essences of Religion*, translated by Ralph Mannheim (New York: Harper and Row, 1967). All page references to this work will be cited in parentheses immediately following the quoted or paraphrased passage.

[4] The edition on which I base my exposition of Stirner's ideas was edited and introduced by John Carroll and translated by Steven T. Byington and published by Jonathan Cape, London, 1971. The translation was first published in 1907. Hereafter, references to this book will be cited in parentheses immediately following the quoted passage.

[5] Karl Marx and Friedrich Engels, *The German Ideology* (Moscow: Progress Publishers, 1964), pp. 481–82.

[6] See David McLellan, *The Young Hegelians and Karl Marx* (London: Macmillan, 1969), pp. 48–80.

[7] See also Meir Amor, "State Persecution and Vulnerability: A Comparative Historical Analysis of Violent Ethnocentrism" (Ph.D. diss., University of Toronto, 1999). After reviewing not only Bauer's views but also several other classical analyses of the status of Jews in Western Christendom, Amor proceeds to criticize their one-sidedness in centering attention on the minority and ignoring the role of the "host" regime, and the general context in which tensions emerge between the majority as "host" and the minority as "guest." To shed light on the phenomena of violence, expulsion, and genocide perpetrated against ethnic minorities, Amor employs the historical experiences of the Jews as prototypical and then explores parallels in the experiences of the Armenians and the East Asians in Africa.

[8] Karl Marx, *Early Writings*, translated and edited by T. B. Battomore (London: C. A. Watts, 1963), p. 4.

CHAPTER 4

MARX

We have seen that Bauer demands of the Jews that they renounce their Judaism and that Christians, too, should give up their faith in order to emancipate themselves, become true citizens, and thereby enter the modern epoch. In response, Marx observes that Bauer has considered the so-called Jewish Question from only one aspect. For Marx, it was by no means sufficient to ask, who should emancipate? and who should be emancipated? because a third question of moment needed to be addressed: *What kind of emancipation are we talking about?* In Marx's critique of Bauer we see that as early as 1843, Marx was beginning to develop a theoretical position of his own, a position diverging significantly from that of the other Left Hegelians.

Marx sees it as an error on Bauer's part that he criticizes the Christian state but not the state as such. Bauer had failed to examine the relation of political emancipation to *human emancipation*. Bauer had asked the Jews why they supposed they had a right to political emancipation, that is, to citizenship in a Christian state, before they have given up their Judaism. But Marx asks the converse question: For the aim of achieving *political* emancipation, can the Jew be required to abandon Judaism, or Christians be asked to abolish their faith? Marx is thus challenging the notion that in gaining citizenship citizens should have to pay the price of giving up their religious beliefs and practices.

In Germany, Marx observes, where the many autonomous principalities are all *Christian* states, none of them is a political state in the constitutional sense in which such a state had already existed in the United States and in France. In the German states, therefore, the Jewish Question is a theological one, for the Jew finds himself in religious opposition to the state, which proclaims Christianity as its foundation. The German state is thus a theologian *ex professo*, which means that Bauer's critique is really a critique of theology—a double-edged criticism, of both Jewish and Christian theology.

In France, in contrast, which is a *constitutional* state, the Jewish Question is a constitutional question: of the *incompleteness of political emancipation*. Marx means that in France, despite the Declaration of the Rights of Man and the Code Napoleon's granting of equal rights to all citizens, the Jews were often regarded and treated as second-class citizens or even noncitizens. In France, although constitutionally there was no official state religion, the vast majority of the citizens were Christian, so there was the semblance of a state religion. Hence, the relation of the French state to the Jews also retained at the time a semblance of religious-theological opposition.

It followed, for Marx, that it was only in the free states of America that the so-called Jewish Question tended to lose its theological significance and become a truly *secular* question. It was quite evident to Marx that where freedom of religion was concerned, the political state appeared in its purest form in America, where the state ceased, constitutionally, to maintain a theological attitude toward the religion of its citizens and adopted a secular, political attitude.

Marx cites a work by Gustave Beaumont, who had visited America together with his friend Alexis de Tocqueville. On religion in America, Beaumont observed: "There is not in the United States, either a state religion or a religion declared to be that of a majority, or a predominance of one religion over another. The state remains aloof from all religions."[1] In no state of North America, Beaumont observed, does one find the imposition of a "religious belief or practice as a condition of political rights." And Marx, quoting still another important sentence of Beaumont's, says, and yet "no one in the United States believes that a man without religion can be an honest man" (9). On the authority of Beaumont, Tocqueville, and an Englishman, Thomas Hamilton, Marx observed what is still true today: "And North America is pre-eminently the country of religiosity" (9).

Marx thus used the example of America to make a significant point: "If we find in the country that has attained full political emancipation, that religion not only continues to exist, but is *fresh* and *vigorous*, this is proof that the existence of religion is not at all opposed to the perfection of the state. But since the existence of religion is the existence of a defect, the source of the defect must be sought in the nature of the state itself" (10). In Marx's argument that follows, we hear the beginnings of what he was later to call his "materialist conception of history," using the term *materialist* in a sense quite distinct from that of his predecessors. For as we have seen, it was at about this time that he exposed what he regarded as a major defect in Feuerbach's and in all previous forms of materialism—the defect being that they conceived of the human being as a primarily passive object, thus overlooking the active and creative side of human nature, which, Marx acknowledged, was discovered and highlighted by the great Idealist philosophers.

It is this new outlook that Marx expresses when he says that in pondering the relation of religion to the state, we have to recognize that religion is not the basis but the manifestation of secular narrowness. "That is why," Marx clarified,

> we explain the religious constraints upon free citizens by the secular constraints upon them. We do not claim [as does Bauer] that they must transcend this religious narrowness in order to get rid of their secular limitations. We claim that they will transcend their religious narrowness once they have overcome their secular limitations. We do not turn secular questions into theological questions; we turn theological questions into secular ones.... The question of the *relation between political emancipation and religion* becomes for us a question of the *relation between political emancipation and human emancipation*. We criticize the religious failings of the political state by criticizing the political state in its *secular* form, disregarding its religious failings. We express in human terms the contradiction between the state and a *particular religion*, for example, *Judaism*, by showing the contradiction between the state and particular *secular elements*, between the state and *religion in general* and between the state and its general presuppositions. (10)

To grasp adequately what Marx is saying here, we have to keep his example of America in mind. How does a state emancipate itself from religion? By emancipating itself from the imposition of a *state religion*; that is, by giving official recognition to *no* religion, and by affirming itself purely as a state based on constitutionally determined civil laws granting equal civil rights to all its citizens. But in anticipation of his mature social theory, Marx adds that even this high level of political liberty falls short, in his judgment, of the fuller human emancipation that he envisioned.

Already at this stage of Marx's intellectual development, he had come to believe that his vision compelled him to come to grips with the question of private property and its role in the human condition. As is well known, Marx regarded private property and, in particular, private ownership of the basic means of production, as an institution that divided humanity against itself. True human community, he supposed, required the abolition of private property and the institution of communal property in its place. In the context of his debate with Bauer over the Jewish Question, he wants therefore to expose what he regards as the limitations of the existing political state, even the most democratic and liberal. He again cites Thomas Hamilton, who reported that in several American states property qualifications for electors and representatives were abolished. Hamilton had correctly interpreted this policy from a political standpoint: The people had gained a victory over property owners and financial wealth. So Marx wants to underscore that as welcome as such widenings of political democracy are, they fall short of his ideal because what is presupposed in eliminating property qualifications is that private property will remain intact.

In his rebuttal of Bauer, then, Marx worked hard to clarify the concept of political emancipation. A secular, constitutional state, such as America's, is a higher form of state than the Christian states of the Germanies. Why? Because the American form leaves religion in existence while privileging no specific one. Still, for Marx, the liberation of the state from religion is, of course, neither the liberation of humanity from religion nor full human liberation from the prevalent class-structured form of society based on private property. So Marx says:

> We do not say to the Jews, therefore, as does Bauer, you cannot be emancipated politically without emancipating yourselves completely from Judaism. We say rather: it is because you can be emancipated politically without renouncing Judaism completely and absolutely, that *political emancipation* itself is not *human* emancipation. If you want to be politically emancipated without emancipating yourselves humanly, the inadequacy and the contradiction is not entirely in yourselves but in the *nature* and the *category* of political emancipation. (21)

In opposition to Bauer, then, and for all of Marx's positing of a communistic ideal, we need to observe that Marx fully recognized the virtues of political liberty and civil rights, and the highest form in which they expressed themselves in America. Political, liberal, and civil rights, Marx had shown Bauer, do not at all presuppose the abolition of religion. So now, to further repudiate Bauer's thesis, Marx turns his attention to "rights of man" as distinct from the "rights of the citizen." Among the "rights of man" is the freedom of conscience, the right to practice a chosen religion. The privilege of faith is expressly recognized as a fundamental liberty. Marx cites article 10 of the Declaration of the Rights of Man and of the Citizen (1791): "No one is to be disturbed on account of his opinions, even religious opinions." Guaranteed as a fundamental right is "the liberty of every man to practice the religion to which he adheres." The Declaration of 1793 not only reaffirms the liberty of religious observance but also reminds the reader, as it were, that "the necessity of enunciating these *rights* presupposes ... the recent memory of despotism." Marx then turns again to the United States, citing the Constitution of Pennsylvania, which declared that all men have received the natural right to worship the Almighty "according to the dictates of their conscience, and no one can be legally compelled to follow, establish or support against his will any religion or religious ministry" (23). The same right and freedom of conscience was guaranteed in other American states. Contra Bauer, then, whose views had never transcended the standpoint of the Christian state, Marx hammers home the point that far from proscribing religion, the highest and most democratic form of the state recognizes freedom of conscience and the privilege of faith as a natural and universal human right. One acquires this right, and others so necessary to the dignity and freedom of the individual, simply by becoming a member of civil society.

Bauer had claimed that the Jew is not only unfit to acquire equal civil rights but unfit as well to acquire the rights of man. "As long as he remains Jewish," wrote Bauer, "the limited nature which makes him a Jew must prevail over the human nature which should associate him, as a man, with other men; and it will isolate him from everyone who is not a Jew" (24). To this Marx responds effectively by noting that "liberty as a right of man [i.e., as a human right] is not founded upon the relations between man and man, but rather upon the separation of man from man. It is the right of such separation" (25).

In the remainder of Marx's rejoinder to Bauer, he proceeds to clarify why he believes that private property is a manifestation of egoism and therefore a barrier to be overcome if humans wish to achieve a higher form of community. The assurance of the basic civil and human rights found in both the American Constitution and the French Declaration of the Rights of Man, is, for Marx, essential and to be highly valued. But from the standpoint of his ideal, Marx believed that the egoistic side of the human being, as represented in the institution of private property, ensures that the only bond between citizens will remain cold, formally contractual, and self-interested.

Marx parenthetically remarks on the hypocrisy and opportunistic abridgment of certain rights and liberties during the French Revolution and afterward. He ridicules policies in which the right to certain liberties such as freedom of the press ceases to be a right as soon as it comes into conflict with the aims or interests of the "political liberators." Theoretically, in a constitutional polity, the basic rights and freedoms of the individual are the *end*, which is to be protected by the government as the *means*. So Marx disappointedly wonders "why it is in the minds of [so-called] political liberators that the relation is inverted, so that the end appears as the means and the means as the end?" (27)

The young Marx concludes his short, pithy essay by summarizing the achievements of political emancipation in the constitutional polities of his time: "Man was not liberated from religion; he received religious liberty. He was not liberated from property; he received the liberty to own property. He was not liberated from the egoism of business; he received the liberty to engage in business" (29).

THE YOUNG MARX ON RELIGION

If we now proceed to other early writings of Marx in which he presents his view of religion, we shall see how he strives to go beyond the mere criticisms of religion of his erstwhile colleagues in the Young Hegelian circle. As we cite some of his aphorisms concerning the religious experience, we shall see that although he accepts the view of religion as a symptom of self-alienation, he goes on to propose a relatively new idea, that certain definite social conditions evoke in humans the need for a religious experience.

Marx found Feuerbach's analysis of religion convincing as far as it went, but in his judgment it had not gone far enough, or rather deep enough. Feuerbach's analysis had remained on the psychological level and had ignored what Marx now regarded as key sociological questions: *Why* do people project their desires for perfection onto hypothetical beings, products of their imagination? What are the *social* conditions that prompt people to externalize their own powers and to attribute them to supernatural beings? Marx's reply to these questions was that religion is largely the consequence of *social alienation*—that, historically, humanity has been divided against itself by internal class cleavages. The domination, oppression, and exploitation of humans by humans have perpetuated the need for religion.

Now Marx knew that besides being divided by classes, the human species was divided against itself in several other ways as well—tribally, ethnically, nationally, and so on. He also knew that there had been precapitalist forms of domination that were harshly oppressive and murderous. Indeed, Hegel had described history as a "slaughter-bench." But Marx, primarily interested in the dynamic present, had already at this early stage of his intellectual development recognized certain key features of the capitalist system—as is evident from his *Economic and Philosophic Manuscripts of 1844*. Those features persuaded him that there was something especially harsh and dehumanizing about the new system that had been developing since the Industrial Revolution. Marx was quite familiar with contemporary descriptions of the conditions of the British working class. Already in the 1830s some factories in Manchester employed as many as fifteen hundred workers, who labored sixty-nine hours a week at mind-numbing, repetitive operations requiring neither skill, knowledge, nor judgment. The new capitalist-industrial division of labor suggested to Marx that the master trend of the system was the polarization of society, with a rapidly growing unskilled proletariat on the one hand, and on the other, a class of capitalist entrepreneurs into whose hands the major means of production were being concentrated. Moreover, the working conditions in the factories and the living conditions in the factory towns were regarded by observers as varied as

Charles Dickens, Alexis de Tocqueville, and Friedrich Engels as a great moral outrage.

In order, therefore, to appreciate fully why the young Marx centered attention on capitalism (he coined the term) and regarded it as the primary source in his time of an alienation that fostered the yearning for an illusory happiness, we need to remind ourselves of what capitalism meant for the industrial working class of the time.

In his famous book, *The Condition of the Working Class in England*, Friedrich Engels takes us by the hand and guides us through every major town—London, Manchester, Birmingham, and so on. Perhaps one passage will suffice to convey what urban-industrial life was like at the time:

> Every great city has one or more slums, where the working class is crowded together. True, poverty often dwells in hidden alleys close to the palaces of the rich; but, in general, a separate territory has been assigned to it, where, removed from the sight of the happier classes, it may struggle along as it can. These slums are pretty equally arranged in all the great towns of England, the worst houses in the worst quarters of the towns; usually one or two-storied cottages in long rows, perhaps with cellars used as dwellings, almost always irregularly built. These houses of three or four rooms and a kitchen form throughout England ... the general dwellings of the working-class. The streets are generally unpaved, rough, dirty, filled with vegetable and animal refuse, without sewers or gutters, but supplied with foul, stagnant pools instead. Moreover, ventilation is impeded by the bad, confused method of building of the whole quarter, and since many human beings here live crowded into a small space, the atmosphere that prevails in these working-men's quarters may readily be imagined. (59-60)

Although London was not primarily an industrial town, its slums were no less disgusting: "Heaps of garbage and ashes lie in all directions, and the foul liquids emptied before the doors gather in stinking pools. Here live the poorest of the poor, the worst paid workers with thieves and the victims of prostitution indiscriminately huddled together ... sinking daily deeper, losing daily more and more of their power to resist the demoralizing influence of want, filth, and evil surroundings."[2]

Such were the conditions that aroused in Marx a passionate repudiation of the capitalist system. He had come to believe that the historical failure of humans to recognize themselves in the imaginary divine beings they had created had now found a new hiding place. For just as the analysis of idolatry revealed the self-delusion and loss of conscious freedom of the idolator, the analysis of capitalism revealed a new form of alienation, as a sign of the loss of freedom.

All the conditions described here, and their manifold consequences, Marx writes, "are contained in the definition that the worker is related to

the *product of his labor* as an *alien* object. For on this premise it is clear
that the more the worker spends himself, the more powerful the alien objective world becomes which he creates over against himself."[3] The worker has no control over the production process or its results. His labor is an
alienating activity because the whole process is external to him and his
human needs:

> In his work, therefore, he does not affirm himself but denies himself,
> does not feel content but unhappy, does not develop freely his physical
> and mental energy but mortifies his body and ruins his mind. The
> worker therefore only feels himself outside his work, and in his work
> feels outside himself. He is at home when he is not working, and when
> he is working he is not at home. His labor is therefore not voluntary,
> but coerced; it is *forced labor*. It is therefore not the satisfaction of [an
> inner] need; it is merely a *means* to satisfy needs external to it. Its
> alien character emerges clearly in the fact that as soon as no physical
> or other compulsion exists, labor is shunned like the plague. (72)

Writing in the optative mood of the early nineteenth century, Marx
envisioned the abolition of such alienating conditions and the creation of
a higher form of human community. In that light we can more readily
grasp Marx's intention in criticizing religion. Religious criticism, he
writes, "has plucked the imaginary flowers from the chain, not in order
that man shall bear the chain without... consolation, but so that he shall
cast off the chain and pluck the living flower. The criticism of religion dis-
illusions man so that he will think, act and fashion his reality as a man
who has lost his illusions and regained his reason."[4]

NOTES

[1]Karl Marx, *Early Writings*, edited and translated by T. B. Bottomore (London:
C. A. Watts, 1963), p. 9. Hereafter, all references to this book will be cited in
parentheses immediately following the quoted passage.

[2]Friedrich Engels, *The Condition of the Working Class in England* (Moscow: Foreign Languages Publishing House, 1953), pp. 59–61.

[3]Karl Marx, *Economic and Philosophic Manuscripts of 1844* (Moscow: Foreign
Languages Publishing House, 1961), p. 70. Hereafter, all references to this work
will be cited in parentheses immediately following the quoted passage.

[4]Marx, *Early Writings*, p. 44.

CHAPTER 5

NIETZSCHE

No thinker in the history of modern philosophy, with the possible exception of Max Stirner, has launched as radical an assault upon Western values as has Friedrich Nietzsche (1844–1900). Therein lies his importance as a philosopher—in challenging the religious, moral and intellectual foundations of Western society. On the whole, his challenge may be characterized as negative and critical, in that it aims to tear down the old table of values.

The mature Nietzsche, as is well known, looked upon Christianity as a major source of the decadent and antilife outlook of the West. Although his father and grandfathers on both sides had been Lutheran ministers,[1] and although Nietzsche was the heir of a long line of Lutheran pastors reaching back to the early seventeenth century, he ceased to be a believing Christian while still in his teens. In 1862, in an essay called "Fate and History," he set down the grounds for his doubts, stating that history and science are the only reliable means of pursuing truth and knowledge.

When Nietzsche enrolled in the university in Bonn, he eventually chose to study classical philology under the tutelage of the distinguished Friedrich Ritschl, who was greatly impressed with the young man's brilliance. It was during his stay at Bonn that Nietzsche abandoned the study of theology, a discipline, he decided, that was devoted to the investigation of a primitive superstition, namely, Christianity. He now declared himself to be a "freethinker." In contrast, however, to his atheistic predecessors from the time of the Enlightenment, Nietzsche held that "freedom" meant not only throwing off a yoke but taking on a new and heavier one in its place. He had lost patience with the so-called liberal-minded unbeliever who thought he could deny the existence of a divine Lawgiver but nevertheless accept the validity of the Law handed down by human beings. Nietzsche now began to sense that insofar as God has ceased to exist for a multitude of human beings, life as such has been deprived of its traditional meaning. In such circumstances, humanity was liable to degenerate under the impact of its basic meaninglessness.

Although Nietzsche distinguished himself early as a brilliant philologist, he held a rather modest view of the importance of that subject and often even deprecated it as the study of dead books. That attitude turned him away from philology and toward philosophy. At about this time (1866), he discovered Friedrich Albert Lange's *History of Materialism*, a work that influenced him profoundly, pushing him farther in the direction of philosophical materialism. By now Nietzsche had left Bonn and followed Ritschl to Leipzig, where the young classical philologist so impressed Ritschl that he successfully recommended Nietzsche, then only twenty-four, for a vacant professorship at Basel University. The Leipzig years (1865–69) also witnessed the emergence in Nietzsche's writings of at least two notable ideas that eventually contributed to the formation of his mature views. Following an intensive study of Homer and Hesiod, and the role of the mythological "contest" in Greek culture, Nietzsche began to recognize just how central the concept of *agon*, or competition, was in the development of Greek culture.

When Nietzsche had carefully read and pondered *The Origin of Species* and *The Descent of Man*, the validity of Darwin's theory appeared to him to have been demonstrated. Nietzsche accepted the fundamentals of the Darwinian thesis, that humanity had evolved from earlier animal forms in a purely natural manner, through chance and accident. Earlier evolutionary theories had still left open the possibility of a "purpose" in evolution; but Darwin had mobilized massive evidence in support of his view that "higher" animals and humans have come into being entirely by fortuitous variations in individuals. Before Darwin had presented his convincing hypothesis, it was not too difficult to discern some directing agency in the unfolding of natural and even historical events. After Darwin, however, that became increasingly difficult. The need for a conscious, creative being seemed unnecessary, since what had formerly appeared to be order could now be explained as random change. "Natural Selection" was a natural process free of metaphysical implication. Hence, Nietzsche now denied the existence of order in the universe. "The entire character of the world," he wrote, "is ... in all eternity chaos, not in the sense of an absence of necessity, but of an absence of order, arrangement [*Gliederung*], form, beauty, wisdom, and whatever other terms there are for our aesthetic anthropomorphisms. ... Let us beware of saying that there are laws in nature. There are only necessities: there is nobody who commands, nobody who obeys, nobody who trespasses."[2] It is in this general context that we encounter the first occurrence of Nietzsche's most famous utterance: "God is dead: but given the way of humanity, his shadow will remain on the walls of caves for thousands of years. And we—we still have to conquer his shadow as well" (109).

Nietzsche's view of the world as chaotic was certainly reinforced by his reading of Darwin, and the chaotic nature of the universe remained a basic element of his philosophical outlook. The Darwinian theory complemented and confirmed a view of reality that Nietzsche had already begun to form in his youth. From the time of his reading of F. A. Lange's *History of Materialism*, Nietzsche had come to regard all metaphysical ideas as mere ideas and nothing more. There was no such thing as a supersensible reality with which humans could somehow get in touch. Darwinism implied for Nietzsche that the planet Earth was devoid of any transcendental meaning. Nietzsche thus regarded his own era as "nihilistic": all traditional values and meanings had ceased to make sense, and philosophy was in a state of crisis, faced as it was with an inherently meaningless universe.

For Nietzsche, then, there are socially constructed moralities, but no Morality. His sociological conception of moralities is similar to that of Émile Durkheim, as we shall see in a later chapter. For Nietzsche, to obey morally is to obey a certain code. Morality is convention and custom. In *Human, All Too Human* (96), for example, Nietzsche asserts that to be moral, virtuous, or ethical means, merely, to obey a long-established tradition or law. The "good" are those who follow the customs readily; the "evil," those who resist custom and tradition for whatever reason. In *Assorted Opinions and Maxims* (89), Nietzsche maintains that custom is, in essence, that which is good for the *community*. In a formulation from which Durkheim would not have dissented, Nietzsche wrote: "The origin of custom may be traced to two ideas: 'the community is worth more than the individual' and 'a long-lasting advantage is to be preferred over a fleeting one'; from which the conclusion is drawn that the long-lasting advantage of the community must take unconditional precedence over the advantage of the individual." The chief problem with such formulations is that they tend to justify whatever practices a given society engages in. This amoral or morally relative conception of things refuses to recognize transhistorical or transcultural criteria by which to evaluate the customs and political practices of a given society. And in the absence of such criteria, one is left with a moral relativism that renders one intellectually defenseless against, for example, oppressive, murderous, and genocidal tyrannies. It appears that Nietzsche never comes to grips with this danger.

By the time Nietzsche had completed his *Dawn* or *Daybreak* (1881), he appears to have got no farther than trying to show that the so-called higher qualities of humans—those for which a transcendental origin had been traditionally claimed—were simply the transformation of "lower" qualities, those that humans have in common with other members of the animal kingdom. Nietzsche now begins to speak of the "will to power," which somehow appeared to him to offer the widest scope for human development. This suggests that by the time of the *Dawn*, Nietzsche had not advanced beyond the notion that morality emerged from the desire for power and the fear of disobedience, a quasi-Hobbesian idea. His various aphorisms on the subject in the *Dawn* (e.g., 104, 112, 142, 174) are a reworking of Hobbes's proposition that the international arena is in a "state of nature," "a war of each against all," because it lacks a common power, a Leviathan.

Other statements in the *Dawn* indicate that Nietzsche did in fact hold implicit standards by which to evaluate human conduct, though he refused to call those standards moral. He again denies both morality and immorality, but then says he does not deny "that countless people *feel* themselves to be immoral, but that there is any true reason so to feel. Understandably, I do not deny—unless I am a fool—that many actions called immoral ought to be avoided and opposed, or that many actions called moral ought to be done and promoted—but I think that the former should be avoided and the latter promoted *for other reasons than hitherto*" (103). But, alas, Nietzsche not only fails to inform us which actions should be opposed and which promoted but also fails to tell us what his "other reasons than hitherto" are. Some students of Nietzsche's thought have suggested that he did in fact have "standards," but that they were *aesthetic*, rather than ethical, from which it follows that desirable and undesirable actions are for Nietzsche merely a matter of *taste*—his taste!

And, yet, there is at least one aphorism in the *Dawn* that appears to be a conspicuous departure from his general view, that reason and faith in reason ought to be rejected as a merely metaphysical idea. In aphorism 96 he urges his fellow Europeans to accomplish what was done several thousand years ago in India, "in accordance with the commandments of reason":

> There are today among the various nations of Europe perhaps ten to twenty million people who no longer "believe in God"—is it too much to demand that they should *give a sign* to one another? Once they have thus come to *recognize* one another, they will also have made themselves known to others—they will at once become a power in Europe and, happily, a power *between* the nations! Between the classes! Between rich and poor! Between rulers and subjects! Between the most unpeaceful and the most peaceful people. (96)

If we take this statement at face value, it is remarkable for what it reveals, at least at this stage of Nietzsche's thinking. It reveals that peace between the nations and classes was for Nietzsche an ideal. But as Nietzsche denies morality and immorality, how would he justify the pursuit of this ideal? Nietzsche's statement is remarkable for another reason. That he should have rested his hopes for the future of Europe on the millions of people who no longer "believe in God" strikes one as the height of naïveté. Presumably, Nietzsche was referring to the large numbers of

Europeans who attended church irregularly or not at all, who, perhaps, preferred civil marriage ceremonies to church weddings, who refrained from baptizing their children, and so on. In a word, Nietzsche made his surmise on the basis of the secular atmosphere of western Europe's urban social life. If there were, in fact, millions of such people, one need not doubt that most of them were decent individuals who would have approved of Nietzsche's ideal. But, one wonders, did Nietzsche somehow come to believe that secularism, materialism, and atheism are preconditions for the solution of social problems? As Dostoyevsky had so powerfully demonstrated in his great philosophical novels, it is quite possible for someone who has lost his faith to believe—as did, say, Raskolnikov in *Crime and Punishment*—that if God is dead, everything is permitted. The danger of such consequences of moral nihilism Nietzsche nowhere addresses. Moreover, the history of twentieth-century totalitarian regimes has also shown that the most militantly atheistic regimes were also the most genocidal.

In *The Gay Science* one finds in embryo several of Nietzsche's mature ideas: the "will to power," the "higher type" or "superman," and the "eternal recurrence." "The strongest and most evil spirits," wrote Nietzsche,

> have so far done the most to advance humanity: again and again they reignited the passions that were falling to sleep—every ordered society puts the passions to sleep—and they reawakened again and again the meaning of comparison, of contradiction, of the pleasure in what is new, daring, untried; they forced men to pit opinion against opinion, ideal against ideal. In most cases [they accomplished this] by force of arms, by destroying boundary markers, by violating pieties—but also by means of new religions and moralities. (*The Gay Science*, 4)

In *The Gay Science* we hear once again that there are only "moralities," but no Morality. Because Morality has for Nietzsche lost its transcendental origin and sanction, it can have no everlasting and universal worth. To regain such worth it must emerge as the consequence of necessity felt by those who frame it. And who are the future framers? In one of his most militantly rhetorical statements Nietzsche writes:

> I welcome all signs that a more manly, warlike age is about to dawn, which will restore honor to courage above all. Then that age will pave the way for one yet higher, and it will gather the strength that the higher age will find necessary—the age that will carry heroism into the pursuit of knowledge and that will *wage wars* for the sake of ideas and their consequences. To that end we now need many valiant human beings ... who are determined to seek in all things what must be *overcome* in them. . . . For, believe me, the secret of harvesting from existence the greatest fruitfulness and enjoyment, is to *live dangerously*. (*The Gay Science*, 283)

Walter Kaufmann and R. J. Hollingdale have sought to defend Nietzsche, arguing that his war rhetoric simply expresses the same idea he had held as a schoolboy, inspired by Heraclitus's philosophical insight, that strife is a necessary component of life and the creative process. As a result of the careful research of Kaufmann and Hollingdale, the following characteristics of Nietzsche's outlook are beyond doubt. He was neither a racist nor a German nationalist, nor an anti-Semite. On the contrary, in both his published writings and his notes he attacks anti-Semitism several times and goes out of his way to praise Jews, Judaism, and the Hebrew Bible, the so-called Old Testament. Thanks to Kaufmann's work, we now understand how the blatant distortions of Nietzsche's work came about. During the years of Nietzsche's insanity and incapacity and after his death, his sister Elizabeth became the executor of his literary estate. Together with her husband, a notorious Jew-hater named Bernhard Förster, Elizabeth "edited" and tampered with Nietzsche's writings, interpreting his "will to power" and his war rhetoric so as to make him appear as a proto-Nazi theorist. Kaufmann and Hollingdale therefore suggest that while Nietzsche's words may have been unwisely chosen, thus lending themselves to distortion, his real meaning is that the "new" philosopher of the higher type must be not only a thinker but a "warrior" as well, aggressively living his philosophy and showing the way. Nevertheless, the fact that Nietzsche's examples of "higher types" of the past are most often individuals like Alcibiades, Julius Caesar, Cesare Borgia, and Napoleon raises serious doubt that he had merely philosophers in mind.

THUS SPOKE ZARATHUSTRA

Nietzsche chose "Zarathustra"—but not the historical Zarathustra who founded Zoroastrianism—as the "higher-type" protagonist and prophet of the new philosophy with which Nietzsche wished to replace the old. Nietzsche's Zarathustra is endowed with *great health*—indeed, a new health, stronger, tougher, more audacious, and also more joyful than any previous health. As a higher type, Zarathustra sees farther and possesses greater capabilities than any other human being. In him humanity has been overcome, and the concept of a "superman" has become so superlative a reality that whatever has so far been considered great in humanity lies beneath the superman at an infinite distance. Nietzsche's protagonist is confronted by a Dionysian task, and the indispensable condition for such a task is "the hardness of the hammer, the joy even in destroying. The imperative, 'become hard!', the most fundamental certainty *that all creators are hard*, is the distinctive feature of the Dionysian nature" (*Ecce Homo*, "Thus Spoke Zarathustra," 8). Humanity is the raw material, the "stone," as it were, which Zarathustra the prophet will strive to sculpt into a higher type.

To understand the role of Dionysus in Nietzsche's outlook we need to refer to his first book, *The Birth of Tragedy*, where he proposed that the development of the Greek genius was determined by the Apollinian-Dionysian duality. This was especially true of Greek tragedy. Then Socrates entered the picture, and the older duality was undermined and replaced with a new one, the Dionysian-Socratic. Socrates' aesthetic principle held that "to be beautiful a thing must be intelligible." Art, for Socrates, was no exception to the principle that "knowledge is virtue." It was under the influence of this newer doctrine, Nietzsche maintained, that Socrates' contemporary Euripides began to measure all the separate elements of drama—language, character, choir music, structure—and to organize them according to the Socratic principle. It was this intrusion of Socratic *reason* that led, after Sophocles, to the degeneration of Greek tragedy. Dionysian passion had been crushed by Socratic reason, and the great, creative art of Greek drama was wrecked as a consequence. The powerful tendency in Nietzsche to think in dualisms suggests why he chose Zarathustra as his superprotagonist.

Among the great founders of the world religions, it was Zarathustra (Zoroaster) who had founded a dualistic religion based on the strife between the antagonistic principles of light and darkness, good and evil, Ormazd and Ahriman. It appears that the people whom the prophet addressed in ancient Iran were in transition from a nomadic or seminomadic way of life to an existence as tillers of the soil. The prophet prohibited the idolatry of the nomadic life and taught that there is a great god and master of the world, who is the creator and provider of all life on earth. He is the good god, the god of light, Ormazd. Anyone who opposes the light and the good participates in the work of Ahriman, the god of evil and darkness, and the leader of demonic forces.

Now we come to an important point in the historical Zarathustra's doctrine that might be pertinent to Nietzsche's appropriation of the name Zarathustra for his protagonist. In the momentous struggle between the two gods, Ormazd and Ahriman, humans are obliged to stand on the side of the god of light and goodness. When they sow and plant and build and bring fertility to the desert and wilderness, they thereby strengthen the powers of Ormazd over those of Ahriman. The more the people engage in such constructive activities, the more they increase the power of good over evil, light over darkness. The tillers of the soil and the herdsmen are the workers of light who expand the good in the world. However, the tent-dwelling nomads, who do nothing to fructify the earth but, on the contrary, often plunder the fruit of the peasants' toil, are those who strengthen the forces of evil. Thus Zarathustra taught that one ought to treat with affection the useful, nonpredatory, domesticated animals, especially the ox that pulls the plow and, of course, the quiet and peaceful cow that nourishes the human being with milk. To the extent, then, that human beings are productive and constructive, the spirit of Ormazd is victorious and that of Ahriman is vanquished. The final victory, however, of Good over Evil will be achieved by Ormazd himself, thus creating the kingdom of one supreme God over the world. Zarathustra's doctrine tends in that way to transcend the original dualism in favor of the total victory of goodness and light.

As we now turn to Nietzsche's protagonist, it appears that Nietzsche, too, abandoned his original duality. For, as we have seen, in *The Birth of Tragedy* he had argued that the older Apollinian-Dionysian dualism was supplanted by the Dionysian-Socratic opposition in which Dionysian passion was overwhelmed by Socratic reason with the consequence that the greatness of Greek drama was thus undermined. Clearly, Nietzsche did not look with favor upon this development, since he regarded Dionysian passion as *the* fundamental element of the creative process. And as we have seen in *Ecce Homo*, his final reflections on the nature of his protagonist, he states that Zarathustra was faced with a Dionysian task that required, above all, a *Dionysian nature*. This suggests that, like the historical Zarathustra, Nietzsche abandoned his original dualism. In his case, however, Dionysus defeats both Apollo and Socrates—that is, the deity of dark passion overpowers the forces of the sun god, and reason is no longer to be regarded as the supreme principle and standard of value. Nietzsche's Zarathustra is first and foremost Dionysian! Accordingly, in *Thus Spoke Zarathustra*, Nietzsche temporarily abandoned his aphoristic method, which, despite its shortcoming, exhibited an "Apollinian," measured thoughtfulness, and replaced it with self-styled Dionysian dithyrambs. Nietzsche, disliking the system-building of the philosophers who preceded him, employed aphorisms to avoid even the impression that he was trying to build a system. But the main shortcoming of the aphoristic method is that it leaves ideas undeveloped. However, the dithyrambs of *Zarathustra* also exhibited a shortcoming, which, as we shall see, Nietzsche himself eventually recognized.

In sum, Nietzsche aims in his *Zarathustra* to accomplish both a negative and a positive task: to topple the twin pillars of Western ethics, the Platonic and the Christian legacies, and to put in their place a new, strong, and hard philosophical foundation for life. What is the nature of Nietzsche's positive message? He speaks frequently of the now familiar death of God, and he proclaims the need for a superman. The traditional faith is lost, he repeatedly claims, so it is up to human beings themselves to give their lives meaning. How? By raising themselves above the animals and the all-too-human. What, then, is the new, "superior" meaning that Nietzsche offers us in his *Zarathustra*? That meaning, such as it is, lies in the very few "higher types" who will raise themselves above the all-too-human mass. Throughout, Nietzsche's protagonist shows nothing but contempt for the human "herd" and sees his mission in luring the few away from the herd.

Nietzsche was not entirely pleased, as I have said, with the way he had presented his "thought experiments" in *Zarathustra*. The poetic style had failed, he came to believe, to convey his ideas as clearly as he would have liked. *Beyond Good and Evil* was therefore designed to elaborate and clarify *Zarathustra*, just as *On the Genealogy of Morals*, published a year later (1887), was to perform the same service for *Beyond Good and Evil*.

BEYOND GOOD AND EVIL

Beyond Good and Evil maintains the strong Dionysian motif of *Zarathustra*, the proclamation of the will to power as the will to life, and the emphasis on the need to free the passions and instincts from the crippling influences of the old virtues. The central theme is the same as before: the old virtues have to be overcome, and that is the role and privilege of the very few who are very strong. One should shed the bad taste of wanting to agree with the multitude about the "good," and especially about the "common good," for whatever is common always has little value.

Nietzsche has no use for the modern philosophers among his contemporaries, the prolific scribbling slaves of the democratic taste who find the cause of all human misery in the social system. They foster in the herd a yearning for a green-pasture happiness, a new society offering security and comfort—a life free of risks and dangers. Catering to the masses, these democratic theorists speak incessantly of the "equality of rights"; they sympathize with all who suffer, and they dangle before the people the promise of abolishing all misery. All such doctrines are simply a translation of Christian eschatology into secular terms, with the consequent weakening of the human will to life. For the Christian faith was, from the start, a denial of the freedom, pride, and self-confidence of the human spirit. Like all religious neuroses, it has made dangerous and debilitating, antilife demands—fasting, sexual abstinence, and other forms of self-denial. Christianity broke the strong and healthy by casting suspicion on the joy in beauty, and by devaluing the haughty, manly, conquering, and domineering qualities of the human being—all the qualities and instincts of the highest type of man. The church has inverted these old noble values and has put in their place a suspicion and a hatred of the healthy human passions.

The will to power and life in the healthy and strong "higher type" presupposes that one's drives and passions are given free play, so that a man's sexuality reaches up into the heights of his spirit. The real test of a man's maturity therefore consists in finding again the seriousness one had as a child at play. It is in music, above all the arts, that the passions and emotions enjoy themselves. The big mistake of the past, which continues to plague the present, is to look at the joy of the passions from a sickly moral standpoint. It is time to gain the courage to proclaim that the so-called evil passions are what is best in us.

Together with this salient Dionysian motif one finds a corresponding deprecation of reason. When philosophers claim to provide a "rational foundation for morality," they fail to recognize that what they have actually given us is merely a sophisticated version of the common faith in the prevalent morality. Nietzsche rejects all metaphysics—all standpoints outside of the Earth—and he regards reason as just another metaphysic. For him, philosophy still confronts the age-old problem of instinct versus reason. In the evaluation of things, he asks, which deserves more authority, instinct or rationality? And, of course, he favors Dionysus over Socrates.

In praising the instincts and demanding they be given free play, and in rejecting both reason and morality as means of guiding the instincts, it is certain that Nietzsche does not mean the instincts should be left entirely uncontrolled. It is certain because while he wants to liberate the instincts he also speaks of "self-mastery" as the highest ideal. So if, for Nietzsche, it is neither reason nor morality that must guide the instincts, what element of the psyche must fulfill that function? That element is, most likely, what Nietzsche would call the Apollinian faculty of the psyche—an *aesthetic* faculty enabling us to distinguish between balance, harmony, and beauty, and their opposites. The implication is clear: If the Apollinian faculty is to be the sole regulator of the will to power and life, then whether it is "properly" regulated is, for Nietzsche, strictly a matter of *taste*. As a philosopher, he thus writes from an aesthetic point of view, which he conceives as beyond good and evil. Aesthetics, apparently, is to replace ethics!?

Nietzsche was aware of his provocative use of "herd" and "herd *instinct*," but he held that these were appropriate epithets with which to express his view: What European morality calls "good" is nothing other than the instinct of the herd animal in man, which has prevailed over other instincts. Prior to the emergence of this morality, Nietzsche proposes an older, higher morality was predominant, namely, the noble "master morality" that already in antiquity had been inverted and fused with an emerging "slave morality." To understand how this inversion occurred, we have to wait for *On the Genealogy of Morals*, where Nietzsche for the first time presents his thesis coherently. Since Nietzsche believed a "higher" morality had once held sway, it might be possible, he assumed, to reestablish a noble morality *after* the herd morality has been extinguished once and for all. The task would be far from easy, however, in the face of the huge stumbling blocks standing in the way—Christianity and its direct heir, the democratic movement.

For Nietzsche, democracy is not only a decadent political movement but a pronounced diminution of human beings, lowering their value and turning them into mediocrities. New philosophers must therefore arise who are sufficiently strong and original to begin the process of reinverting the herd-values and re-creating the higher values opposed to the herd. The new, genuine philosophers, writes Nietzsche, are to be "*commanders and legislators*: they say, 'thus it *shall* be!' They first determine the Wither and For What of Man, and then make use of the preliminary work of all philosophical laborers, all who have overcome the past. Reaching for the future with a creative hand, everything that is and has been becomes for them an instrument, a hammer. Their 'knowing' is creating, their creating is a giving of laws, their will to truth is—a will to power" (211). In such passages one hears a loud authoritarian chord. If Nietzsche's "new" philosophers are to be "commanders and legislators," then his vision is quite similar to that of Plato in the *Republic*, whose philosophers were to hold a monopoly of political power. Plato's Philosopher-Guardians were to be a ruling class or ruling elite in the full sense, since Plato gave them a monopolistic control over the major means of political administration and means of violence. In contrast, the largest class, the vast majority of the populace in Plato's scheme—the producers or farmers—were assigned no political role whatsoever. Since Nietzsche shares Plato's strong antipathy for democracy, we may reasonably infer that when Nietzsche speaks of genuine philosophers as commanders whose will to truth is a will to *power*, he, too, envisions his "higher-type" philosophers as kings who, like Plato's Guardians, will also possess the physical means of realizing their will against the resistance of the populace.

That Nietzsche's conception of the will to power implies domination is also borne out by the contrast he draws between the old philosophers and the new, genuine ones whom he envisions: In the past the task of philosophers amounted to little more than being the bad conscience of their time, but the genuine philosophers of the future will embody such greatness that they will be "beyond good and evil" (212). Even Walter Kaufmann, who normally defends Nietzsche, interpreting his rhetoric generously, comments that "the element of snobbery and the infatuation with 'dominating' and 'looking down' are perhaps more obvious than Nietzsche's perpetual sublimation and spiritualization of these and other similar qualities."[3] It is rather doubtful, however, that Nietzsche's theory can be interpreted as "spiritual," if by that is meant that it has no political implications. As Nietzsche perceived Europe's "herd" religion at the time, it was experiencing a profound crisis, which, he believed, opened the possibility of supplanting it eventually with a new, philosophico-religious movement based on his conception of the "master morality."

It is true that Nietzsche viewed the prevailing morality as a form of spiritual revenge against the powerful masters. The moral judgments of the "herd" are malice spiritualized. This is the central idea of his *Genealogy*, to be considered in the next section. But it is also true that

Nietzsche sees an order of rank among individuals: The higher and rarer types should command while the lower ranks obey. That is why he rejects political equality; for it is immoral, he says, to suppose that what is right for the one is also right for the other. Europe, he asserts more than once, has been plunged into a semibarbarism by the democratic mingling of classes and peoples.

Nietzsche never shows any sign of trying to examine the merits of democracy objectively. Typically, his aphorisms are mere assertions unaccompanied by any explanation. A glaring example is provided by his utterances concerning women. Nietzsche sees a fundamental antagonism between the sexes, an eternally hostile tension. One must think about women, he says, as the Orientals do, as property that can be locked up and as creatures predestined for service. Thinkers who advocate equal rights, equal education, and equal obligations for women are therefore too shallow to serve as the higher philosophers of the future era. In no age, Nietzsche continues, have women been accorded as much respect by men as in the present democratic age, which proves that the notion of emancipating women is yet another product of the dominant herd mentality. The first and last profession of women is to give birth to strong children (231–39).

It needs to be underscored again that Nietzsche rather immodestly conceived of his aristocratic philosophy as the central element of what he envisioned as a new, post-herd religion and morality. Aristocracy, for Nietzsche, has always embodied what is noble in man, and would do so again in the future. The aristocratic societies have brought out the best in man because they believed in an order of rank and in differences of value between one man and another, and because they also believed in the necessity of slavery in one form or another. One must not have illusions about aristocratic societies and the nature of the men who constituted them: They were barbarians in the terrible sense of the term, predators who possessed an enormous strength of will and an insatiable lust for power, and who threw themselves upon weaker, more civilized and peaceful peoples. In the early periods of history, the noble caste was always the barbarian caste whose predominance rested not only on their physical strength and prowess but also on their definition of themselves as the "good." The chief feature of a healthy aristocracy is that it experiences itself as fully justified to rule and dominate. It therefore accepts with a good conscience "the sacrifice of an untold number of human beings who, *for its sake*, must be lowered and turned into incomplete human beings, into slaves and instruments. Their [the aristocrats'] basic faith has to be that society exists not for its own sake but only as the foundation and scaffolding on which a select type of being is able to raise itself to its higher task and, in general, to a higher state of being" (258).

Among aristocrats—that is, higher men who are similar in strength and in value standards—it may be good manners to refrain mutually from injury, violence, and exploitation; but as soon as such manners are extended to the society as a whole, thus becoming its fundamental moral principle, they result in a denial of life and in deterioration and decay. Exploitation, injury, and violence are not manifestations of imperfect, corrupt, or primitive societies; they are the essence of anything that lives—consequences of the will to power, which is, after all, the will to life. And to understand the will to life realistically, one must resist sentimentality and weakness: Life is, in its essence, the appropriation, injury, and overpowering of what is "alien" and weaker.

Beyond Good and Evil is the work in which Nietzsche had first introduced his now famous terms *master morality* and *slave morality*, which he explicates more fully in his *Genealogy*. These key terms are what Max Weber called *ideal types*. Nietzsche employs these conceptual constructs to explain how the ideas of "good," "bad," and "evil" had first emerged—to explain the origins of Western morality. In what is undoubtedly his major contribution to our understanding of such origins, he proposes that the moral distinction of values first appeared in both the dominant and dominated groups. When the ruling group determined what is "good," the term referred to its own exalted status, to its superiority over the servile, lower orders who were despised. In the "master morality," the opposition of "good" and "bad" meant roughly the same as "noble" and "contemptible," respectively. The dominant, noble man who is, above all, a courageous man of war, feels contempt for the dominated and servile because they are, in his view, fearful and cowardly, allowing themselves to be maltreated. The noble type of man experiences himself as the creator of values who needs only his own approval and that of his peers. From the standpoint of the dominated, however, the nobles—especially those who ride roughshod over the poor and weak and fail to exhibit the qualities associated with noblesse oblige—are soon perceived as "evil."

The noble virtues of strength, courage, and hardness emerge of necessity from the life circumstances of the masters who have to stick together if they want to prevail. They must stay united or run the risk of being destroyed either by hostile neighbors or by their own oppressed masses. Experience teaches the noble warrior caste to which qualities it owes its success and triumphs, and it is those qualities that are cultivated and called virtues. The noble soul is, above all, egoistic, holding the conviction that he and his peers are superior, and that those other beings, inferior by nature, must subordinate and sacrifice themselves. Nietzsche, of course, favors and admires the master morality whose noble qualities he hopes to see in the "higher men" of the future. In that regard, Nietzsche speaks of the "problem of those who are waiting" and says, "Strokes of luck and much that is incalculable are necessary if a higher man, in whom the solution of a problem lies dormant, is to get around to action in time" (274). So the coming of the "higher man" is a matter of luck, and Nietzsche's expectation of such an event turns out to be an act of faith.

ON THE GENEALOGY OF MORALS

Nietzsche described *Beyond Good and Evil* as a clarification of *Zarathustra*, and *On the Genealogy of Morals* as performing the same task for *Beyond Good and Evil*. It is in the *Genealogy* that we find the most coherent and lucid account of Nietzsche's theory of ethics and morality. The *Genealogy* is a brilliant and original work in which Nietzsche most convincingly employs social psychology, philosophy, and classical philology to trace Western values to their roots.

The basic question addressed in the *Genealogy* is where and how the Western concepts of good and evil had originated. The method Nietzsche employs is historical-sociological, in that he addresses this question: What were the social conditions in which human beings first formed value judgments of good and evil? It is clear, as we shall see in due course, that for Nietzsche the social origin of the values "good" and "evil" has definite implications for the validity of those values. Nietzsche's criterion for assessing the value of "values" is whether they further or hinder the will to power and life. So his first task is to analyze the social circumstances in which Western values emerged and developed. And, of course, in providing such an analysis Nietzsche intends to call into question the transcendent validity of what he has contemptuously dubbed the "slave morality."

Nietzsche begins with the question of what the concept of "good" had meant originally. The judgment "good," as we have seen, originated not with those to whom actions were done but, on the contrary, with the good themselves, with the noble, powerful, high-stationed, and high-minded who looked upon themselves and their actions as good in contradistinction to the low, common, and plebeian. It was the experience of the feeling of the nobility, as the dominant and higher ruling order in relation to a lower order, that first gave rise to the antithesis "good" and "bad." In ancient Greece, for example, the nobility as a class was designated by such phrases as "the good" (*agathoi*), "the best men" (*aristoi beltistoi*), "the great and the good" (*kaloi kagathoi*), and the like.

It follows from the noble origin of the concept "good" that originally it had nothing to do with unegoistic actions. When, then, did "good" and "unegoistic" become linked? Only with the decline of the nobility. For Nietzsche, a historical analysis therefore makes it plain that "noble" or "aristocratic," in the social sense, was the basic source from which "good," in the sense of possessing a soul of a higher order, had developed. This process, from the nobility's point of view, also accounts for how "common," "plebeian," and "low" were transformed into the concept "bad." From Nietzsche's philological studies he gained the insight that although the Greek nobles most often designated themselves by their superiority in power, they also called themselves "the truthful." That is how they were described by the Megarian poet Theognis, who wrote in the sixth century B.C.E. The root of the Greek word for this, *esthlos*, denotes one who possesses reality, one who is actual or true. This is then given a subjective turn so that it is exclusively the nobleman who tells the truth in contrast to the common man who lies—perhaps out of fear of telling his master what he really thinks of him.

When, however, the highest stratum in society is the priestly caste, the concept denoting political superiority carries with it the connotation of the superiority of soul. The "pure" and "impure" enter the picture as designations of social station. But "pure" from the outset merely referred to those who washed themselves, who forbade and avoided certain foods that caused skin and other ailments, who did not sleep with women of the lower strata, and so on. Although the priests as a caste may have roots in the noble strata, the priestly mode of evaluation can develop into the antithesis of aristocratic values, which becomes more likely when the priests and noble warriors stand in zealous opposition to one another and refuse to compromise. The knightly noble values presupposed great health and a powerful physicality required for war, plundering expeditions, hunting, and anything else that entailed vigorous, adventurous, and joyful activity. The priestly noble mode of evaluation, owing to the specialization of the priests in "sacred" functions, soon turns in another direction. As a caste, they lose their physical prowess and war skills, becoming relatively weak and even powerless. Priests, for Nietzsche, are the most bitter enemies of anyone whom they oppose, and it is precisely because of their impotence that their hatred and vengefulness reach monstrous proportions. Nietzsche calls the Jews a priestly people par excellence and describes in the most dramatic terms the historical role of the Jews in inverting the noble values:

> All that has been done on earth against "the noble," "the powerful," "the masters," "the rulers," is not even worth talking about when compared with what the *Jews* have done against them. The Jews, that priestly people, who in opposing their enemies and conquerors gained satisfaction only through a radical revaluation of their enemies' values, that is to say, through an act of the *most spiritual revenge*. . . . It was the Jews who, with awe-inspiring consistency, dared to invert the aristocratic value-equation (good = noble = powerful = beautiful = happy = beloved of God) and to cling to this inversion with their teeth, the teeth of the most abysmal hatred (the hatred due to impotence), establishing the principle that "the wretched alone are the good; the poor, powerless, lowly alone are the good; the suffering,

deprived, sick, ugly, alone are pious, alone are blessed by God—
blessedness is for them alone; and you, the powerful and noble, are, on
the contrary, the evil, the cruel, the lustful, the insatiable, the godless
to all eternity; and you shall be for all eternity the unblessed, ac-
cursed, and damned!"... With regard to the tremendous and immea-
surably fateful initiative which the Jews have taken, through this
most far-reaching of all declarations of war, I recall the proposition I
arrived at on an earlier occasion (*Beyond Good and Evil*, 195)—that
the slave revolt in morality begins with the Jews, a revolt which has a
two-thousand-year history behind it and which is no longer so obvious
because it has been victorious. (*Genealogy*, I, 7)

How, according to Nietzsche, does the slave revolt in morality give
birth to countervalues? It does so through *ressentiment*, a psychological
process by which the weak, unable to react against the strong in the form
of deeds, compensate themselves with a spiritual revenge. Ressentiment
entails a negation and repudiation of the masters' values, a saying of No!,
which eventually becomes the creative act of inverting those values and
substituting new values for them. The new values arise out of opposition
to a hostile, oppressive, external world.

In the morality of ressentiment the "good man" of the other morality, that is, the noble, powerful man or ruler, is transformed into the source
of *evil*. Nietzsche acknowledges that from the standpoint of the weak and
oppressed, who know the noble and powerful only as enemies, there is
good reason to regard them as evil. Nietzsche also observes that mutual
respect, suspicion, and jealousy hold the noble warriors in check in their
relations with one another, but not in relation to outsiders. Against
strangers and enemies, including their servile subjects, the "good" and
the "noble" become enraged beasts of prey who find their feats of murder,
arson, rape, and torture exhilarating, and who take pride in the new material they thus provide for the poet's song and praise. Nietzsche compares the attitude of the men of ressentiment to that of lambs who dislike
great birds of prey, and who call them evil and themselves, good. The
"lambs" are the majority, the weak and the oppressed of every kind, clad
in the ostentatious garb of virtue, as if their weakness were willed and
chosen and as if weakness were meritorious.

For Nietzsche, humanity has been engaged in a fearful struggle for
thousands of years, a struggle between two opposing value systems: "good
and bad" versus "good and evil." From the time of the Roman Empire the
symbol of this struggle has been "Rome against Judea, Judea against
Rome"; and no event has been more significant than this deadly con-
frontation. Rome looked upon the Jew as a dangerous antipode, and
rightly so, says Nietzsche, "provided one has a right to regard the future
salvation of the human race as contingent upon the unconditional domi-
nance of aristocratic values, Roman values" (*Genealogy*, 16). It is such

passages that suggest an interpretation quite different from those scholars who maintain that Nietzsche's conceptions of the "will to power" and "higher specimens" refer primarily to artists, poets, and philosophers. If Nietzsche links the salvation of the human race to a reaffirmation of Roman values, and if he regards such values as "beyond good and evil," then he does, apparently, espouse the doctrine "might is right." The Romans, says Nietzsche, were the mighty and noble, and "nobody mightier and nobler has yet existed on earth or even been dreamed of" (*Genealogy*, 16).

Power and might, then, do appear to be the paramount values which Nietzsche admires and which the ressentiment of the Jews, that people of "unequaled popular moral genius," has negated and inverted. Which of these, Nietzsche asks, Rome or Judea, has won for the present? The answer for him is beyond doubt. Consider, he says, to whom one bows down in Rome itself, and not only in Rome but in over half the earth. Nietzsche understood that in a sense Judaism, from the time of the Hebrews' enslavement in Egypt, had developed as a negation and inversion of oppressors' ideals; and that Jesus' repudiation of force and violence in Matthew 5:38ff. may also be understood in that light: as a continuation and accentuation of the inversion process—a rejection of Roman (i.e., pagan) ideals of war, power, might, and domination. Thus three Jews, says Nietzsche, Jesus, Peter, and Paul, proclaimed the countervalues that led to the victory of Judea over Rome.

But Nietzsche is contemptuous of the New Testament, the texts of which embody the most extreme form of the "slave morality." And, interestingly, he admires the Old Testament, for though it is largely the product of a slave revolt in morals, it has nevertheless preserved noble elements: "great human beings, a heroic landscape," "the incomparable naiveté of the strong heart," and "people, things and speeches in an incomparably grand style" (*Beyond Good and Evil*, 52). In contrast, Nietzsche says:

> I do not like the "*New Testament*," as should be plain. I find it almost disturbing that in my taste concerning this most highly esteemed and over-rated work, I should stand alone. (The taste of two millennia is against me.) But it can't be helped! "Here I stand, I cannot do otherwise." I have the courage of my bad taste. The *Old* Testament, that is something different: all honor to the Old Testament! There I find great human beings, a heroic landscape, and something that is rarest in the world, the incomparable naiveté of the *strong heart*; furthermore, I find a people. In the New one, in contrast, I find nothing but petty sectarianism, mere rococo of the soul, mere tortuous phrases, nooks, queer things, the air of the conventicle, not to forget an occasional whiff of bucolic sweetness, which belongs to the epoch (*and* to the Roman province) and which is not so much Jewish as Hellenistic. (*Genealogy*, II, 22)

Let us note how often *taste* is mentioned and stressed. We must, then, take Nietzsche at his word. It is a matter of taste, an aesthetic criterion, that has determined his attitude toward the two testaments.

Guilt, Bad Conscience, and Ascetic Ideals

The second essay in the *Genealogy* is concerned with the social origin of guilt and the bad conscience; and in the third essay Nietzsche proposes that asceticism is part and parcel of that belief in nothingness ("God") that has produced the antilife phenomena of guilt and bad conscience.

The ascetic ideal, says Nietzsche, has infected every area and has created a sick animal—the sickest of animals. The sick represent the greatest danger to the healthy. It is the sick, those who are failures from the start, the weak and the inferior, who undermine life. And yet they presume to monopolize virtue, employing a variety of devious ways by which to tyrannize over the healthy. The sickly are the unfortunate men of ressentiment: physically and mentally defective, they seek revenge against the fortunate and strong. They have poisoned the consciences of the fortunate with their own misery. They want the fortunate, higher specimens to be ashamed of their good fortune and to consider it disgraceful to be fortunate in the face of so much misery. Proclaiming once again his aristocratic doctrine, Nietzsche declares: Away with this "inverted world"! He urges the higher types to grasp their task rightly: They must not allow themselves to be degraded to the status of an instrument of the inferior. The higher and the lower ought to be eternally separate. It is the higher whose right to exist is a thousand times greater, for they are the warranty of the future (*Genealogy*, III, 14).

For Nietzsche, guilt, the bad conscience, and the overarching ascetic ideal are primarily the product of Christian morality. Far from having improved humanity, Christian "medications" have merely tamed, emasculated, and discouraged humanity, thus actually harming it. The ascetic priest has ruined humanity's health wherever he has come to power. This is the context in which Nietzsche coolly declares, "I do not like the 'New Testament'....Why? Precisely because it is permeated throughout by the values of the ascetic ideal. It lacks any trace of good breeding, as is evident in the fuss those pious little men make over petty vices" (*Genealogy*, III, 22). Under Christian influence, asceticism has even penetrated ostensibly secular enterprises like science. Scientists and scholars are far from being free spirits. Actually, Nietzsche asserts, they are metaphysicians, for they still have faith in truth. Science rests on a metaphysical value, the absolute value of truth.

Here as elsewhere in his remarks on science, Nietzsche is among the first to have made an original observation: that there is no such thing as a presuppositionless science. Science is only a *means*, and therefore presupposes certain values that give it direction. It is a metaphysical faith that underlies the value we place on science, a faith that goes back millennia to the Christian doctrine that God is truth, and beyond that to the Greeks who believed that truth is divine. Philosophers, both ancient and modern, Nietzsche avers, have been oblivious to the fact that science itself requires justification. Philosophy's failure in this regard came about because it was dominated by the ascetic ideal, because truth was posited as the highest form of being (as in Plato) or as God (as in Christianity). In a word, the failure came about because truth was not allowed to become a problem (*Genealogy*, III, 24). The will to truth requires a critique, and the value of truth must be experimentally called into question; for once the God of the ascetic ideal is denied, a new problem inevitably arises, the value of truth. Nietzsche thus advances the fundamental insight that science itself never creates values but, on the contrary, requires a value-creating power in the service of which it can be justified. (Max Weber, as we shall see, accepted the validity of this insight.)

It is not science but *art* that for Nietzsche is fundamentally opposed to the ascetic ideal. For it is in art that the biologically rooted, creative impulses express themselves most freely. Reflecting on the various epochs of history, Nietzsche speaks with disdain of those ages in which learned, ascetic mandarins stepped into the foreground. In such ages the emotions grow cool, dialectics replaces instinct, seriousness is imprinted on faces and gestures, and life is impoverished. "The predominance of mandarins," he writes, "never signifies anything good; nor do the rise of democracy, international peace courts in place of war, equal rights for women, the religion of pity, and whatever other symptoms of declining life there are" (*Genealogy*, III, 25). There are Nietzsche scholars, as we observed earlier, who strive to save Nietzsche from himself by arguing that his war rhetoric and his admiration for noble-warrior values should be taken not literally but in the sublimated, creative, artistic sense. But is there any really good reason to deny that he had intended such passages to be taken literally? Nietzsche's utterances, taken as a whole, strongly suggest that as a nineteenth-century man, he held the view of war as a glorious event, an opportunity to reinvigorate the instincts and to breathe new life into the values of the "master morality." If he had lived to witness the horrors of the twentieth century, he might, perhaps, have thought and written differently.

THE ANTI-CHRIST

In this work Nietzsche analyzes the New Testament in considerable detail, explaining more clearly than in any of his previous writings the reason for his anti-Christian attitude. In an earlier work, *Twilight of the Idols*, Nietzsche explained the reason for his ill will toward the "morality-and-ideal swindle" of the Socratic schools. Nietzsche despises Platonism because it represents the *décadence* (he always uses the French word) of the Greek instinct. For Nietzsche, the leading Athenian intellectual of the time was neither Socrates nor Plato but Thucydides, who never deceived either himself or others in dealing with reality. Platonism, in contrast, shares the fundamental defect of the Christian world of ideas—cowardice when confronted with reality and the consequent flight into the Ideal. In order to understand Nietzsche's standpoint in his bitter "higher criticism" of the New Testament, we need to summarize his critique rather carefully.

For Nietzsche, the word *Christianity* is misleading because there was in reality only one Christian, and he died on the cross. It is false and hypocritical to posit faith in redemption through Christ as the distinguishing feature of a Christian, since only those who, in *practice*, live a life such as the one Jesus had lived deserve to be called Christians. Being Christian is not merely a matter of belief or a state of mind; it is a matter of doing and *not* doing certain things. Have there been any true Christians during the past two millennia? How could there have been, when the church has always spoken of *faith* and has presented to its adherents a world of ideas containing nothing that so much as touches upon *reality*? Christ lived and died in an exemplary way as a demonstration of his teaching. His disciples, however, transformed his death into an affair requiring "retribution," "punishment," "revenge," and "judgment"—products of a bitter ressentiment.

Nietzsche proposes that it was primarily Paul who was responsible for beginning the transformation. With Paul, the real meaning of Jesus' exemplary life and death was totally obliterated and replaced with a "horrible paganism" in which God gave his son, an innocent man, for the sins of the guilty. Neither the reality nor the historical truth became the foundation of the new religion, but rather a falsified history in which the entire Old Testament drama of Israel was interpreted as the prehistory of Christianity. Paul shifted the meaning of Christ's life and death from the real world to the beyond—to the *"lie of the 'resurrected' Jesus"* (sec. 42). By thus ignoring the redeemer's *life*, Paul made of his hallucination on the road to Damascus the "proof" that the redeemer was still alive. Nietzsche even doubts that Paul had such a hallucination and suspects that in his "priestly" quest for power, Paul simply devised new teachings as a means of creating a spiritual tyranny over the masses.

The original and actual meaning of Jesus' life was thus shifted away from life and into the "beyond," into nothingness. This was accomplished by means of a big lie of personal immortality, a doctrine contrary to reason, opposing all the instincts *for* life. Life after death became the "meaning" of life. Christianity thus owed its victory to the doctrine of the immortal soul, in which everyone is equal to everyone else, and in which the salvation of every single individual may claim to be of everlasting moment. In thus appealing to egoism and personal vanity, Christianity was able to win over to its side the underprivileged and rebellious-minded masses who wanted to believe that the "world revolves around *me*" (sec. 43). This is the source of that poisonous "democratic" doctrine of equal rights for all. From the time of Paul, Christianity has waged a war against the social distances between man and man, thus forging out of the ressentiment of the masses its chief weapon against everything noble, joyful, and high-spirited on earth, against happiness in the one and only world that exists. The Christian doctrine of the "equality of souls" is ultimately responsible for the modern, sickly state of affairs in which no one any longer has the courage to claim special privileges or the right to rule. The aristocratic outlook (the "master morality") has been permanently undermined by the Christian revolt against everything elevated. The gospel of the humble and lowly, says Nietzsche, makes everyone low.

Nietzsche detests the Gospels for their pretense of holiness. They say, "Judge not!" but they send to hell everything that stands in their way. In glorifying God, they actually glorify themselves. They have appropriated "morality" as a means of seducing mankind and leading it by the nose. What poses as humility is in reality the arrogance and megalomania of the self-chosen *Electi*, the so-called good and just who are on the side of "truth" and who relegate everyone else to the other side. Nietzsche provides numerous examples of the vengeful inversion of noble values that one finds in the Gospels and in Paul's letters.

In Nietzsche's view, then, there are in the New Testament only "bad," that is, contemptible traits. Everything in it is cowardice and self-deception in the face of life. When given opponents like Paul and the Gospel authors, the Scribes and Pharisees gain advantage. Hated in such an intense and indecent fashion, they must have been worth something. Why were they hated? Was it for their hypocrisy? No, says Nietzsche, it was their privileged status that evoked so intense a reaction. The "first Christians" were rebels against everything privileged.

For Nietzsche, of course, there is no God in history, in nature, or above nature. His primary aim in *The Anti-Christ*, therefore, is not to deny the existence of God but to propose that the Christian conception of God is a harmful illusion, a "crime against life." And if the existence of such a God were proved to exist, he would believe in him even less. "God," as Paul created him, is a denial of God, since his doctrine of faith gave birth to a religion that at no point comes in contact with actuality. All the concepts associated with Faith—sin, guilt, punishment, grace, forgiveness, redemption—are lies that were created to destroy the real, causal sense in human beings. The church has inculcated an idée fixe that turns humans into weak and sickly creatures who fear their own bodies and combat instinctual health as a satanic temptation.

All priestly power structures, Nietzsche avers, foster the "holy lie" that the priest is the only reliable authority for what is right and what is wrong. Nietzsche cites the Law-Book of Manu as a breath of fresh air, as fundamentally different from any sort of Bible, in that the laws are the means "by which the noble orders, the philosophers and the warriors, keep the multitude under control; noble values everywhere, a feeling of perfection, an affirmation of life, a triumphant feeling of well-being in oneself and towards life—the *sun* shines on the entire book" (sec. 56).

We will notice in this passage that it is the philosophers and warriors who keep the multitude under control. This bears a remarkable resemblance to Plato's scheme in the *Republic*, except that Plato's philosopher-kings do not share in the full affirmation of life, since Plato deprives them of both family and property and subjects them to an extremely ascetic way of life. Yet despite Nietzsche's detestation of Plato, Nietzsche nevertheless adopts a similar three-class system, claiming that such a system is inherent and natural in any healthy human society. Nature, he says, separates from one another the predominantly spiritual, muscular, and mediocre types, the last being the majority and the first, the ruling elite. As is the case in Plato's *Republic*, Nietzsche's highest caste also consists of the very few. And lo and behold, as Nietzsche proceeds to describe his highest, spiritual caste, he, too, subjects them to severe "self-constraint": with them "asceticism becomes nature, need, instinct" (sec. 57). They rule because of who they are, and their pursuit of knowledge is itself a form of asceticism. The second caste consists of the noble warriors who are the guardians of law and order. Finally, there is the vast majority of the populace, those who engage in agriculture, crafts, and trade, and who are in no way capable of anything other than mediocrity in ability and desires. This three-class scheme is therefore virtually identical to that in Plato's *Republic*.

Nietzsche asserts that the order of rank and castes he has prescribed follows the supreme law of nature and life itself. The separation of ranks is necessary not only for the preservation of society but also for enabling higher and higher types to emerge. "Inequality of rights," he declares, "is a precondition for the general existence of rights" (sec. 57). Nietzsche, going farther, asserts that specialization is for the mediocre a natural instinct, bringing them a kind of happiness that comes from serving as a cog and fulfilling a single function. Nietzsche apparently had failed to recognize that his entire scheme rests on specialization: the spiritual elite specializes in knowledge, the second class in war, and the third in economic tasks. Plato, however, allowed for the gifted from the third class to rise into the first and second; whereas Nietzsche says nothing about the real and high probability that some of those who possess the greatest promise of becoming "higher types" in the respective human endeavors and arts find themselves precisely in the third class consisting of the vast majority of the populace. Nietzsche's antidemocratic bias blinded him to the "higher-type" promise of individuals in the populace who, by means of education in an open, democratic society, realize their promise. In his diatribes against the "herd," the "mob," and the "demos," Nietzsche also failed to see that there is no good reason to believe that the one or the few, when they are in power, are always wiser and better than the many. That, he should have recognized, is the ultimate reason for democracy, and the reason for its superiority to other political systems—even for Nietzsche's own aim of bringing "higher types" to the fore.

For Nietzsche, as we have seen, there are no transcendent ethical and moral principles. Since God is dead or there is no God, the Bible may no longer be regarded as the source of such revealed principles. As for "reason," it is an illusion originally fostered by Plato's Socrates, that through reason and dialogue we can not only know reality but also improve it in accordance with fundamental truths. Thought, for Nietzsche, can no longer pretend to operate in the realm of truth and validity claims. Nietzsche thus leaves us with his own peculiar, beyond-good-and-evil aestheticism, which enthrones *taste* as the sole means of arbitrating between values. His aristocratic, politicized aestheticism seems to have prevented him from considering the likelihood that his yearning for "higher specimens" and his contempt for the "herd" were simply manifestations of his snobbish prejudices.

NOTES

[1] For biographical details I rely on R. J. Hollingdale's superb study, *Nietzsche: The Man and His Philosophy* (Baton Rouge: Louisiana State University Press, 1965).

[2] Friedrich Nietzsche, *The Gay Science*, aphorism 109 (New York: Vintage Books, 1974). Throughout, numbers in parentheses refer to aphorisms, not pages.

[3] Friedrich Nietzsche, *Beyond Good and Evil*, translated with commentary by Walter Kaufmann (New York: Vintage Books, 1966), p. 140 n. 37. My discussion of Nietzsche's other writings is based on Friedrich Nietzsche, *Sämtliche Werke, Kritische Studienausgabe in 15 Banden*, (Complete Works, Critical Edition in 15 Volumes) edited by Giorgio Colli and Mazzino Martinari (Berlin: Deutscher Taschenbuch Verlag/Walter de Gruyter, 1988).

CHAPTER 6

MAX WEBER

We learn from Marianne Weber's biography of her husband that it was in 1903 that he began writing his most famous work up to that time, *The Protestant Ethic and the Spirit of Capitalism*, and that he had completed the first part before beginning his travels in the United States in the summer of 1904. A year later he completed the second part, which reveals the influence of his American experience.

In order to gain an adequate grasp of Weber's aim in this classic study, we need to understand the distinctive method he employed. In German it is called *Verstehensoziologie*, which may be translated as "interpretive sociology." The central aim of this method is to grasp the meanings that the individual actors themselves attribute to their actions. Weber strives to understand individuals as they understand themselves. However, an equally essential element of this approach is a concern with the causes and consequences of actions that were motivated by the self-understandings of the individuals concerned. In Weber's classic study an application of this method meant that he had to examine the religious and moral values of the "carriers" of the Protestant ethic, as well as the consequences of the actions motivated by that ethic. Weber also applies this method in his studies of the world religions—the religions of China, India, and ancient Israel.

Throughout Weber's studies of the world religions, as we shall see, he strives to convey adequately the intrinsic theory and practice of each religion. Weber, however, is interested not only in the religions themselves but also in their relevance for other social institutions. Indeed, he is interested in the historical role a particular religion has played in imparting a certain character to a given society and culture. In *The Protestant Ethic*, for example, he expressly set out to illuminate only one causal sequence, namely, the influence of religious consciousness on everyday economic life in the West. In later works Weber began but never completed the task of also tracing the opposite causal sequence—the influence of economic and other material and historical conditions on the development of religious and ethical ideas. In *The Protestant Ethic*, however, he concerned himself primarily with the practical impulses toward action that derived from the religious values of the ascetic Protestant sects.

Another important element of Weber's method of studying the world religions is his focus on the social and historical roles of key strata: in China it is the Confucian literati or mandarins; in India it is the Brahmans; in ancient Israel it is the Hebrew prophets. Buddhism, for Weber, was propagated by itinerant, mendicant monks; Islam by world-conquering warriors; postexilic Judaism by the religion of civic "pariahs"; and Christianity by itinerant, urban artisans.

Still another element of Weber's method is the concept he called the *ideal type*, which he consciously employed for the first time in *The Protestant Ethic*. Examples are "spirit of capitalism" and its opposite, "traditionalism." Rather than attempting at the outset to provide formal definitions of the "ascetic Protestant ethic" and the "spirit of capitalism," Weber makes their respective meanings quite clear by means of increasingly rich and vivid illustrations as he progresses in his investigation. Moreover, Weber strives to assess the causal influence of such ideal-type concepts by examining the historical role of their carriers. And since he proposes to attribute significant historical influence to religious ideas, he buttresses his propositions with copious evidence and references. For example, one finds in the endnotes of *The Protestant Ethic* a virtual treatise on the philological origin of the modern conception of a "calling." And in the second, unchanged version of this work the footnote apparatus was considerably enlarged and supplemented by responses to critics like Lujo Brentano and Werner Sombart whom he had not dealt with earlier. In *The Protestant Ethic* in particular, Weber found it necessary to provide fully the scholarly sources and evidence on which he based his argument. It was especially necessary because his thesis was novel and even surprising, and because his careful qualifications of his thesis were at first not completely absorbed.

One more essential element of Weber's methodology is quite evident in *The Protestant Ethic*. For it is there that he demonstrates in practice what he means by "objectivity." He demonstrates how analysis and evaluation or "fact" and "value" can be separated within the framework of a scholarly investigation. Throughout, Weber refrains from making judgments on the value of the various religious and ethical ideas he analyzes; nor does he anywhere attempt to rank the diverse conceptions of the Divine and its role. Thus Weber presents the theological content of Catholicism and Protestantism with the same fairness that one would expect from a scholar whose primary aim is the pursuit of historical truth and knowledge. And, as we shall see, Weber's objectivity is equally evident in his subsequent studies of the world religions. With this background in

mind we can begin to consider Weber's major contributions to the sociology
of religion.

THE PROTESTANT ETHIC AND THE SPIRIT OF CAPITALISM

Weber opens this work with a discussion of a phenomenon that had long
been noted: that if one examines the occupational statistics of any European country containing substantial numbers of Catholics and Protestants, one finds a predominance of Protestants among owners of capital,
among the higher levels of skilled labor, and among technically trained
personnel and leaders of industrial enterprises. Wherever citizens have
had the formal freedom to choose their occupations as capitalism ex-
panded, one finds the same predominance of Protestants in the ownership of capital, in management, and in the higher ranks of labor in
modern industrial and commercial enterprises.

Weber immediately acknowledges that this phenomenon may in
part be explained not by religious affiliation as the cause but rather as
the effect of economic conditions. He notes, for instance, that it was precisely in areas of the old empire which were most highly developed economically and favored by natural resources that a majority went over to
Protestantism in the time of the Reformation in the sixteenth century.
For Weber, this raised the question of why the most highly developed
economic areas were especially favorable to a revolution in the church.

One factor, no doubt, was the emergence and growth of new economic processes that strengthened the tendency to question the sanctity
of religious tradition and perhaps all traditional authority. Weber notes,
however, that the Reformation meant not the elimination of the church's
control over everyday life but the introduction of a new form of control to
replace the earlier one. Moreover, the earlier, Catholic form of control
was relatively lax and a comparatively light burden, in contrast to the
rule of Calvinism, which penetrated all spheres of private and public life
and was strictly enforced and infinitely burdensome. So how does one explain that in the most economically advanced countries, such as Switzer-
land, Scotland, the Netherlands, and for a time in England itself, the
rising bourgeois middle classes not only failed to resist the new tyranny
of Puritanism but even zealously embraced it?

Returning to the occupational statistics, Weber observes that the
Catholics in Germany, a religious minority, showed a strong tendency to
remain in the traditional crafts, whereas the Protestants preferred entry
into industry to fill the upper ranks of skilled labor and administration.
This fact was especially striking because it ran counter to a tendency observed throughout history. When religious and ethnic minorities were
excluded from political influence, they sought opportunities in the economy.

But the Catholics in Germany showed no such propensity. On the other hand, certain branches of the Protestant movement exhibited a form of economic rationalism that was especially well suited to the nature of modern capitalism. Weber thus begins the unfolding of his thesis by proposing that the principal explanation for the different economic propensities of Catholics and Protestants must be sought in the character of their religious beliefs and not merely in their historical-political situations.

Weber recognized that the Protestants of his own time exhibited certain hedonistic characteristics, such as wishing to eat well. He insists, however, that things were quite different in the past. "The English, Dutch, and American Puritans," he writes, "were characterized by the exact opposite of the joy of living, a fact which is indeed, as we shall see, most important for our present study."[1] To this historical fact Weber adds another, that many of the greatest capitalist entrepreneurs have come from Protestant clergymen's families, and the representatives of the most spiritual forms of Protestant, Christian piety have sprung from commercial circles.

Facts such as these cannot therefore be explained by allegedly materialistic motives of Puritan businessmen, or by a rejection of their ascetic upbringing. The affinity of commerce and piety was characteristic of the most important churches and sects in the history of Protestantism, and especially of Calvinism. Even in Germany, where Protestantism was predominantly Lutheran, Calvinism exhibited the strong tendency to promote the spirit of capitalism. Weber cites the role of the Quakers in England and North America, and the Mennonites in Germany and the Netherlands. With considerable originality he therefore proposes that if any inner motivational relationship is to be found between Protestantism and modern capitalistic culture, it is not to be sought in materialistic or hedonistic motives but in the purely religious motives of ascetic Protestantism. In a word, Weber is proposing that a definite connection exists between the conspicuous commercial superiority of certain Protestant denominations and their piety. And in order to buttress this proposition, Weber has to clarify the ideal-type construct he calls "the spirit of capitalism."

THE SPIRIT OF CAPITALISM

For Weber, an "ideal-type" concept is an indispensable analytical tool in the study of history and in the social sciences. It is a deliberately constructed concept arrived at by accentuating certain aspects of social reality, and it is employed for heuristic purposes. In his essays on the methodology of the social sciences Weber gives the example of "handicraft" production to illustrate what he means by an ideal-type construct. Creating an ideal type of "handicraft" as a precapitalist form of production becomes heuristically useful in contrast to another ideal type, "capitalist" production. Both ideal types become useful in helping us to grasp the essential features and characteristic uniqueness of the respective forms of production and their significant differences.

In order, therefore, to understand the motives, values, and attitudes of the early modern capitalist entrepreneur, Weber creates the ideal-type concept "spirit of capitalism" to contrast it with the precapitalist or "traditional" attitude of, say, the typical Renaissance merchant prince. For Weber, this is a more effective way of approaching the phenomenon he wishes to illuminate than by trying to provide a formal definition of the ethos of capitalism.

He thus selects some of the most famous sayings of Benjamin Franklin, which express in almost classical purity what Weber means by the "spirit of capitalism." "Remember," says Franklin,

> that time is money, that credit is money, that money is of the prolific, generating nature. Money can beget money, and its offspring can beget more, and so on. After industry and frugality, nothing contributes more to the raising of a young man in the world than punctuality and justice in all his dealings; therefore never keep borrowed money an hour beyond the time you promised, lest a disappointment shut up your friend's purse for ever.
>
> The most trifling actions that affect a man's credit are to be regarded. The sound of your hammer at five in the morning, or eight at night, heard by a creditor, makes him easy six months longer; but if he sees you at a billiard table, or hears your voice at a tavern, when you should be at work, he sends for his money the next day....
>
> It shows, besides, that you are mindful of what you owe; it makes you appear a careful as well as honest man, and that still increases your credit. (49–50)

Weber, quoting more from Franklin in the same vein, wishes to contrast the spirit of these utterances with that of earlier men of commerce. As Weber interprets Franklin's sayings, what he is preaching to young men is not simply a means of making one's way in the world "but a peculiar ethic. The infraction of its rules is treated not as foolishness but as forgetfulness of *duty*. That is the essence of the matter. It is not mere business astuteness, that sort of thing is common enough, *it is an ethos*. This is the quality that interests us" (51, italics added).

To strengthen his claim, Weber proceeds to contrast the spirit of Franklin's statements with those of Jacob Fugger, representing the precapitalist, *traditional* view. When Fugger was urged to retire, "since he had made enough money and should let others have a chance," he rejected the advice as pusillanimity and responded that "he wanted to make money as long as he could" (51). The spirit of Fugger's statement Weber perceives as fundamentally different from that of Franklin's. Fugger's was an expression of "commercial daring and a personal inclination morally neutral," whereas Franklin's "takes on the character of an ethically colored maxim for the conduct of life" (51–52). Franklin, in a word, expressed the spirit or ethos of *modern* capitalism, that of western Europe and America, which contrasts with the spirit of the earlier, premodern forms of commerce and capitalism: "Capitalism," Weber writes, "existed in China, India, Babylon, in the classical world, and in the Middle Ages. But in all these cases ... this particular ethos [expressed by Franklin] was lacking" (52).

Weber acknowledges, however, that Franklin's moral attitude carries with it a utilitarian coloring. Honesty, punctuality, industriousness, and frugality are useful virtues because they assure credit. But Weber sees more than strict utilitarianism in Franklin's outlook. In his autobiography Franklin attributed his recognition of the utility of virtue to a divine revelation that was intended to lead him in the path of righteousness. The highest form of the ethic espoused by Franklin is the earning of more and more money combined with a strict self-denial of the joys and pleasures of life. The pursuit of money in this ascetic ethos becomes "so purely an end in itself, that from the point of view of the happiness of, or utility to, the single individual, it appears entirely transcendental and absolutely irrational" (53). The "spirit of capitalism" therefore refers to a new set of values and attitudes in which the making of money or the pursuit of profit becomes the ultimate purpose of life. Economic acquisition is no longer regarded as it was traditionally in the premodern era, as the means to the satisfaction of one's material needs, or the gaining of honor and prestige. Weber discerns in the ethos preached by Franklin—and this, of course, is of central importance to Weber's thesis—a definite religious element; for we have to remember that Benjamin Franklin had been brought up by a strict Calvinist father. Weber writes:

> If we thus ask, *why* should "money be made out of men," Benjamin Franklin himself, although he was a colorless deist, answers in his Autobiography with a quotation from the Bible, which his strict Calvinist father drummed into him again and again in his youth: "Seest Thou a man diligent in his business? He shall stand before Kings" (Proverbs, 22: 29). The earning of money within the modern economic order is, so long as it is done legally, the result and expression of virtue and proficiency in a *calling*; and this virtue and proficiency are, as it is now not difficult to see, the real Alpha and Omega of Franklin's ethic. (53–54)

Now in order to grasp Weber's thesis adequately, we need to understand his qualifications of it. He is *not* saying that the ethos expressed by Franklin appeared only under capitalist conditions or that the ethos is a product of capitalist, economic conditions. To refute such a view it is enough to point to the fact that in the Massachusetts of Franklin's birth the ethos or spirit of capitalism in the sense described here was present *before* a capitalistic system had actually emerged there. Furthermore, even though some of the southern states of the United States had been founded by large capitalists for business motives, those states remained far less developed economically than the New England colonies founded by preachers and seminary graduates—joined by small merchants, craftsmen, and yeomen—for religious reasons. This historical fact not only refutes naive theories of economic determinism but also brings Weber closer to his main point: that the spirit of capitalism had religious roots, and that this new spirit had to fight its way to supremacy against a wide array of hostile *traditional* forces. In both antiquity and the Middle Ages the espousal of Franklin's attitude would have been regarded as the lowest form of avarice and would have elicited contempt. As Weber explains, the unscrupulous pursuit of selfish interests by making money is as old as history. The difference between the capitalistic and precapitalistic spirits is not to be found in the greed for gold and profit. The difference lies, rather, in the fact that the ruthless acquisition of premodern capitalism was bound to no ethical norms whatsoever.

TRADITIONALISM

For Weber, then, the "spirit of capitalism" refers to a new, religiously rooted ethical standard of economic conduct that, in order to prevail, had to struggle against and overcome its most powerful opponent, "traditionalism"—the ideal-type concept Weber counterposes to the "spirit of capitalism." Weber illustrates the "traditional" system of values by beginning with the attitude of laborers. In agriculture, for instance, given the uncertainty of weather conditions, the gathering of the harvest as speedily as possible is a paramount consideration. Employers of agricultural laborers had therefore often instituted piece rates in the hope that this would give workers an incentive to work faster and thereby earn more. But the raising of piece rates often had the opposite effect of decreasing the amount of a laborer's work. In Weber's example, "A man who at the rate of 1 mark per acre mowed $2\frac{1}{2}$ acres per day and earned $2\frac{1}{2}$ marks, when the rate was raised to 1.25 marks per acre mowed not 3 acres, as he might easily have done, thus earning 3.75 marks, but only 2 acres, so that he could still earn the $2\frac{1}{2}$ marks to which he was accustomed. The opportunity of earning more was less attractive than that of working less" (60). That is what

Weber means by "traditionalism" as applied to the attitude of laborers. Weber, as a distinguished economic historian, observes that wherever emerging modern capitalism had attempted to raise productivity by increasing its intensity, it encountered the stubborn traditional attitude of precapitalist labor.

Another old and opposite article of faith proposed that *low* wages increased the productivity of labor—that people work only because they are poor. So Weber observes that wherever production required skill, care for expensive machinery, sharp attention to the productive process, or initiative, low wages had an effect opposite to what was intended. Weber thus argues that modern rational capitalism required a nontraditional attitude on the part of labor, an attitude that labor should be performed as if it were an absolute end in itself, a *calling*. Neither high wages nor low wages alone could overcome the traditional attitude of labor. Human beings do not *naturally* allow themselves to be subjected to the kind of labor required by modern, capitalist, factory production. The new, nontraditional attitude that was required could be evoked only by a long and arduous process of religio-moral education.

Weber notes in that regard that young women of a pietistic background were especially receptive to such an education. It was among them that one found the ability to concentrate mentally, a sense of responsibility toward their work, a rational calculation of the probability of increasing their earnings the harder they worked, and a cool self-control and frugality, all of which contributed to an enormous increase in their productivity. Historical experience thus appeared to demonstrate that the probability of overcoming traditionalism was greatest when the individuals concerned had received the moral education characteristic of the ascetic Protestant sects. Weber calls attention to the fact that in the early stages of capitalist development in the eighteenth century, the Methodist workers were disliked and even persecuted by their comrades. The primary reason for this hostility was not their religious peculiarities but—as the recurring destruction of their tools suggests—their willingness to subject themselves to the rigors of factory production. We see, then, the difference, for Weber, between the traditional attitude of labor and the religiously rooted attitude of labor that suited the needs and interests of the emerging, early modern capitalism.

We need to understand, therefore, that Weber's ideal-type concept "spirit of capitalism" refers to the spirit of *modern* capitalism, with "spirit" signifying an antitraditional attitude among early capitalist entrepreneurs as well as among laborers. Among entrepreneurs it manifested itself in an attitude that seeks profit rationally and systematically in the manner suggested by Franklin's sayings; among laborers, the "spirit" expressed itself in a religiously rooted motivation to adapt willingly to the harsh inflexibility of factory production.

So if we have followed Weber's argument up to this point, there should be no confusion as to the meaning of his thesis. The title of his famous book is *not The Protestant Ethic and the Rise of Capitalism* but *The Protestant Ethic and the Spirit of Capitalism*. Weber is certainly not saying that the Protestant ethic had somehow given rise to capitalism, for if he had said that, he would have been easily refuted and would have made a fool of himself besides. Weber and all good economic historians knew that certain forms of capitalism had preceded the Reformation. Weber is not even saying that the Protestant ethic gave rise to modern, rational capitalism. Then what is he saying? Weber is proposing that the "spirit of capitalism" was rooted in ascetic Protestant values that served to impart to early capitalism a dynamic, energizing quality that it might not have possessed and exhibited in the absence of those values.

This brings us to this question: Who were the pioneering entrepreneurs of early modern capitalism? The historical evidence is clear. In the early stages it was not the members of the old and established commercial aristocracy who were the bearers of the "spirit of capitalism." It was, rather, the rising groups of the lower, industrial middle classes. In a footnote, Weber reinforces the point: "The rising middle and small bourgeoisie, from which the entrepreneurs were principally recruited, were for the most part here [i.e., in the Netherlands] and elsewhere typical representatives both of capitalistic ethics and of Calvinistic religion" (200 n. 23). Even in the nineteenth century the classical representatives of the "spirit of capitalism" in England and Germany "were not the elegant gentlemen of Liverpool and Hamburg, with their commercial fortunes handed down for generations, but the self-made parvenus of Manchester and Westphalia, who often rose from very modest circumstances. As early as the 16th century the situation was similar; the industries which arose at that time were mostly created by parvenus" (65).

It was precisely the new men of the lower middle classes who challenged and eventually transformed the older capitalistic organization, which was *traditional* in all respects. To illustrate the change, Weber cites the putting-out system in the textile industry, which had been entirely traditional until some young men went out to the country, carefully chose weavers for their employ, and turned peasants into wage laborers whose work was strictly supervised. At the same time the new type of capitalist entrepreneur introduced the principle of low prices and large turnover. The rationalization of the productive process in that way meant that those in the industry who could not follow suit had to go out of business. The old traditional system thus eventually collapsed under the pressure of a bitter competitive struggle. The new young men thus made respectable fortunes, but owing to their Protestant upbringing lived ascetically and frugally, reinvesting every penny of profit in their businesses. That is the way the new "spirit of capitalism" had begun its work, gaining momentum despite the flood of mistrust, hatred, and moral indignation that regularly opposed itself to those early innovators. The strength of character the innovators required in order to withstand such hostility was derived, Weber avers, from their religio-ethical outlook.

In examining further the radical opposition between the traditional view of moneymaking and the new "spirit of capitalism," Weber stresses the fact that the dominant traditional doctrine regarded capitalistic acquisition as moral turpitude and gave it no positive ethical sanction. The wealthy commercial circles themselves recognized the danger of colliding with the church's doctrine on usury and jeopardizing their chances of salvation. The evidence shows that as they were dying they gave huge sums to religious institutions as conscience money and, at times, gave back to their former debtors the usurious sums unjustly taken from them.

So the key question, for Weber, is this: How did the capitalistic activities that were either condemned, or at best barely tolerated from an ethical standpoint, turn into a positively sanctioned calling? What needs to be explained in order to answer that question is a curious fact: In say, fourteenth- and fifteenth-century Florence, the money and capital market for all the great political powers of the time, capitalistic activity was considered morally base, but in the backwoods of eighteenth-century Pennsylvania, where there was scarcely a sign of large enterprise, and small businesses were threatened, for lack of money, to fall back into barter, capitalistic activity not only received full moral approval but also became a morally dutiful obligation fulfilled as a *calling*.

LUTHER'S CONCEPTION OF THE CALLING

When one reads Weber's *Protestant Ethic and the Spirit of Capitalism* carefully, one soon comes to realize that the "Protestant ethic" in the title refers directly neither to Luther's doctrine nor even to Calvin's. For Weber, the ascetic Protestant ethic refers to the Calvinist doctrine as it was reinterpreted in the course of several generations after Calvin. Luther, however, had nevertheless inadvertently made a significant contribution to the "Protestant ethic" when he translated the Bible into German.

Weber notes that in the German word *Beruf*, and even more clearly in the English word *calling*, there is a religious connotation of a task set by God. The word with this connotation is found in the languages of Protestant peoples but not in those of Catholic peoples. Nor does the word with that connotation appear in the languages of classical antiquity. So it appears to be true that the word *Beruf*, with the religious connotation, first appeared in Luther's translation of the book Jesus (or Joshua) Sirach (xi:20, 21), and that it rapidly took on that meaning in the everyday

speech of all Protestant peoples. Prior to Luther's translation there was
not even the suggestion of such a meaning in any of the European languages. The closest one came to such a meaning in any language—Weber
points out in a footnote—was in the Hebrew word *melachah* (204 n. 1).

Like the new meaning of the word *calling*, the idea was unques-
tionably new:

> the valuation of the fulfillment of duty in worldly affairs as the highest
> form which the moral activity of the individual could assume. This it
> was which inevitably gave everyday worldly activity a religious signif-
> icance, and which first created the conception of a calling in this sense.
> The conception of the calling thus brings out that central dogma of all
> Protestant denominations.... The only way of living acceptably to God
> was not to surpass worldly morality in monastic asceticism, but solely
> through the fulfillment of the obligations imposed upon the individual
> by his position in the world. That was his calling (80).

In this new conception of a "calling," the monastic life was regarded
not only as devoid of value but as a selfish renunciation of worldly duties.
In contrast, labor in a calling in the economic life of society became an expression of brotherly love. This was proved by the observation that in the
division of labor everyone is compelled to work for others. In time, this
was replaced by the more general view that the fulfillment of worldly duties is in all circumstances the only way to live acceptably to God. This
new moral justification of worldly activity was one of the most significant
consequences of the Reformation, and especially of Luther's part in it.

But that is where Luther's contribution ends, for he certainly would
have repudiated the "spirit of capitalism" as we now understand the
phrase. Indeed, in his many statements against usury or the charging of
interest in any form, and in his doctrine of the sterility of money, Luther
is "definitely backward" even compared with late Scholasticism, from a
capitalistic standpoint (83). For Luther, especially after the peasant up-
risings, the objective social order of things in which the individual has
been placed becomes more and more a manifestation of God's will. His
emphasis on the providential element led increasingly to a traditional
interpretation based on the idea of Providence: The individual should remain in the station in which God has placed him and accept the limits
thus imposed. Weber observes that although Luther's traditionalism was
originally the result of Pauline indifference, it soon became an intense
belief in divine Providence "which identified absolute obedience to God's
will, with absolute acceptance of things as they were" (85).

Luther's concept of a calling thus remained traditional. In his theology the overwhelming emphasis on the centrality of faith led him and his
followers to suspect the tendency to ascetic self-discipline as leading to

the belief in salvation by works. Hence, in Weber's view, although Luther gave the word *Beruf* a moral coloring, his conception of the calling remained traditionalistic and made little or no contribution to the idea of the calling as understood by the post-Calvinist, ascetic Protestant denominations. One must therefore look elsewhere for the source of the idea of a calling as the fulfillment of a religiously motivated task in the practical life of this world.

THE RELIGIOUS FOUNDATIONS OF WORLDLY ASCETICISM

Weber discerned four major forms of ascetic Protestantism: (1) Calvinism and the form it assumed in western Europe in the seventeenth century; (2) Pietism; (3) Methodism; and (4) the sects that grew out of the Baptist movement. None of these was totally separated from the others, and even their distinction from the nonascetic churches of the Reformation was never entirely clear. Methodism first arose in the mid–eighteenth century in the context of the established Church of England and was originally intended as a reaffirmation of the ascetic spirit, not as the formation of a new church. Only in its later development in America did it separate itself from the Anglican Church. Pietism first broke away from the Calvinist movement in England and especially in Holland but by the end of the seventeenth century was absorbed by the Lutheran movement. The staunchest leaders of the ascetic movement were eventually called "Puritans," which included such sects as the Independents, Congregationalists, Baptists, and Quakers, all of which found themselves in opposition to the Anglican Church. The Mennonites were also a part of the ascetic movement. There were significant dogmatic differences among the sects, with regard to predestination and other issues, which precluded the possibility of unifying them in one church. On the other hand, there were great similarities among them, which account for their having been lumped together in the ambiguous category of Puritanism.

CALVINISM

Clearly, the doctrine of predestination may be considered Calvinism's most characteristic dogma, which was elevated to canonical authority by the great synods of the seventeenth century. Weber cites the Westminster Confession of 1647, in which the full implications of the doctrine of predestination were explicitly spelled out:

> Chapter IX (of free will), No. 3. Man, by his fall into a state of sin, hath wholly lost all ability of will to any spiritual good accompanying salvation. So that a natural man, being altogether averse from that Good, and dead in sin, is not able, by his own strength, to convert himself, or to prepare himself thereunto.

Chapter III (of God's Eternal Decree), No. 3. By the decree of God, for the manifestation of His glory, some men and angels are predestined unto everlasting life, and others foreordained to everlasting death.

Chapter X (of Effectual Calling), No. 1. All those whom God has predestined unto life, and those only, He is pleased in His appointed and accepted time effectively to call, by His word and spirit (out of that state of sin and death, in which they are by nature)...taking away their heart of stone, and giving unto them a heart of flesh; renewing their wills, and by His almighty power determining them to that which is good. (99–100)

Clearly, this doctrine, which nullified the free will of humanity and inculcated the notion that it is entirely God's grace that determines whether one will be among the saved or damned, was a heavy and terrifying psychological burden. Adherents were taught that good works are worthless for the attainment of salvation and any effort to learn one's destiny was an attempt to force God's secrets, a pagan act. Weber cites John Milton's opinion of this doctrine: "Though I may be sent to Hell for it, such a God will never command my respect." But Weber reminds us, "We are here concerned not with evaluation, but the historical significance of the dogma" (101).

In beginning to explore the historical significance of the predestination dogma, Weber observes that for the church fathers of Lutheranism, it was an article of faith that grace was revocable and could be "won again by penitent humility and faithful trust in the word of God and in the sacraments" (102). With Calvin, in contrast, the rigidity of the doctrine increased. Everything of flesh is separated from God by an unbridgeable chasm and deserves only eternal death if he has not decreed otherwise. Only a small portion of humanity is saved, and the rest are damned. To assume that human meritorious acts play a part in determining their destiny would be to suppose that God's decrees are subject to change by human influence, an unthinkable condition for Calvin. Thus God the Father of the New Testament, the kind and merciful Deity who rejoices over the repentance and atonement of a sinner, is replaced by a transcendental, cosmic being who regulates the smallest details of the cosmos from eternity. The Calvinist's God's decrees cannot change, so those to whom he has granted grace cannot lose it, and those to whom he has denied grace can do nothing to gain it.

From a psychological point of view, Weber observes, the extreme inhumanity of the doctrine surely created in the Puritan individual an unprecedented inner loneliness. One could not help oneself, nor could anyone else help one—no priest, no sacraments, no church, for the church included the damned. Yet everyone was subject to the church and had to obey God's commandments, not in order to attain salvation—which was impossible in any case—but for the glory of God. Indeed, not even God nor Christ could help the lonely individual, for Christ, in the Calvinist doctrine, died only for the elect. It was strictly for their benefit that God had decreed Jesus' martyrdom from eternity. Calvinism thus totally eliminated salvation through the church and the sacraments, which distinguished it absolutely from Catholicism. The genuine Puritan, viewing the Catholic sacraments as magic and superstition, pure and simple, even buried their loved ones without ritual "in order that no superstition, no trust in the effects of magical and sacramental forces on salvation, should creep in" (105). In their reaction against Catholicism, the Calvinist branches of the ascetic Protestant movement eventually eliminated the private confession and thus increased further the isolation of the individual by doing away with the periodical discharge of the emotional sense and pain of sin.

The question, then, for Weber, is how the inner torment of Calvin's doctrine was borne by the three or four generations of his followers, for whom the afterlife was more important than the interests of this world. For the vast majority, the question of their state of grace became an absolutely dominant preoccupation. In the course of the several generations after Calvin, some of the sectarian pastors tended to reinterpret Calvin's doctrine, toning it down and even abandoning it. Wherever the doctrine of predestination was retained, however, the question could not be avoided whether there were infallible criteria by which membership in the *electi* could be known. To those who raised that question, Weber explains, two mutually connected types of pastoral advice were given:

> On the one hand it is held to be an absolute duty to consider oneself chosen, and to combat all doubt as temptations of the devil, since lack of self-confidence is the result of insufficient faith, hence of imperfect grace. The exhortation of the apostle to make fast one's own call is here interpreted as a duty to attain certainty of one's own election and justification in the daily struggle of life. In the place of the humble sinners to whom Luther promises grace if they trust themselves to God in penitent faith are bred those self-confident saints whom we can rediscover in the hard Puritan merchants of the heroic age of capitalism and in isolated instances down to the present. On the other hand, in order to attain that self-confidence intense worldly activity is recommended as the most suitable means. It and it alone disperses religious doubts and gives the certainty of grace. (112)

So in the course of the hundred or more years after Calvin, his doctrine was reinterpreted to mean that though good works are useless for the attainment of salvation they are nonetheless indispensable as a possible sign of election. Good works are the means not of gaining salvation but of ridding oneself of the fear of damnation. In practice, the Calvinist came to believe that God helps those who help themselves. The Calvinist thus created his own salvation—that is, the conviction of it. The Calvinist could not hope to atone for his weak, impious, or sinful thoughts and acts by compensating with good acts at other times as could the Catholic or even the Lutheran. The God of Calvinism required not single good works but rather "a life of good works combined into a unified system. There was no place for the very human Catholic cycle of sin, repentance, atonement, release, followed by renewed sin" (117). The actions of the typical Calvinist were subjected to a consistent method for moral conduct in life as a whole. "It is no accident," therefore, as Weber observes, "that the name Methodists stuck to the participants in the last great revival of Puritan ideas in the 18th century" (117). In the course of its development, Calvinism thus substituted for the traditional, spiritual aristocracy of monks outside of and above the world, "the spiritual aristocracy of the predestined saints of God within the world" (121). Hence, what is essential for an understanding of Weber's thesis is recognizing the most important result of ascetic Protestantism: a systematic, rational, and moral ordering of life as a whole.

PIETISM

The doctrine of predestination is also the starting point for the ascetic movement that came to be known as Pietism. Eventually, however, as Pietism penetrated Lutheran denominations, its emphasis on rational asceticism came to be regarded as a foreign element. The Lutheran conception of salvation through the forgiveness of sins soon replaced the systematic, rational struggle to attain certain knowledge of salvation. The Lutheran need to feel reconciliation and community with God in the present meant, for Weber, that Lutheranism could not develop as powerful a motive to rationalize worldly activity as could the Calvinist in his preoccupation with the question of his destiny in the beyond.

METHODISM

Corresponding to Continental Pietism in combining emotionalism with asceticism was the Anglo-American movement that came to be called Methodism. As the name itself suggests, the characteristic of the movement's adherents that most impressed contemporaries was the methodical nature of their conduct for the purpose of attaining certainty of salvation. This remained from the beginning the central inspiration of the movement.

Under Moravian and Lutheran influences John Wesley, the founder of Methodism, lent the movement a pronounced emotional character. Departing from orthodox Calvinism, which regarded everything emotional as suspect, Wesley's doctrine taught that the only sound basis for the certainty of salvation was the *feeling* of absolute certainty of forgiveness. In addition, Wesley proposed the doctrine of sanctification, according to which one can be reborn by virtue of the divine grace already working in the individual in this life. One is reborn by attaining "sanctification," an awareness of now being free of sin due to forgiveness and a sudden, spiritual transformation. Such a transformation always should be sought, and though it should be expected only late in life, it eventually provides the Methodist with a serene confidence in salvation that replaces the sullen anxiety of the strict Calvinist.

Wesley demanded righteous conduct from his followers and, like the other Calvinist denominations, stressed that works can never be the cause of salvation but only, perhaps, a sign of one's state of grace. Though righteous conduct alone was not enough, and the *feeling* of grace was, in addition, necessary, Wesley insisted that he who performed no good works was not a true believer. What followed the emotional experience of conversion for the Methodist was not a pious enjoyment of community with God but a rational struggle for perfection. Even when the emotional excitement occasionally assumed the form of a powerful enthusiasm, it never made the rational pursuit of perfection superfluous. Weber concludes that for the purpose of his thesis, nothing more needs to be said about Methodism because "it added nothing new to the development of the idea of the calling" (143).

THE BAPTIST SECTS

A key element of the Baptist or Anabaptist denominations was the doctrine that only adults who have personally gained their own faith should be baptized. The ascetic Protestant denominations thus rejected the Catholic baptism of infants. Among the Baptists and Mennonites, there was a return to the early Christian pneumatic or spiritual doctrines. Menno Simons wished his followers to become the true blameless church of Christ consisting, like the early apostolic community, of those personally awakened and called by Christ. A common denominator of the Baptist groups was the doctrine that what God had revealed to the prophets and apostles was not all that he would reveal. They held the strong belief in the continuing life of the Word not as a text but as the Holy Spirit working in daily life, speaking to any individual who is willing to listen. From the idea of the continuing revelation, the Quakers developed the well-known doctrine of the primary significance of the inner message of the Spirit in one's conscience. Thus the "Baptist denominations along with the Predestinationists, especially the strict Calvinists, carried out the most radical devaluation of all sacraments as means of salvation, and thus accomplished the religious rationalization of the world in its most extreme form" (147). What became the common ground of these Protestant sects was the belief that only an unconditional submission to God, speaking through one's conscience, and a corresponding moral conduct in everyday practical life, could justify considering oneself reborn and saved. For Weber, this conception gave "conduct in worldly callings a character which was of the greatest significance for the development of the spirit of capitalism" (151). And Weber reminds us that in the "judgment of the 17th century the specific form of the worldly asceticism of the Baptists and especially the Quakers, lay in the practical adoption of this maxim: 'honesty is the best policy'" (151).

ASCETICISM AND THE SPIRIT OF CAPITALISM

Just as Weber employed the preachments of Benjamin Franklin to illustrate the ideal-type "spirit of capitalism," Weber will now employ Richard Baxter to illustrate the ideal-typical, ascetic Protestant ethic, treated as a single totality. Weber chooses Baxter because the English side of Puritanism provides the most consistent religious ground for the idea of the calling.

Weber begins by considering Baxter's *Saints' Everlasting Rest* and his *Christian Directory*, where he asserts that the pursuit of wealth is not only senseless as compared with the paramount importance of striving to bring in the kingdom of God but also morally suspect. At first glance, Baxter thus appears to have turned against the acquisition of worldly goods more sharply than Calvin, who even permitted the clergy to employ their resources profitably.

For Weber, however, the true ethical meaning of Baxter's strictures requires a deeper analysis. Baxter's real moral objection is to the *enjoyment* of wealth and the resulting idleness and temptations of the flesh, and distraction from the pursuit of a righteous life. It is this danger that makes the pursuit of wealth morally objectionable. The saints' everlasting rest is in the next world, but here on earth there is to be neither rest nor enjoyment but only activity to enhance the glory of God. Weber therefore proposes that if we now listen carefully to Baxter in that light, we hear utterances that anticipate Franklin's and bear a remarkable affinity with his "spirit of capitalism." "Waste of time," says Baxter, is the deadliest of sins. Human life is too short and precious to distract oneself from making sure of one's election. Time is wasted and lost through sociability, idle talk, and luxury. Even more sleep than is necessary for health deserves moral condemnation. Weber acknowledges that Baxter does not yet say, as did Franklin, that time is money, but Baxter does imply it. For he states that time is as precious and valuable as it is because every hour wasted is lost to labor for the glory of God.

Thus contemplation in idleness is also reprehensible if it is at the expense of one's daily work. For contemplation pleases God less than the active fulfillment of his will in a calling. Besides, the Sabbath is provided for rest and contemplation.

Baxter's writings are dominated by the repeatedly almost passionate preaching of hard, continuous, physical or mental labor. Labor is the approved ascetic means of defense against all the temptations that jeopardize one's salvation. As applied to sexuality, Puritan asceticism meant that even in marriage sexual intercourse was permitted only as the means willed by God to fulfill his commandment: "Be fruitful and multiply." To combat sexual temptations the pastoral advice is the same as that given for combating religious doubts and feelings of moral unworthiness: "Work hard in your calling." Labor, for Baxter, comes to be considered the telos of life. St. Paul's view "he who works not, shall not eat" holds unconditionally for everyone, since unwillingness to work is a sign of the lack of grace.

Weber compares the medieval view with that of Baxter. Thomas Aquinas, for example, interpreted Paul's statement to mean that labor is necessary only for the sustenance of the individual and the community. When that is achieved, the precept ceases to make sense. For Baxter, however, there are no exceptions to the moral duty to labor. Even the wealthy shall not eat without working, for though they do not need to labor to provide for their own needs, they, like the poor, must obey God's commandment. God's providence has ordained a calling for everyone without exception, a calling that one should profess and in which one should labor. Weber calls attention to the subtle but fundamental difference between the Lutheran view of the calling, a fate to which one must submit and make the best of, and the ascetic Protestant view in which one strives to fulfill God's commandment to the individual to work for the divine glory. The Lutheran realm of ideas never freed itself from Pauline indifference. But in the Puritan view, the economy and especially the division of labor lead to good consequences for the society and change it for the better. Anticipating Adam Smith's famous discussion of the division of labor, Baxter argues that specialization of occupation is what makes the development of skill possible, and that the quantitative and qualitative improvements in production serve the common good, or the good of the greatest number.

Weber acknowledges that the motivation here is utilitarian and thus the common standpoint of much of the secular literature of the time. But Weber also discerns a characteristic Puritan element in Baxter's statement that "outside of a well-marked calling the accomplishments of a man are only casual and irregular, and he spends more time in idleness than in work...therefore a certain calling is best for everyone" (161). Baxter goes further and places a positive sanction on private profitableness: "If God shows you a way in which you may lawfully get more than in another way (without wrong to your soul or to any other), if you refuse this, and choose the less gainful way, you cross one of the ends of your calling, and you refuse to be God's steward, and accept His gifts and use them for Him when He requireth it: You may labor to be rich for God, though not for the flesh and sin" (162).

Thus expressing the characteristic ascetic Protestant doctrine, Baxter views wealth as ethically reprehensible only insofar as it tempts one to idleness and the sinful enjoyment of life. But wealth as the fruit of the morally dutiful performance of a calling is not only permissible but actually enjoined. In that way the Puritan's interpretation of profit-making as providential legitimized the activities of the businessman. Puritan asceticism thus granted to the sober, middle-class, self-made man the highest ethical appreciation.

Puritanism was more profoundly inspired by the Hebrew Bible, the so-called Old Testament, than was the Catholicism of the time. Following Baxter's advice, Puritans compared their state of grace with that of the outstanding figures of the Bible, and in the process treated the Scriptures as the source of inspiration and statutes to live by. Among the canonical books of the Hebrew Bible, the Puritans regarded the Book of Job as of greatest moment. For on the one hand, it contained a conception of an almighty cosmic deity beyond all human comprehension, a conception closely related to that of Calvinism; on the other hand, it offered certainty to the Puritan mind that God would bless his own in this life in the material sense. For the Puritans, moreover, only the purely historical-ceremonial precepts of the Mosaic Law, which applied only to the ancient Hebrews, had lost their validity. In all other respects the Law had

> always been valid as an expression of the natural law and must hence be retained. This made it possible [Weber explains], on the one hand, to eliminate elements which could not be reconciled with modern life. But still, through its numerous related features, the Old Testament morality was able to give a powerful impetus to that spirit of self-righteous and sober legality which was so characteristic of the worldly asceticism of this form of Protestantism. (165)

The Puritan idea of the calling, then, with the extraordinary value it assigned to ascetic conduct, was bound, Weber avers, to influence the development of a capitalistic way of life. Puritan asceticism repudiated, with all its force, the spontaneous enjoyment of life. We gain real insight into the Puritan mind from their resistance to royal legislation permitting sport and other popular amusements on Sunday after church hours. The feudal and monarchical powers in England sought to protect the pleasure seekers against the rising, antiauthoritarian, Puritan middle-class morality. In opposition to those powers, however, the Puritans steadfastly upheld the paramountcy of ascetic conduct.

However, the Puritan ideals by no means implied a narrow-minded contempt for culture. Especially where science was concerned, the great leaders of the Puritan movement were thoroughly familiar with the cultural achievements of the Renaissance. But the situation was quite different where the nonscientific literature was concerned. "Here," Weber remarks, "asceticism descended like a frost on the life of 'merrie old England'" (168). The Puritan's fierce "hatred of everything that smacked of superstition, of all survivals of magical or sacramental salvation, applied to the Christmas festivities and the May Pole and all spontaneous religious art" (168). As against artistic tendencies, the Puritan always favored sober utility, which had definite implications for the emerging modern capitalistic economy. "This was especially true," Weber observes, "in the case of decoration of the person, for instance clothing. That powerful tendency toward uniformity of life, which today so immensely aids the capitalistic interest in the standardization of production, had its ideal foundation in the repudiation of all idolatry of the flesh" (169).

For the Puritan, then, the pursuit of wealth as an end in itself was highly reprehensible,

> but the attainment of it as the fruit of labor in a calling was a sign of God's blessing. And even more important: the religious valuation of restless, continuous, systematic work in a worldly calling, as the highest means to asceticism, and at the same time the surest and most evident proof of rebirth and genuine faith, must have been the most powerful conceivable lever for the expansion of that attitude toward life which we have here called the spirit of capitalism. (172)

When acquisitive activity is thus positively sanctioned, and a severe limitation is morally imposed upon consumption, there is an unavoidable practical result: Capital is accumulated due to the ascetic compulsion to save. The restraints on the consumption and enjoyment of wealth served to increase it, making it available for productive investment as capital. In time, however, the Puritan ethic became a specifically bourgeois, economic ethic. As long as the businessman remained within the bounds of legality, and as long as his moral conduct was unblemished and the use to which he put his wealth was unobjectionable, he could feel himself fulfilling a divine duty and standing in the fullness of God's grace. And where labor was concerned, the Puritan ideology as it was inculcated in the working class—for example, Methodism—provided the entrepreneur with conscientious, loyal, and industrious laborers who looked upon their labor and station in life as the fulfillment of a purpose willed by God. Finally, the Puritan ideology gave the successful and wealthy Puritan, bourgeois entrepreneur a "comforting assurance that the unequal distribution of goods in the world was a special dispensation of Divine Providence" (177).

If, therefore, we reread Franklin's preachments, we can see clearly that the attitude Weber called the "spirit of capitalism" is the same as that shown to be the content of Puritan worldly asceticism. However, once capitalism gained a momentum of its own and became victorious, it no longer needed the support of the Puritan ideology. So Weber concludes his great essay with this famous insight:

> The Puritan wanted to work in a calling; we are forced to do so. For when monasticism was carried out of the monastic cells into everyday life, and began to dominate worldly morality, it did its part in building the tremendous cosmos of the modern economic order. This order is now bound to the technical and economic conditions of machine production which today determine the lives of all the individuals who are born into this mechanism, not only those directly concerned with economic acquisition, with irresistible force. Perhaps it will so determine them until the last ton of fossilized coal is burnt. In Baxter's view the care for external goods should only lie on the shoulders of the "saint like a light cloak, which can be thrown aside at any moment." But fate decreed that the cloak should become an iron cage. (181)

And because Weber's subtle, extraordinarily complex, and carefully qualified thesis was poorly understood and even totally misunderstood, he concludes with a cautionary, methodological remark:

> Here we have only attempted to trace the fact and the direction of its [ascetic Protestantism] influence to their motives in one, though a very important point. But it would also further be necessary to investigate how Protestant asceticism was in turn influenced in its development and its character by the totality of social conditions, especially economic. The modern man is in general, even with the best will, unable to give religious ideas a significance for culture and national character which they deserve. But it is, of course, not my aim to substitute for a one-sided materialistic an equally one-sided spiritualistic causal interpretation of culture and of history. Each is equally possible, but each, if it does not serve as the preparation, but as the conclusion of an investigation, accomplishes equally little in the interest of historical truth. (183)

WEBER'S TRAVELS IN AMERICA AND THEIR CONFIRMATION OF HIS THESIS

The first fact that struck Weber during his travels in the United States was the exceptionally high rate of church affiliation, despite the great financial burden that such affiliation entailed, especially for the poor. As Weber examined the role of religion in the United States more closely, he recognized that religious affiliation offered definite advantages in social relations and in business life.

Weber relates an experience he had on a long railroad journey in 1904, when he remarked to a salesman sitting next to him, that he was impressed by the church-mindedness of American culture. "Sir," the salesman responded, "for my part everybody may believe or not believe as he pleases; but if I saw a farmer or businessman not belonging to any church at all, I wouldn't trust him with fifty cents. Why pay me, if he doesn't believe in anything?"[2] Weber soon learned that baptism and belonging to a definite Baptist denomination was a virtual precondition for success in business. Baptism earned one the patronage of an entire community, and admission to a congregation was viewed as an absolute guarantee of the moral qualities of a gentleman, especially the qualities required in business. "In general," Weber observed, "*only* those men had success in business who belonged to Methodist or Baptist or other *sects* or sect-like conventicles. When a sect member moved to a different place, or if he was a traveling salesman, he carried the certificate of his congregation with him; and thereby he found not only easy contact with sect members but, above all, he found credit everywhere" (305). Sect membership certified the moral qualities and especially the business morals of the individual.

Weber distinguishes between the concepts of "church" and "sect." A "church" is a broad religious-social organization into which one is "born," and which may include righteous and unrighteous alike. "Membership in a church," writes Weber, is "in principle obligatory and hence proves nothing with regard to the member's qualities. A sect, however, is a voluntary association of only those who, according to the principle, are religiously and morally qualified" (306). In the United States at that time, expulsion from one's sect for moral offenses meant "economically, loss of credit and, socially, being declassed" (306). At the time of Weber's travels in America, the *kind* of sect or denomination to which one belonged was not the main consideration. It did not matter whether one was an Adventist, Quaker, Christian Scientist, or whatever. The decisive factor was that one be "admitted to membership by 'ballot,' after an *examination* and an ethical *probation* ... [testing] the virtues which are at a premium for the this-worldly asceticism of Protestantism and hence, for the ancient Puritan tradition" (307).

Weber's main aim in this essay was to demonstrate that there survived in the United States of the time the derivatives of a religious regulation of life, which continued to provide definite social and economic advantages to businessmen who were sect members. The Protestant sects were the social contexts in which the breeding of strong traits took place, through the necessity of having to prove one-self and to hold one's own in the circle of one's fellow members. One proved oneself by means of a certain methodical, rational way of life, expressed in the morally dutiful pursuit of a calling. This had paved the way to the emergence of the "spirit of capitalism." Premium was placed on "proving" oneself before God in the sense of gaining confidence of one's salvation, and "proving" oneself before men by holding one's own—continuing to command respect within one's sect. Weber's American experience thus tended to confirm his thesis that "only the methodical way of life of the ascetic sects could legitimate and put a halo around the economic 'individualist' impulses of the modern capitalist ethos"[3] (322).

CRITICISMS OF THE WEBER THESIS

As we reflect on the thesis and ask whom Weber had selected to illustrate the ethical injunctions of ascetic Protestantism, the answer is: never its founder! This led some of Weber's early critics to wonder whether, in Weber's view, Calvin was a Calvinist. Well, if it had in fact been Weber's position—and some of his critics have thus wrongly interpreted him—that Calvin's religious doctrine was of *direct* importance in generating the capitalist spirit, then, of course, it would have been methodologically impermissible to use anyone but Calvin. But Weber does something else, as we have seen; he employs Richard Baxter (1615–91), John Wesley (1703–91), and Benjamin Franklin (1706–90), all having lived a hundred or more years after Calvin. Clearly, Weber employed these historical figures not to show what Calvin was in the middle of the sixteenth century but to show what Calvinism had become in the course of its development. Furthermore, he showed what it had become not in isolation from other social conditions but under the influence of economic and other developments. That is why the thinkers Weber cited embodied elements of both Protestant asceticism *and* the capitalist spirit.

What Weber was proposing, then, is that two, relatively autonomous developments embraced one another at a given historical moment to contribute to the modern, rational capitalist spirit. There was a definite "elective affinity" between the values of a new religious movement and the values of the new, middle-class entrepreneurs who were also adherents of the ascetic Protestant sects.

Some critics who have failed to read Weber with sufficient care have asserted that in his use of Franklin, Baxter, and Wesley, seventeenth- and eighteenth-century figures, Weber had neglected the impact on religion of economic and political developments, which from the time of Calvin had modified the original doctrine. But, of course, Weber had understood this problem and, indeed, promised to study the causal influences in that direction. However, because he never lived to fulfill that promise, he left himself open to such criticisms. He once remarked ironically that had he accomplished the entire project, he would have been accused of capitulating to a Marxian-materialist position, just as he was now charged with fostering an idealistic interpretation of history.

Some of the earliest criticisms of the Weber thesis pertain to matters of historical fact. In his *Anfänge des Kapitalismus*, Lujo Brentano argued that some of the developments Weber attributed to ascetic Protestantism had already appeared during the Renaissance, and R. H. Tawney agreed that "Brentano's criticism that the political thought of the Renaissance was as powerful a solvent of traditional restraints as the teaching of Calvin is not without weight."[4] Other historians have also objected to Weber's assignment of antitraditional values primarily to ascetic Protestantism. They have argued that such values were more general than Weber's essay suggests, and that they were common to Catholic as well as to Protestant writers. In spite of all such objections, however, most critics acknowledge that Weber was right in discerning a definite affinity between the ascetic Protestant ethic and the ethos of modern capitalism.

Recent criticisms include at least one that attempts to undermine the foundation of Weber's thesis and to discredit it entirely. Malcolm H. MacKinnon has asserted that Weber's thesis is wrong and defective for two reasons: "First, there is no crisis of proof in dogmatic Calvinism that tenders an absolute guarantee of assurance from the use of good works and introspection. Second, works in dogma and pastoral advice have nothing to do with earthly toil, but are spiritual duties that call for the enactment of the Law."[5] Regarding the first of the alleged errors, it should be entirely clear from our exposition of Weber's analysis that he nowhere even faintly suggests that the post-Calvinist, Puritan divines provided an "absolute guarantee" of salvation. What Weber suggested instead is that the ideal-typical ascetic Protestant individual pursued his calling in a morally dutiful manner to bolster his self-confidence. He lived in the hope that his worldly success might be a *sign* of his election. The second purported error of Weber is his alleged failure to recognize that "works" in the Puritan texts refers to religious-moral, and not to secular, activities.

In response, David Zaret argues that MacKinnon has been insufficiently objective in his sampling of relevant passages from the Puritan texts. When one corrects this methodological error, it becomes evident, says Zaret, that the Calvinist and Puritan "doctrines contained the essential elements that Weber attributed to the Protestant ethic" (270).

Guy Oakes also deals with MacKinnon's critique, in an especially interesting and effective way. He says, let us suppose for a moment that the two claims of MacKinnon's critique are sound. Even if they were sound, Oakes avers, that would be "irrelevant to the validity of Weber's argument, which depends not upon the correct interpretation of theological doctrines but upon the *consequences* of these doctrines for a revolution in the conduct of life" (290). "In the final analysis," Oakes continues, "the validity of Weber's argument in the *Protestant Ethic* depends on the following question: Can it be shown that the ethos of inner-worldly [i.e., this-worldly] asceticism was incorporated into the lives of religious non-professionals, and did this ethos become secularized as the spirit of capitalism?" (291). This question cannot, of course, be answered even by the most intensive examination of theological texts. Hence, even if Weber erred in his reading of Calvin and the post-Calvinist literature, that does not necessarily mean that his explanation of the relation of the Protestant ethic to the spirit of capitalism is invalid. As Oakes explains,

> This is because, as Weber himself noted, his explanation does not turn on the intrinsic meaning of elite theological doctrines, but on the interpretation and application of these doctrines *in the lives* of lay religious actors. The validity of Weber's explanation depends on how the Puritan "civic strata"—artisans, traders, entrepreneurs: men of the "middling" or "industrious" sort—interpreted religious doctrine, the consequences these interpretations produced for their understanding of their moral obligations, and the impact of this understanding on their conduct. (292)

If, therefore, it is conduct and consequences that are the criteria by which to evaluate the validity of Weber's thesis, then, Oakes argues convincingly, it is Weber's "The Protestant Sects and the Spirit of Capitalism" that we need to consider. And, indeed, as we have seen in our exposition of that essay, there can be no doubt that as late as the time of Weber's travels in the United States, Quakers, Baptists, and Methodists gained economic advantages from their religiously determined honesty in business and their sectarian affiliations. That accounts for the old saw about the Quakers, who came to America to do good and soon found themselves doing well. And as we have also heard Tocqueville's remarks about the relation of religion to commerce in America of the 1830s there appears to be no good reason to question Weber's central claim concerning that relation.

In sum, one can say with full confidence that the Weber thesis is a brilliantly conceived, subtle and complex, counterintuitive exercise in *Verstehensoziologie*, in which Weber had successfully grasped the meanings and motives of the early, ascetic Protestant entrepreneurs. That means that Weber succeeded in understanding these historical actors as they understood themselves.

NOTES

[1] Max Weber, *The Protestant Ethic and the Spirit of Capitalism*, translated by Talcott Parsons and introduced by Anthony Giddens (London and New York: Routledge, 1995), p. 41. Hereafter, all page references to this work will be cited in parentheses immediately following the quoted passage.

[2] H. H. Gerth and C. Wright Mills, eds., *From Max Weber: Essays in Sociology* (London: Routledge and Kegan Paul, 1948), p. 303, "The Protestant Sects and the Spirit of Capitalism." Hereafter, all page references to this volume will be cited in parentheses immediately following the quoted passage.

[3] It is noteworthy that an earlier distinguished traveler in America, Alexis de Tocqueville, anticipated Weber's thesis by noting the connection between religion and commerce in the United States. "Americans," he wrote, "follow their religion from interest." American preachers, Tocqueville observed in the 1830s, are always "referring to the earth, and it is only with great difficulty that they can divert their attention from it." Describing their discourses, Tocqueville continues: "It is often difficult to ascertain...whether the principal object of religion is to procure eternal felicity in the other world or prosperity in this" (*Democracy in America* [New York: Knopf, 1948], vol. 2, p. 127).

America, Tocqueville observed, was uniquely Puritan and bourgeois. He noted the predominantly Puritan background of the independent merchants and entrepreneurs. The values of Puritanism, on the one hand, and of commerce and industry, on the other, appeared to be not only compatible but mutually reinforcing. Although Tocqueville includes other elements that contributed to the pronounced practical temperament of Americans, he mentions first their "strictly Puritanical origin [and] their exclusively commercial habits" (36–37). These people, wrote Tocqueville, spend "every day of the week in making money and Sunday in going to church" (83).

[4] See Tawney's foreword to Weber's *Protestant Ethic and the Spirit of Capitalism* (New York: Scribner, 1958), p. 8.

[5] See Malcolm MacKinnon's "The Longevity of the Thesis: A Critique of the Critics," in *Weber's Protestant Ethic: Origins, Evidence, Contexts*, edited by Hartmut Lehmann and Guenther Roth (Cambridge: Cambridge University Press, 1993), p. 212. Hereafter, all page references to this work will be cited in parentheses immediately following the quoted passage.

CHAPTER 7

MAX WEBER ON THE WORLD RELIGIONS

If one had to summarize Max Weber's conception of the religious experience from the earliest phases of human society to those of the modern era, it would resemble something like the following schematic view. In the earliest phases, magical and religious powers and the social duties attached to the belief in them were among the most essential conditions shaping the conduct of social life. Almost everywhere history exhibited a similar process: the gradual transformation of an earlier belief in spirits, demons, and impersonal, supradivine forces (e.g., the Greek *moira*, fate) into a *religion of salvation*, that is, a religious outlook that negates the world in its existing condition and inculcates a doctrine according to which liberation from suffering is attainable in another world.

As human beings begin to reflect more carefully on the human condition, they come to feel that the existing world ought to be or can become a meaningfully ordered cosmos. They begin to raise questions concerning the relationship between good fortune and merit. They observe that too often the innocent suffer and the wicked prosper, and they seek an explanation of this phenomenon, as well as the reason for suffering and death. In attempting to address such questions by means of reason, they create a "theodicy," a defense of the Divine's goodness and omnipotence in spite of the existence of evil. This process of intellectual reflection on the human condition, and on the implications for religious experiences and doctrines, is what Weber calls *rationalization*, the process that dissolves magical notions and increasingly "disenchants" the world.

In the transition from magic to doctrine, and the gradual disintegration of the magical image of the world, Weber discerned two tendencies in the world religions: one toward the *rational* mastery of the world, and the other toward otherworldly, *mystical* experiences. The rationalization process, which Weber regards as characteristic of the West, advances on many paths, and its development encompasses and permeates all of the institutions of Western civilization—the economy, the state, law, science, art, and music.

Although as we shall see, Weber proposed that one finds certain important beginnings of the rationalization process in ancient Judaism, it is the ancient Greeks, for Weber, who first developed a *methodical way of thinking*. All the institutions of Western society have been decisively shaped by that way of thinking, which was joined by a *methodical way of life* oriented to practical purposes. In accounting for that way of life, Weber assigned considerable causal weight, as we have seen, to ascetic Protestantism. For Weber, it was the union of the Greek theoretical with Protestant practical rationalism that separated modern Western society from antiquity, and it was the special character of both forms of rationalism that distinguished modern Western society from the civilizations of the East. There were, of course, certain processes of rationalization in the East as well, but neither the scientific, the political, the economic, nor the artistic institutions took the path that is peculiar to the West. In contrast to the thoroughgoing rationalization or "disenchantment" of the West, the East remained an "enchanted garden."

Weber looked upon his recognition of the fundamentally different characters of East and West as one of his most important discoveries and contributions to our knowledge. Consequently, his original inquiry into the relationship between religion and economics grew into an even broader inquiry into the special character of Western society that distinguished it so sharply from Eastern society: Why is it only in the West that one finds the development of rational-experimental science, rational harmonic music, and architecture and plastic arts that employ rational methods? Why only in the West do we find government by professionally trained officials and specialists, parliaments, political parties, and states with rational bodies of law? And, finally, the chief and related question for Weber: Why only in the West did the most fateful force in modern life—namely, *capitalism*—develop indigenously?

These are the questions that impelled Weber to transcend any single academic field and to come to grips with the worldwide scale of reality that concerned him.

THE RELIGION OF CHINA

Interested as he was in the economic and social consequences of Chinese religion, Weber had to begin his study by illuminating the most distinctive features of Chinese social structure. And since the central, historical-sociological question for Weber was why capitalism had not developed indigenously in China, he asks us to face two peculiar facts: (1) A great increase of wealth in precious metals led to the emergence of a money economy, but this not only failed to undermine the traditional forces, it strengthened them; (2) although imperial China experienced an enormous growth in population, it, too, failed to stimulate capitalist development. In a word, both the increase in precious metals and growth in population were associated with a *stationary* economy. There was, then, something about the structure of the society and its culture that formed insuperable obstacles to capitalist development.

To explain the nature of those obstacles, Weber had to analyze in some detail the major features of the imperial Chinese political system. Montesquieu was among the first to recognize the distinctive political structure of certain Asian societies. He coined the ideal-type concept *Oriental despotism* to characterize certain Asian political systems. Weber's studies of China taught him that Montesquieu's ideal-type concept did in fact capture the chief characteristics of the Chinese system.

Montesquieu's concept refers to a highly centralized, agrarian bureaucracy in which *all* power is concentrated in the hands of the supreme ruler. Egypt under the Pharaohs is the historical prototype and an excellent example of such a system. The Pharaoh regarded the entire society as his *oikos* (household)—this is the Greek word Weber used in another context to describe the Pharaoh's attitude—and all his subjects as his domestic servants. In the pure form of Oriental or Asian despotism, only the despot possesses real power in Weber's sense: the ability to realize his will despite and against the resistance of others. There are rich landlords and rich merchants in such systems, who possess power over their subordinates but not in relation to the despot. In these terms, "Oriental despotism" is the opposite of a "feudal system" as an ideal type. Feudalism is a polycentric political system in which each feudal lord does in fact possess real power within his own domain. There was a feudal era in Chinese history, but eventually it was superseded by a centralized imperial structure.

The concept of Asian despotism as applied to China helps Weber bring out the sharp contrasts with the structure of the West. So beginning with the concept of "city," Weber shows that the Chinese city differed fundamentally from that of the West. For although the Chinese city was the usual locus of trade and crafts, it lacked real political autonomy. The Chinese city, unlike the Western, was not a "polis" in the ancient Greek sense, for it was not a "commune" with political privileges of its own. In those terms there was no citizenry in China, in the sense of a self-equipped, military estate such as existed in Western antiquity. In a word, no social forces emerged in Chinese cities that enabled them to attain autonomy. There were periodic revolts of the urban populace, but they always aimed at removing a specific official, or rejecting a new tax, but never at gaining a charter to guarantee the freedom of the city. This proved impossible, Weber explains, because the traditional kinship relations, especially the "sib" (i.e., family or clan), remained intact.

Inhabitants of the Chinese "city" retained their relations to the native place of their sib, the ancestral land and shrine. All important relations with the native village were maintained. Moreover, the prosperity of the Chinese city depended primarily not on an enterprising spirit in economic and political ventures but on the imperial administration of the rivers. River regulation is another central feature of "Asian despotism." Just as the Pharaoh in Egypt was held responsible for the proper administration of the dams and sluice gates of the Nile, the Chinese emperor was responsible for the "regulation of the waters." In China as in ancient Egypt, the need to control the rivers and to distribute the waters for artificial irrigation was a precondition for the adequate working of the economy.

The Chinese emperor, however, unlike the Pharaoh, was regarded not as a deity but as the chief magician who had learned the secrets of the timeless impersonal forces governing the cosmos harmoniously. Thus, the

> laws of nature and of rites were fused into the unity of *Tao*. Not a supramundane lord creator, but a *supradivine, impersonal, forever identical and eternal existence was felt to be the ultimate and supreme.* This was to sanction the validity of the eternal order and its timeless existence. The impersonal power of heaven did not "speak" to man. It revealed itself in the regimen on earth, in the firm order of nature and tradition which were part of the cosmic order, and, as elsewhere, it revealed itself in what occurred to man. The welfare of the subjects documented heavenly contentment and the correct functioning of the order. All bad events were symptomatic of disturbance in the providential harmony of heaven and earth through magical forces.[1]

In this conception of things, deities, spirits, and other superhuman beings were stronger than humans but far below the impersonal, supreme power of Heaven, and even below the emperor as chief magician, who studied the "laws" of heaven and learned how to apply them for the welfare of his subjects. Though the spirits remained subordinate, however, they, too, could be magically influenced and might also determine one's fate. The emperor, as chief magician, was seen to possess the magical charisma necessary for him to serve as the supreme ruler. He most probably achieved this status, as did the Pharaohs of Egypt, by the highly significant role he played in river regulation. The Chinese emperor thus ruled by virtue of his charismatic authority. He had to prove himself, as the "Son of Heaven," as a ruler approved by Heaven, the criterion of proof being that his subjects fared well under him. If he failed to prove himself, he lost his charisma. If, for example, "the rivers broke the dikes, or if rain did not fall despite the sacrifices made, it was evidence...that the emperor did not have the charismatic qualities demanded by Heaven" (31). In such cases, the emperor was compelled to do public penance or even to abdicate.

The key public officials in the imperial bureaucracy were the Confucian mandarins or literati. For the most part candidates for such posts were recruited from the ranks of the well-to-do landlords, although occasionally the bright son of a peasant might have qualified for admission to the Confucian schools, where the curriculum consisted primarily of Chinese classical literature and culture. For more than two thousand years the literati were the leading stratum in China. Their social honor rested not on a charisma of magical powers but on their knowledge and expertise in writing and literature. Only those who had distinguished themselves as graduates from the Confucian schools were considered competent to order the imperial administration correctly, and it was they who were assigned to posts in the imperial bureaucracy. The concern for "correct" administration of the state imparted to the literati a far-reaching, practical, political rationalism. In their literature they created the concept of "office," an ethos of "official duty," and a concern with the "public weal." Confucius himself had been an official before he began to live as a teacher and writer.

The emperor and his circle strove to retain the concentration of supreme power in their hands by devising special stratagems in the assignment of posts to the Confucian mandarins. Once they had graduated from the schools successfully, they became officials in the bureaucracy, most often as tax farmers, that is, as officials responsible for the collection of taxes in a certain locale. The term *tax farmers* refers to the fact that they paid themselves for their service by retaining a portion of the revenues as salary. Indeed, there was always tension between the mandarin and the central authorities, the former often tending to squeeze the peasants excessively, thus raising the likelihood of rebellion and banditry, the latter, out of concern for social order, admonishing, punishing, or even replacing such officials.

The central powers sought to prevent the mandarin official from becoming independently powerful in the manner of a feudal lord by prohibiting employment in his home province and by ensuring the transfer of the official to another province or locale every three years. Such devices, together with the fact that as tax collectors the mandarins could hardly endear themselves to the peasants, prevented officials from striking roots in any given area and developing independent power bases of their own. Moreover, since the mandarin was always an "outsider," and was unfamiliar with provincial law based on precedent, he ran the risk of violating sacred traditions. He thus always remained dependent on the instructions of an unofficial adviser, a native man of literary education who was thoroughly familiar with local customs. Finally, the Confucian official was dependent on a number of unofficial assistants whom he had to pay from his own pocket. The mandarins were thus effectively prevented from becoming feudal lords who could throw off the control of the central authorities.

Indeed, it was with the aim of preventing feudalization that the central authority instituted the examination system and the appointment to office on the basis of educational rather than on birth-and-rank qualifications. The Confucian schools aimed for a pedagogy of cultivation. The examinations tested no special skills, as do modern Western examinations for physicians, lawyers, technicians, and state officials. On the contrary, the examinations of the Confucian schools "tested whether or not the candidate's mind was thoroughly steeped in literature and whether or not he possessed the *ways of thought* suitable to a cultured man and resulting from cultivation in literature" (121). Here, however, Weber calls attention to an important historical fact: Although the content of the examinations was purely mundane in nature and represented a test of cultural knowledge, "the popular view of them was very different: it gave them [the examinations] a magical-charismatic meaning. In the eyes of the Chinese masses, a successfully examined candidate and official was by no means a mere applicant for office qualified by knowledge. He was a proved holder of magical qualities, which . . . were attached to the certified mandarin just as much as to an examined or ordained priest of an ecclesiastic institution of grace, or to a magician tried and proved by his guild" (128). In earlier times the mandarins had adversaries in the "great families" of the feudal period who resisted centralization and being pushed out of their positions of power. In the long run, however, the mandarins won out because every drought, eclipse of the sun, defeat in arms, and generally threatening event at once enhanced the prestige of the literati. "For such events," Weber explains, "were considered the result of a breach of tradition and a desertion of the classic way of life, which the literati guarded" (139). When the throne needed advice, it turned quite naturally to the literati.

Confucianism can therefore be seen in one of its main aspects as worldly and rational. There is no word for "religion" in the Chinese language. There were "doctrine" and "rites," without distinguishing whether they are religious or conventional in nature. The official Chinese term for Confucianism was "doctrine of the literati." As Weber observes, the orthodox Confucian "performs his rites for the sake of his fate in this world—for long life, children, wealth, and to a very slight degree for the good of the ancestors, but not at all for the sake of his fate in the 'hereafter'" (144). Confucianism is a system of ethics, an inner-worldly or this-worldly morality for everyday life. However, because of the overarching Chinese belief in Tao and the role of Heaven as an impersonal, supradivine force, Confucianism meant primarily *adjustment to the world*, to its order and conventions. The cosmic order of the world was considered fixed and inviolable, and that included the orders of society.

A key question for Weber, then, was how the predominantly rational and this-worldly Confucians related to the doctrines of Tao and to the magicians. There was, of course, a great gap between the rational and learned Confucians and the masses, a gap that could not be filled by educating them with the classical doctrine. The old folk deities and many new ones had come under the patronage of a priesthood, and they were tolerated because they claimed they had originated with Lao-tzu. "Originally," writes Weber, "the meaning of this doctrine did not differ in the main from that of Confucianism. Later it became antagonistic to Confucianism and was finally considered thoroughly heterodox" (177). "Tao," per se, is an orthodox Confucian concept, referring to the eternal order of the cosmos. With Lao-tzu, however, Tao took on the qualities of mysticism. Tao was the one unchangeable element, and therefore of absolute value. It meant the order as well as the supradivine essence of matter and all being. Tao thus became the supradivine, All-One with which one could unite—as in all contemplative mysticisms—by emptying oneself of all worldly interests and desires until one felt released from the world and united with the supradivine. However, although the Confucians understood Tao as the All-One, they were not mystics; they had no interest in the psychic state called a *unio mystica*.

We now arrive at one of Weber's most important observations about the Confucian literati. Although they were in many respects worldly and rational, they never aimed resolutely at uprooting magic in general and Taoist magic in particular. Magic as a belief and practice was so deeply rooted among the masses that the Confucians tolerated it as a means of social control. Thus the toleration of magic and animism by both the Confucians and the heterodox Taoists became decisive for the continued existence and tremendous power of magic in Chinese life. What magic and animism meant in Chinese social life was that mountains, rocks, valleys, trees, and waters were all considered animated by indwelling spirits. A single rock or tree could protect a whole area against the attacks of evil demons. Even as late as the twentieth century, detours of many miles were made because from the geomancers' viewpoint the construction of a canal, road, or bridge would disturb or violate the spirits, thus constituting a real danger.

So although there certainly were certain definite, rational, and empirical-scientific developments in China, this-worldly rationalism was pretty much confined to the Confucian intellectuals, and science was so encrusted with magical-animistic beliefs that the Chinese world would remain an "enchanted garden." Folk magic and Taoist magic, together with the strong traditionalism of both Confucianism and Taoism, constituted a major obstacle to innovation in general and economic development in particular. This brings us to Weber's conclusion in which he compares Confucianism with Puritanism to explain why China had never developed a modern rational type of capitalism indigenously.

CONFUCIANISM AND PURITANISM

For Weber, as noted earlier, the degree of rationalization that a given religion has undergone may be assessed by using two criteria. The first is the extent to which a religion has divested itself of magic. The second is the degree to which a religion has "systematically unified the relation between God and the world and therewith its own ethical relationship with the world" (226). Employing the first criterion, Weber proposes that it is ascetic Protestantism that has eliminated magic most completely, even to the extent of burying the bodies of loved ones without any formal ceremony to avoid even the semblance of superstition. But, of course, Weber recognized that notwithstanding Puritanism's extraordinary degree of disenchantment, a residue of superstition remained, as was evident in the witch trials that flourished for a time in New England. However, in spite of the residue of superstition, Puritanism had developed an ethical rationalism enjoining its adherents to live and work in this world with a God-fearing attitude and in accordance with God's commandments.

Confucianism, in contrast, tolerated magic and animism. This meant, culturally, that China remained a magical garden in which scientific knowledge was never translated into the technology that is so integral a part of the modern, rational capitalist economy. Puritan ethics, on the other hand, meant that the individual in pursuit of his calling turns his back on traditionalism, lives in tension with the world, and changes it economically and socially. In Confucian ethics, in contrast, one accepted tradition and strove to adapt to Tao, the eternal, impersonal, supradivine force responsible for the harmonious regulation of the universe.

Virtue for the Confucian therefore implied *adjustment* to the world in accordance with the mandate of Heaven. For the ideal Confucian gentleman, grace and dignity were expressed by fulfilling traditional obligations. The Confucian ideal of the harmonious balance of the world as a macrocosm had its counterpart in the individual's ideal conception of the self as a harmoniously balanced personality as a microcosm. The Confucian was rational and worldly in the sense that as a reward for virtue "he expected only long life, health and wealth in the world and beyond death the retention of his good name.... [But] all transcendental anchorage of ethics, all tension between the imperatives of a supra-mundane God and a creatural [*sic*] world, all orientation toward a goal in the beyond, and all conception of radical evil were absent" (228). In a word, orthodox Confucianism had never produced an ethical equivalent to the ascetic Protestant ethic. The Confucian "ethic of unconditional affirmation of and adjustment to the world presupposed the unbroken and continued existence of a purely magical religion" (229). Anticipating the argument he will make in his *Ancient Judaism*, Weber avers that "tension toward the 'world' had never arisen [in China] because, as far as is known, there had never been an ethical prophecy of a supra-mundane God who raised ethical demands" (230).

A true ethical prophecy, Weber explains, creates in individuals a moral motive compelling them to view the world as material to be fashioned ethically in accordance with the God-given norms. But the Confucian ethic lacked any tension between ethical principles and human shortcoming, between religious duty and sociopolitical reality. Moreover, the attachment to one's sib together with familial piety meant that the duties of a Chinese Confucian always consisted of piety toward those who were close to him as kin or as friends. Hence, nepotism was never supplanted in principle by impersonal, rational, formal-legal, contractual relations, as it was in the West. In Weber's words, "The great achievement of ethical religions, above all of the ethical and ascetic sects of Protestantism, was to shatter the fetters of the sib. These religions established the superior community of faith and a common ethical way of life in opposition to the community of blood.... From the economic viewpoint it meant basing business confidence upon the ethical qualities of the individual, proven in his impersonal, vocational work" (237). For Weber, then, the ethics of both Confucianism and Puritanism had their irrational anchorages, the one in magic and the other in an inscrutable, supramundane God. But the Chinese magical garden meant the inviolability of tradition; life conduct was to remain unchangeable if the wrath of the spirits was to be avoided. In contrast, Weber writes, "From the relation between the supra-mundane God and the creaturely wicked, ethically irrational world there resulted ... the absolute unholiness of tradition and the truly endless task of ethically and rationally subduing and mastering the given world.... Here, the task of the rational transformation of the world stood opposed to the Confucian adjustment to the world" (240).

The typical Chinese Confucian used his family's savings to acquire a classical, literary education, pass the examinations, acquire a lucrative post in the imperial bureaucracy, and thus attain the status of a cultivated gentleman. "The typical Puritan," again in contrast,

> earned plenty, spent little, and invested his income as capital in rational capitalist enterprise out of an ascetic compulsion to save. "Rationalism" ... was embodied in both ethics. But only the Puritan rational ethic with its supra-mundane orientation brought economic rationalism to its consistent conclusion. This happened merely because nothing

was further from the conscious Puritan intention. It happened because inner-worldly [i.e., this-worldly] work was simply expressive of the striving for a transcendental goal. (247–48)

Weber recognizes that the Confucian "mentality" and its corresponding practical attitudes were codetermined, as he has shown, by the political and economic conditions of the Chinese imperial system. Yet in view of the effectiveness of ideas in history, he concludes that "one can hardly fail to ascribe to those attitudes effects strongly counteractive to capitalist development" (249).

THE RELIGION OF INDIA

In his studies of Hinduism and the other religious movements on the Indian subcontinent, Weber continues to address the question of why the modern, rational type of capitalism had never developed there indigenously. This question seemed all the more interesting and important to him in light of the fact that India possessed many of the material and intellectual elements that are preconditions of capitalism. For centuries urban development in India paralleled that of the West in many respects. Moreover, the Indians appear to have originated the rational number system, the zero, arithmetic, and algebra. In contrast to China, India also cultivated rational-empirical sciences. The Indian administration of justice could have been adapted to capitalistic purposes, and Indian handicrafts and occupational specialization were also highly developed. So Weber sets himself the task, as he did with regard to China, of inquiring into the role of Indian religion, *as one factor among many* that might have prevented capitalist development.

The first phenomenon that strikes the student of Indian society is the salience of the caste system. We learn the names of the four major castes from the *Laws of Manu*: Brahmans (priests), Kshatriyas (warriors), Vaishyas (commoners or merchants), and Shudras (peasants). In the course of Indian history, however, thousands of subcastes emerged. I shall explore the significance of the caste system in a later context.

The expansion of Hinduism was accomplished in opposition to folk, animistic beliefs and in conflict with earlier salvation religions. With the propagation of Hinduism the ruling stratum of an animistic, tribal territory began to adopt certain specific Hindu customs—abstention from beef, the absolute refusal to butcher cows, total abstinence from intoxicating liquids. In addition, certain purification practices of good Hindu castes were adopted, and the animistic spirits were reinterpreted and given the names of Hindu gods and goddesses.

As Hinduism continued to spread through missionary work, castes also proliferated. With the increase in population and the growing demand for labor in the wealthier developing areas, numerous unclean and "lower" services were required, which the well-to-do, resident population refused to take over. Such services and occupations therefore fell into the hands of alien workers who even settled in urban areas, forming "guest-occupational" communities of their own. Frequently, the guest-people were regarded as ritually impure and therefore excluded from intermarriage and commensalism with the host-people. But the so-called impure guest-people gained economic security thereby, since the village or city owed them a definite compensation for their services and, in effect, reserved for the guests a monopoly in their respective occupations.

In time, the guest-people began to claim and accept certain religious services from the Brahmans who specialized in serving the impure castes. The guests had thus shed their "pariah" status and become a legitimate caste, however underprivileged, rather than remaining an alien people. Furthermore, the members of the new caste soon formed associations, like quasi–trade unions, making possible the legitimate defense of their interests.

"Caste" in India remained a matter of social rank, and the central position of the Brahmans in Hinduism rested primarily on the fact that it was in relation to the Brahmans that social rank was determined. Castes are, in principle, hereditary and endogamous. So one important consequence of the caste system is that it precludes the kind of fraternization that is presupposed in commensalism. Hence, even where there were no conflicts of economic interest, a profound estrangement usually existed between castes. A caste is a closed status group whose social honor is looked upon as higher or lower than that of other castes.

Originally, the Brahmans were magicians who had learned the sacred magical formulae and ritualistic practices. The historical ascendancy of the Brahmans was connected with the growing significance of magic in all spheres of life. Since their knowledge was held to be a secret monopoly, their sons acquired the monopoly automatically through heredity. The decisive source of the power of a full Brahman was his expert knowledge of the Vedas, a knowledge viewed as charismatic. A Brahman acquired full stature by becoming the spiritual adviser to a prince. A prince without a Brahman could hardly be regarded as a king, and a Brahman without a king could hardly be regarded as a full Brahman.

As Weber begins to assess the effects of the caste system and other factors on the economy, he cites an observation Marx had made on the causes of the stationary character of the Indian economy: "Karl Marx has characterized the peculiar position of the artisan in the Indian village— his dependence on fixed payment in kind instead of production for the market—as the reason for the specific 'stability' of the Asian peoples. In this Marx was correct."[2] Weber adds, however, that "not only the position of the village artisan but also the caste order as a whole must be viewed as the bearer of stability." But Weber cautions us not to exaggerate the role of caste, since despite the caste barriers, and the prohibition of commensalism between members of diverse castes, they were in fact often brought together to work side by side in workshops. What Weber wants therefore to argue is that it is not any specific factor or even one set of factors that served as obstacles to capitalist development but rather the "spirit" embedded in the whole system. It was again, as in the case of China, religious traditionalism that carried most of the causal weight as an obstacle.

Hinduism rested on two basic principles: the *samsara* belief in the transmigration of souls and the related *karma* doctrine of compensation. It was believed that each ethically relevant act has unavoidable consequences for the fate of the individual—the doctrine of karma. The idea of compensation was connected to the individual's fate in the caste order. All ritual and ethical merits and faults of the individual formed a kind of account book in which a surplus of merits or faults determined the destiny of the soul at rebirth. In these terms, an individual's fate was his own doing. Every individual was locked into an endless series of ever new lives and deaths, and he determined his own fate solely by his own deeds and misdeeds. That was the most consistent form of the karma doctrine. Therefore, the very caste status of an individual could not be viewed as accidental. The individual is born into the caste he deserves due to his conduct in a previous life. The karma doctrine thus produced an ethically determined cosmos, the most consistent theodicy ever created in history: Individuals are reborn only in accordance with their just deserts. Order and rank of the castes is eternal: One can become a Kshatriya or even a Brahman, but rebirth can also drag one down into the life of a "worm in the intestines of a dog." Strict fulfillment of caste obligations in the present life was therefore considered the way to earn a more honorific birth.

Another element of the strong *traditionalistic* spirit of Hinduism was the dread of the magical evil of innovation. Even at the time of Weber's writing, the typical peasant could hardly be persuaded to fertilize the soil because it was against custom. Furthermore, Hinduism placed the highest premium on caste loyalty. The Hindu salvation doctrine promises higher rebirth to the artisan who abides by prescribed traditions, never deceiving as to quality and never demanding higher pay. Hinduism's strikingly strong traditionalism finds its explanation, for Weber, in the great promises for future rebirth that were at stake for the low castes whenever their members deviated from the customs and duties of their caste. What is therefore distinctive of Hinduism is the combination of the karma doctrine with the caste structure.

To explain this distinctiveness Weber proposes that ethnic factors alongside economic and status factors were important. Although the historical evidence is less than clear, the conventional historical view at the time suggested that an antagonism between the Arya and the Dasyu had appeared in the ancient Vedic period. The name Arya refers to the distinguished, while the Dasyu was the dark-colored enemy of the invading Aryan conquerors. Weber rejects racialist theories, but he believes that ethnic and color differences appear to have mattered, so that interethnic marriage never attained full social approval.

Industrial specialization advanced largely owing to the incoming guest-peoples. But in the cities the ethnic strangeness of the guest artisans led to segregation, often preventing the multitude of craftsmen from organizing themselves in the manner of the artisans and craftsmen of the guilds in the West. It followed that the ethnic and caste differences also prevented the free fraternization of the Indian urban inhabitants, thus forming an obstacle to the creation of citizen militias like those of the ancient polis or of the rising towns of the late medieval West.

To clarify further what he means by the traditionalistic "spirit" of Indian religions, Weber proceeds first to summarize the nature of orthodox Hinduism, and then the nature of the heterodox soteriologies, that is, the soul-saving doctrines of Jainism and Buddhism.

ORTHODOX HINDUISM

The holy technique of yoga was an integral element of orthodox Hinduism, a technique derived from the ancient magical experience of autohypnosis and the resulting psychological states induced by the regulation and temporary stoppages of breathing and its effects on brain functions. The emotional and mental effects of such practices were valued as holy. Yoga gained more influence than any similar technique. Eventually, the practitioners of the technique, the yogins, formed an association of magicians without Vedic education, and the Brahmans refused to recognize them as their peers. Interpreted intellectually, yoga technique supposes that the grasp of the divine or supradivine is an irrational psychic experience having nothing to do with rational knowledge. Hence, classical Brahmanical doctrine never completely accepted the legitimacy of the technique, for the Brahmans regard the gaining of knowledge as the chief means of grasping the divine or supradivine. The salvation-seeking Brahman believed that right knowledge was the source of magical powers. The supreme good could be achieved only through a higher knowledge: *gnosis*.

In contrast to yoga technique, which sought miraculous power such as suspending gravitation and gaining the ability to float, classical Brahmanical contemplation sought the blissful rapture of a gnostic comprehension of the divine. For the classical Brahmans, all holy techniques were intellectualized to achieve one of two purposes: (1) through the emptying of consciousness, to make room for the holy; or (2) through intense concentrated meditation, to achieve a state experienced not as emotion but as mystically acquired knowledge. In the long run, however, the Brahmans never succeeded completely in rejecting as heterodox the other world-fleeing techniques, in which the individual strove to free himself from the world of the senses, from anxieties, passions, drives, and the concerns of everyday life, thereby preparing himself for a final state of rest and unity with the divine.

And yet the so-called final state was not really a final state of eternal salvation. Why not? Because all the salvation technologies of India, whether orthodox or heterodox, entail a withdrawal not only from the everyday world but even from "paradise" and the world of the godly. Karma implied that residence in paradise can only be for a finite time, and the moment the surplus of merits is used up, one must inevitably enter again the cycle of rebirth on earth. Furthermore, to grasp fully the Hindu conception of the impersonal, supradivine force (similar to the Chinese Tao and the Greek Moira), we need to understand that in contrast to the Jewish, Christian, and Muslim conception of an Almighty God, Creator of the universe, the gods in Hinduism are subject to the magical influence of properly exercised ritual. "In this sense," Weber observes, "they [the gods] are inferior, not superior, to the wise man who knows how to coerce them" (167). Brahmanical salvation strove always for absolute salvation, which had to be more than a temporary residence with the gods. The quest for salvation was not so much a matter of escaping from suffering or the imperfections of the world as escaping from everything transitory.

In the Brahmans' intellectual outlook, transitoriness was characteristic of everything, whether it was earthly, heavenly, or hellish. The cosmos is an eternal, meaningless "wheel" of recurring births and deaths ceaselessly rolling on through all eternity. Only two *non*transitory realities were discoverable in it: the eternal order itself and those beings who might succeed in escaping the cycle of ongoing rebirths, namely, the *souls*. The central question, then, for all Hindu philosophy was this: How could souls be extricated from the cycle of karma—how could they be liberated from the causality binding them to the cycle? Given the two absolute doctrines of Hindu philosophy, samsara (the migration of souls) and karma, the one and only real meaning of "salvation" became an escape from the wheel of rebirth. This necessarily worked toward the enhancement of the religious individualism characteristic of all mystical holy-seeking; the individual, in the last analysis, can only help himself. In contrast to the Puritan belief in election by divine grace, the Brahmanical doctrine left it entirely to the individual to seek his own nontransitory destiny.

Brahmanical gnostic mysticism, Weber observes, thus produced no ethic for life in *this* world. The Upanishads contain nothing or almost nothing of what is considered to be ethics in the West. Hence, the entire soteriological (soul-saving) significance of Brahmanical, gnostic mysticism was the ideal of dissolving the unfortunate and tragic linkage of spirit and matter, dissolving the "materialization" of the "I." Eventually, this dematerialization of the "I" was designated as *nirvana*. Nirvana and similar states of bliss were not necessarily understood as otherworldly, in the sense that they can be entered upon only after death. Quite the contrary, they were sought in the present life by means of diverse gnostic techniques.

The Bhagavadgita and the religious form that emerged from it also preserved the Brahmanical-intellectual character of religious experience. Bhagavata religion retained the centrality of gnosis and the notion of a holy aristocracy of mystical knowledge. Only the wise were holy. In the end, the caste structure and the gnostic character of the varieties of Hindu religious experience, Weber avers, carried with them an absolute relativizing of ethics. Ethics was relative in that it varied with caste membership. The equal and independent value of the various spheres of life in this world had to result, says Weber, from "their equal devaluation as soon as ultimate questions of salvation [through gnosis] were at stake" (190). For Weber, the varieties of Hindu religion may therefore be characterized in the following terms: "Reality and magic, action, reasoning and mood, dreamy gnosis and sharp conscious feelings are found with and within one another, because ultimately all remain equally unreal and insubstantial against the sole reality of divine being" (191).

Weber reminds us again that beneath the official Brahmanical religion there had always existed folk beliefs and practices, including popular orgiasticism consisting of alcoholic, sexual, and meat orgies, magical compulsion of spirits, and more. So Brahmanical Hinduism, finding it expedient to make substantial concessions to the popular religion, often departed from its orthodox doctrines. Moreover, two new religious movements emerged, Jainism and Buddhism, which the orthodox Brahmans regarded as heresies. For several hundred years the two heterodoxies became the chief rivals of Hinduism.

JAINISM

The founder of the Jain movement was a Kshatriya noble named Mahavira who died around 600 B.C.E. He rejected the teachings of the Vedas, arguing that they have no significance for salvation. This new movement accentuated the view that salvation depends solely on the asceticism of the individual: salvation is attained by gaining freedom from the wheel of rebirth, by detaching one's self from the world. All souls are equal and eternal divine essences. The gnostic doctrine of Jainism proposed stages in an individual's striving for salvation, the final stage being the "last rebirth," when the soul is fully redeemed and therefore bodyless, soundless, colorless—or, in a word, without contact with matter and without image.

In contrast, to the Buddhist nirvana, however, which meant salvation from existence in general, the Jainistic nirvana referred to "salvation from the body," the source of all lust and the primary constraint on the soul's power. The soul-saving teachings of the Jains demanded a higher degree of asceticism; indeed, it was pushed to the extreme in which one achieves supreme holiness by starving oneself to death. But a Jain must not yearn for either life or death, since either desire is liable to reattach an individual to karma. The doctrine of freeing oneself totally from worldly concerns gave rise to the principle that one should not resist evil.

Jain asceticism assigned supreme importance to *ahimsa*, the absolute prohibition of the killing of living beings. A Jain was permitted to take his own life if he found himself unable to resist his worldly lust, but in no circumstances was he to take another's life, even inadvertently. Although Jainism was therefore staunchly pacifistic, when it became the official religion in certain princely domains, the doctrine was revised to permit Jains to serve as warriors only in just wars of defense. But the orthodox Jain's interpretation of ahimsa often assumed the extremes of lighting no fires for light in the dark lest he might kill moths; straining water before boiling it; going about with his mouth and nose covered with a cloth to prevent the inhalation of minute insects; sweeping every bit of earth with a soft broom before taking a step; leaving his hair uncut for fear of killing lice, and more. This extreme interpretation of ahimsa, Weber shows, had definite economic consequences: "The practice of *ahimsa* led to the exclusion of the Jain from all industrial trades endangering life, hence from all trades which made use of fire, involved work with sharp instruments (wood or stone work); from masonry; and, in general, from the majority of industrial callings. Agriculture was, of course, completely excluded: ploughing, especially, always endangers the lives of worms and insects" (199).

Weber's primary concern being the economic relevance of the religions of India, he now highlights a few features of Jainism that showed similarities to ascetic Protestantism. Jains were allowed to acquire considerable wealth but, like the Puritans, were to take no joy in their possessions. Another similarity to the Puritans was the Jain commitment to absolute honesty in business life. The honesty of the Jain trader was so famous that at one time it was estimated that more than half the trade of India passed through Jain hands. It was due to the ritualistic requirements associated with ahimsa that nearly all Jains became traders. Only the trader could truly practice ahimsa. But the Jains, like the Jews of medieval Europe, remained confined to commercial capitalism and failed to create industrial organizations. The Jain social ethic also bore resemblance to that of the Puritans and the Jews, in that the Jains' commandments included the feeding of the hungry, the clothing of the poor, and kindness toward others.

Jainism, at the beginning of its development, ignored the caste system, for the castes had no role, even indirectly, in Jainist soteriology. The genuine Jain monk, preoccupied with his own salvation, served as guru and teacher, leaving the care of the temples and idols to the laity. But the laity, lacking the ritualistic knowledge and skills for such care, increasingly placed it in the hands of the Brahmans. In time, then, the laity submitted to Brahmanical Hinduization, and the caste order now also so imposed itself on the Jains that they were integrated into that order as a predominantly trader caste.

ANCIENT BUDDHISM

The founder of Buddhism was Siddharta, called Gautama, the Buddha. He was born in Nepal at the foot of the Himalayas. He belonged to the noble-warrior Kshatriya caste. Like all Indian philosophy and theology, Buddhism is a salvation religion, if the term *religion* may be used to describe a movement without a deity and without a cult. Buddhism, for Weber, represents the most radical form of salvation-seeking conceivable. Buddhism accepts the karma doctrine but, in its divergence from it, considers not the "personality" but the value of the single act.

What is sought in Buddhism is not salvation in an eternal life but the everlasting tranquillity of death. The legend explaining the reasons for the Buddha's flight from his parents' home gives us insight into the nature of his inspiration: Of what use, he asked, was the splendor of the world and of life when it was unavoidably beset with the evils of sickness, aging, and death; when beholding earthly beauty merely reminds us of the evils and enhances pain? And how senseless is the departure again and again into an infinity of new lives? The absolute senselessness of the ephemeral beauty and happiness in an everlasting cosmos is precisely what devalues the goods of this world. For the Buddha, then, it was not "evil" but ephemeral life that was the obstacle to salvation. Salvation is sought from the senseless process of existence in general. The Buddhist therefore fled "passion" because it made no sense in a cosmos in which all forms of existence are transitory. Even the later, "world-friendly" Mahayana school accepted as proof of the total senselessness of life that it inevitably ended in old age and death.

Interpreted philosophically, the Buddha was saying that in the final analysis, however much humans may try to delude others and themselves, the *will* to life is what ultimately holds life together despite its meaninglessness. It is the will that produces an acceptance of karma. Hence, if one wishes to escape karma, one must destroy the will. How does one attain the illumination necessary for the elimination of will? Only through an incessant meditative absorption of the truth, the giving up of the great illusions from which springs the thirst for life.

Whoever achieves such illumination enjoys bliss in the here and now. "Salvation" is thus sought in a psychic state remote from any activity in the social world, for salvation is an absolutely personal performance of the individual. The tranquillity of salvation can be achieved only by giving up every thirst connecting the individual to the world and the struggle for existence.

It followed that the most effective way to give up the struggle is to become *homeless*—to become an itinerant, mendicant monk, wandering without possessions and work, absolutely abstemious as regards alcohol and sex, practicing vegetarianism, shunning salt, spices, and honey. Although their ethical commandments bore some resemblance to the Decalogue, the Buddhists, with their broader application of the prohibition of killing (ahimsa), extended it to all living beings. In addition, the five cardinal prohibitions for the laity were not to kill, steal, commit adultery, lie, or get drunk. We see, then, why Weber averred that no rational, economic ethic had emerged from ancient Buddhism, which placed no religious premium on a specific economic conduct.

After reviewing the transformation of ancient Buddhism, its diffusion from India and its successful missions in Ceylon (present-day Sri Lanka), China, Korea, Japan, and Tibet (Lamaism), Weber proceeds to assess the economic relevance of the religions of India and of Asia in general. In addition to the caste structure and the guru domination of the masses, Weber brings into relief the spiritual or religious elements that contributed to the extraordinary economic and social traditionalism of Hinduism. In all the intellectual strata, there was, above all, the dogma of the unalterability of the world order, a dogma common to both the orthodox and heterodox bodies of thought.

The devaluation of the world common to all the soteriologies led to the paramount ideal of an absolute flight from the world. The highest means of achieving absolute flight was nothing other than mystical contemplation, not active conduct. Gnosis remained the highest and holiest means, despite the varieties of ethical teachings accompanying the diverse versions of the *unio mystica*. No Hindu was prompted by his spiritual outlook to place high value on the rational reconstruction of the world as a means of realizing the divine will. By "salvation," the mass of Hindus understood all events affecting the rebirth cycle as the consequences of their own, individual doings.

In general, Weber observes, there are few ideas transcending practical interests that have not originated in Asia. All the philosophies and soteriologies of Asia have shared one presupposition: that knowledge, whether literary or mystical, is the single absolute path to the highest holiness, here and in the world beyond. Even the knowledge of the "here" was not knowledge of the things of this world, of nature and social life, and the laws that hold for both. Rather, it was a philosophical knowledge concerned with the ultimate meaning of life and the cosmos. It was a knowledge that lay beyond science in the Western sense. Throughout the Asian spiritual outlooks, the conception of knowledge "is not a rational implement of empirical science such as made possible the rational *domination of nature and man* as in the Occident [i.e., in the West]. Rather it is the means of mystical and magical domination over the self and the world: gnosis. It is attained by an intensive training of body and spirit, either through asceticism or, as a rule, through strict, methodologically-ruled meditation" (331).

The fact that Asian knowledge or wisdom remained mystical in character had two consequences. The first was that the mystical soteriologies created a redemption *aristocracy* or *elite*, due to the fact that the capacity for gnosis was regarded as a charisma not accessible to all. The second consequence was that it led to a social and political quietude, a lack of rational concern with "politics" in the Western sense. Both consequences followed almost naturally from the prevalent notion, common to all Asian soteriologies, that the highest form of holiness is an "emptying" from one's self of all the experiences and materials of this world. Asian mysticism assumed the form of the antithesis between "peace" and "restlessness." The first was divine or supradivine; the second, "specifically creature-like, [and] therefore, finally, either illusory or soteriologically valueless, bound by time and space and transitory" (332).

In Asia the power of the religious leaders, of the charismatic strata, grew. But even the most rational of them failed to break the dominion of magic. The "magical spell" therefore remained the core of *mass* religiosity, above all for peasants and laborers but also for the middle classes. This antirational world of magic also necessarily affected everyday, economic life. There were spells

> for achieving all conceivable sorts of inner-earthly values—spells against enemies, erotic or economic rivals, spells designed to win legal cases, spiritual spells ... for forced fulfillment against the debtor, spells for the securing of wealth, for the success of undertakings. All this was either in the gross form of compulsive magic [i.e., compelling the deities by magical means] or in the refined form of persuading a functional god or demon through gifts. With such means the great mass of the non-literary and even the literary Asiatics sought to master everyday life. (336)

So although the Asiatic "drive for gain" was as strong as it was in the West, and pursued by every possible means, including magic, what Asia lacked precisely was the spiritual "factor" that became decisive for capitalist development in the West: a rational, this-worldly ethic of conduct like that of the inner-worldly asceticism of Protestantism.

In the West, the beginnings of a rational, inner-worldly ethic were bound up with the appearance of thinkers and prophets whose conception of the Divine's relation to the world was foreign to Asiatic culture. Moreover, these thinkers, the Hebrew prophets and the Greek philosophers of antiquity, addressed political problems associated with social classes and civic status groups of the city, without which neither Judaism nor Hellenic thought nor Christianity is conceivable (338).

ANCIENT JUDAISM

In contrast to the religions of the Far East, biblical Judaism conceived of the world as neither eternal nor unchangeable but as having been created. The present condition of the world was a result of human actions, first those of the Hebrews, and of God's reaction to their conduct, the criterion being whether they obeyed his commandments or strayed from them. "Hence," Weber explains, "the world was an historical product designed to give way again to the truly God-ordained order. The whole attitude toward life of ancient Jewry was determined by this conception of a future God-guided political and social revolution."[3] Weber's aim in this extraordinary work is to analyze the conditions in ancient Israel that gave rise to its "highly rational religious ethic of social conduct; it was free of magic and all forms of irrational quest for salvation; it was inwardly worlds apart from the paths of salvation offered by Asiatic religions" (4).

Weber begins with an analysis of the ancient Near East and the possible influences on the origins of the Israelite worldview. He recognizes that Egypt was an "essentially negative developmental stimulus." The Hebrews regarded the Egyptian corvée state and its fundamentally despotic nature as an abomination. They detested Egypt as a "house of bondage." Weber also recognizes that the ancient Hebrews were not Bedouins. Ancient Israelite laws showed no trace of Bedouin influence, and, besides, Israelite tradition maintains that the Amalek were the deadly enemies of Israel.

For Weber, the new Israelite worldview that aimed for a radical break with all forms of polytheism originated in the teachings of Moses and the prophets. The new monotheistic ethic rested on the distinctive relation of Israel to God, expressed and guaranteed in a unique historical event—the conclusion of a covenant with Yahweh. The prophets and other devout Hebrews always hearkened back to that great, miraculous event in which God had kept his promise, intervened in history, and liberated the Hebrews from Egyptian bondage. That was proof not only of God's power but of the absolute dependability of his promises.

Israel, then, as the other party to the covenant mediated by Moses, owed a lasting debt of gratitude to serve and worship Yahweh, the Lord of the universe, and to follow his laws strictly. This rational relationship, unknown elsewhere, created an ethical obligation so binding that Jewish tradition regarded "defection from Yahweh as an especially fatal abomination" (119). The markedly rational nature of the relationship lay in the *worldly* character of God's promises to Israel. Not some supernatural paradise was promised, but "that they would have numerous descendants, so that the people should become numerous as the sand of the seashore, and that they should triumph over all enemies, enjoy rain, rich harvests, and secure possessions" (119). What God offered, writes Weber, was "salvation from Egyptian bondage, not from a senseless world out of joint. He promised not transcendent values, but dominion over Canaan, which one was out to conquer, and a good life" (126). If the nation or individuals suffered and God failed to help, that was a sign that some commandment had been violated. Which one?

> Irrational divination-means could not answer this question, only knowledge of the very commandments and soul searching. Thus the idea of *berith* [covenant] flourishing in the truly Yahwistic circles pushed all scrutiny of the divine will toward an at least relatively rational mode of raising and answering the question. Hence, the priestly exhortation under the influence of the intellectual strata turned with great sharpness against soothsayers, augurs, day-choosers, interpreters of signs, conjurors of the dead, defining their ways of consulting the Deity as characteristically pagan. (167)

In that way the devout Hebrews initiated the process of breaking magic's hold upon the world. Weber thus proposed that the new Israelite worldview served to negate and repudiate all forms of polytheism and to put in their place a rational ethic based on the covenant Israel had made with a Presence it felt and conceived as an Almighty, universal God who had heard the cries of the oppressed and had come to their rescue.

If we think of the religions of the ancient Near East in, say, Mesopotamia, Canaan, and Egypt, it would be fair to characterize them as polytheistic. In order therefore to fully appreciate the historical significance of the Israelite, monotheistic outlook, it might be helpful to list the key elements of polytheism as an ideal type and then to contrast it with the Israelite view. Polytheism entails a good deal more than worshiping many gods. The most fundamental feature of polytheistic religions is that the gods do not reign supreme. Throughout we find them dominated by a higher order, an impersonal, supradivine force to which they always remain subject. The superordinate power assumes diverse forms. It is best known to Western readers as fate, the Greek *moira*. The inexorable power of *moira* over humans is most clearly conveyed in Sophocles' *Oedipus Rex*, where Oedipus kills his father in accordance with the prophecy of the oracle, and this despite the father's efforts to foil the prophecy by abandoning Oedipus in his infancy. In the end it is not known whether the oracle was fulfilled despite or because of the precautions taken. Fate had its way.

No less inexorable is the power of *moira* over the gods. In Greek mythology Zeus is the supreme ruler. His power is greater than that of all the other deities combined. Yet he is neither omnipotent nor omniscient. Other gods can oppose and deceive him, and *moira* is so powerful that Zeus is helpless before it. He laments that he cannot save his own son from the death fate has determined. It is simply not within his or any other god's power to avoid what fate has ordained.[4]

In the religions of the Far East one may also discern a supradivine, impersonal force. As we have seen, Weber observed in Chinese religion that it was this force in Taoism that ensured the regularity and felicitous order of the world. Weber also noted that in the religions of India there was the "notion of a supradivine and cosmic all-unity, superordinate to the gods and alone independent of the senseless change and transitoriness of the entire phenomenal world."[5]

When Weber speaks of the Far East as having remained an enchanted or magical garden, we need to understand how magic is related to the supradivine, impersonal force. In polytheistic mythologies and in sacred texts, there are circumstances in which human beings gain the ability, by means of magic, to influence, control, and even coerce the gods. In his studies of China and India and in his essays translated under the title *The Sociology of Religion*, Weber explains this phenomenon: A human magician can coerce the gods because he or she has learned the secret of the workings of the superordinate force, and has learned how to employ and manipulate its powers.[6]

Another element of polytheism is the dependence of the gods on human beings, for they derive their nourishment from the offerings of the sacrificial cult. "Sacrifice," writes Weber, "is a magical instrumentality that in part stands at the immediate service of the coercion of the gods. For the gods [in Hinduism] need the soma juice of the sorcerer-priests, the substance which engenders their ecstasy and enables them to perform their deeds. This is the ancient notion of the Aryans as to why it is possible to coerce the gods by sacrifice."[7]

Still another element of polytheism is the ability of human magicians to achieve divine status, apotheosis. And a final element is the fact that polytheism naturally implies multiple deities and their multiple domains. In Greek mythology, again, the respective domains of Zeus, Poseidon, and Hades are heaven, the sea, and the netherworld.

Taken as a whole, then, it is the polytheistic outlook, consisting of these constituent elements, that the Israelite view combated and sought to replace with the concept of a transcendental, all-powerful, universal, and ethical deity. This was largely accomplished, according to Weber, by the Hebrew prophets through their unrelenting struggle against magic and the other elements of polytheism.

THE HEBREW PROPHETS: THE SETTING

In the eighth century B.C.E., the northern kingdom of Ephraim, or Israel, and the southern kingdom of Judea found themselves in constant jeopardy, caught as they were between the superpowers of the time, Assyria on the one side and Egypt on the other. As Weber remarks, never before had the region witnessed warfare of such frightfulness and magnitude as that practiced by the Assyrian kings. The biblical writings of the period relate just how preoccupied the Israelites were with the fearful concern for their survival in the face of the merciless Assyrian conquerors. It was in this geopolitical context that there emerged in Israel the great Hebrew prophets of social justice, Amos, Hosea, Isaiah, Micah—and later, in the face of the Babylonian menace, Jeremiah and Ezekiel.

These prophets functioned in one of their roles as "political demagogues." They were primarily *speakers* who conceived of the great powers of Assyria, Egypt, and Babylonia as rods of Yahweh's chastisement for Israel's disobedience to his commandments. Had it not been for the menace of these great powers, Weber avers, the prophets would not have emerged. The prophets were an autonomous stratum that often confronted the Israelite kings and the wealthy and powerful, severely criticizing them for their oppression and exploitation of the poor. Occasionally, their admonitions became effective in lessening oppressive conditions.

Typically, the Hebrew prophet spoke on his own, to the public in the marketplace or to the elders at the city gate. The primary prophetic concern was the destiny of the state and the people, a concern that expressed itself in sharp criticism of the overlords. Weber uses the term *demagogue* to describe this prophetic role, but this epithet has to be properly understood. Weber employs the term in its original Greek sense to refer to a speaker who champions the cause of the common people. The demagogue of Periclean democracy, for example, was a secular politician who led the demos through his personal influence. But the phenomenon of religious demagoguery in the manner of the Hebrew prophets appears to be historically unique. Formally, the prophet was a private citizen, so to speak, for he held no official office. And yet, the political authorities paid close attention to the prophets' utterances and activities. Jeremiah's prophecies, for instance, were brought before the king because his message was considered an event of public significance.

Indeed, the political authorities faced the Hebrew "demagogue" with either fear, wrath, or indifference as the situation seemed to warrant. At times, the kings tried to draw a prophet into the royal circle, to co-opt him. At other times, the power holders took harsh action against the social critics. At still other times, members of the royal circle showed open contempt for their critics, as when King Joiakim threw the written prophetic warnings, sheet by sheet, into the fire. When Jeroboam II prohibited prophecy,

Amos reacted by proclaiming God's wrath toward the northern kingdom for its attempt to suppress prophecy. Amos's complaint, Weber remarks, is comparable to that of the modern political critic who demands freedom of speech and the press. For the prophets were more than "speakers." With Jeremiah and his scribe Baruch, the prophetic words were written down in the form of open letters to be read by both the king's circle and the public. Such letters and other prophetic writings constitute, for Weber, "the earliest known example of political pamphlet literature directly addressing itself to contemporary events" (272). Typically, the prophet takes no pleasure from the fact that the catastrophe he anticipated has materialized. He shows neither jubilation nor despair, and alongside his lamentations he offers hope for God's grace and better times.

Although Weber refers to the prophets as political demagogues, he stresses that to understand them as they understood themselves and were understood by their audiences, we must appreciate that their motives were absolutely religious. When Isaiah, for example, in the face of the Assyrian siege of Jerusalem, prophesied that the city would not fall, that was not the result of an assessment of the actual power relations of Assyria and Judea. It was, rather, the result of his assessment of Judea's moral conduct. Of course, the Judeans had sinned but not so egregiously as to deserve the destruction of the city of David. About a hundred years later, Jeremiah, in the face of the Babylonian menace, prophesied that Jerusalem *would* fall. His prophecy, too, was not the result of a realistic assessment of power relations. It was, rather, a matter of his believing that in the light even of Judea's earlier sins—two cases of human sacrifice to the Assyrian god Moloch, under the kings Manasseh and Ahaz—Judea cannot avoid God's severe punishment. The stench, Jeremiah proclaimed, had remained in God's nostrils. Furthermore, the prophets' stand with respect to foreign alliances, notably their constant opposition to an alliance with Egypt, was also determined by purely religious motives.

Just as the prophets' views of foreign policy were not based primarily on political considerations, their attitudes toward domestic issues were not based on their social class background. Their concern for the oppressed, exploited, and poor certainly did not flow from a common, disprivileged background. Quite the contrary, they shared the same attitude despite their diverse social origins. Although they argued passionately in defense of the interests of the "little people," and excoriated the rich and powerful, the great prophets themselves were far from disprivileged. Isaiah was descended from a genteel sib, he moved among distinguished priests and had close relations with King Hezekiah as his councillor and physician, and he was one of the eminent men of Jerusalem. Zephaniah had descended from David and was a great-grandson of Hezekiah. Ezekiel was a distinguished Jerusalem priest. All these men were therefore well-to-do Jerusalemites.

Micah came from a small town, and Jeremiah from a village, but he stemmed from a landed sib of rural priests and possessed sufficient resources for the purchase of land. And even Amos—who was a small stock-breeder and called himself a shepherd who lived on sycamore fruit, the food of the poor—was a highly educated man. Weber thus shows that the social class background of the prophets was certainly not the determinant of their attitudes. That they were not ideologues is also clear from the fact that they were as critical of the common people for failing in their religious duties as they were of the noble landowners for forcibly appropriating and enclosing the land of the poor. In a word, the meaning and motives of the prophets' words and actions were not political in the Greek sense. No Hebrew prophet was a champion of "democratic" ideals, deliberately serving as an ideological spokesman for the impoverished peasants or proletarians.

To the extent that the prophets derived "community" from any source, it was not from the demos. On the contrary, if they received any personal, material support at all, it was from the distinguished, pious families of Judea, where there were sympathetic supporters among the *zekenim*, the elders, who as guardians of the pious traditions held the prophets in high regard. Weber notes that although most prophets spoke out against debt slavery, the pawning of clothes, and the violation of the charity commandments that benefited the poor, the prophets never received support from the peasants.

As for the kings, they never supported the prophets, who were the chief critics of the politically necessary concessions the kings had made in allowing foreign shrines for the wives of their diplomatic marriages. From the time of Solomon and his corvée state, the prophets despised the royal adoption of practices that emanated from Egyptian despotism. Consequently, Solomon had no positive significance for any of the prophets, and it is David who was regarded as the pious ruler. Hosea viewed the kings of the northern kingdom as illegitimate because they had usurped the throne without the will of Yahweh, but no prophet denied the legitimacy of David's descendants. In their reaction to prophetic censure, the kings tolerated the prophets only when they had to, but when they felt sure of themselves, as did Manasseh, who ruled as an Assyrian puppet for fifty years, they resorted to bloody persecution.

Again and again, the prophets spoke out against a reliance on pagan, military technology (horses and chariots) and against political alliances. Dealings with Egypt were especially loathed for religious reasons. Egypt was described as a weak reed that would break and pierce the hand that leaned upon it. The ground of prophetic opposition was again religious not simply because of the dangerous influence of foreign cults on Judean soil but especially because Judah's primary reliance should be on the *berith* (covenant) with Yahweh. Trust in foreign alliances and in advanced military technology indicated a lack of trust in God. As Jeremiah viewed the covenantal relationship with Yahweh, he had ordained as Israel's punishment Nebuchadnezzar's conquest of Judea, and one had to accept the fact that no alliance of any kind could change Israel's God-ordained destiny. "Clearly," writes Weber, "the whole [prophetic] attitude toward internal as well as foreign affairs was purely religious in motivation; nothing bespeaks of political expediencies" (282).

Biblical criticism in Weber's time had introduced the notion of a fundamental dichotomy and even antipathy between the priests and prophets of Israel. Weber, however, regarded that notion as misleading, for the prophets "were by no means always antagonistic to the priests. Isaiah had close relations with the priests of Jerusalem, and Ezekiel was thoroughly priestly in outlook" (282). Weber also makes the point that although Hosea had said of God, "For I desire mercy [*hesed*], and not sacrifice, and the knowledge of God rather than burnt offerings" (6:6), neither he nor any other prophet had repudiated the sacrificial cult per se or attacked the Temple proper. Another example requiring clarification is Jeremiah's having been charged with a capital crime for prophesying that the Temple would share the fate of the shrine in Shiloh, which the Philistines had once destroyed. The authentic meaning of his statement is clarified in Jer. 7:4f. and 11f.: The Temple in itself is useless and will suffer the fate of Shiloh if you do not resolve to change your conduct. The meaning of Jeremiah's critique was not a repudiation of priests in general or of the priestly office. It was a critique of certain priests insofar as they were failing to heed the divine imperatives which the prophet proclaimed as directly inspired by Yahweh.

Moreover, Weber stresses, before we entertain the notion of a basic antagonism between the prophets and priests of Israel, we have to remember that Jeremiah himself came from a priestly family and that he repudiated those whom he called "false prophets" with a passion at least equal to that with which he admonished certain priests. For Jeremiah, Yahweh's covenant was contingent upon the nation's *moral* conduct, so the Temple was no automatic guarantee of the deliverance of Jerusalem. The confidence of certain prophets, notably Hananiah, in the absoluteness of Yahweh's commitment to Israel, Jeremiah branded as false. That is why he accuses Hananiah of making the people "trust in a lie" (28:15). Jeremiah, Weber reminds us, also proclaimed that "circumcision of the heart" (9:24) is more important than circumcision of the flesh. Thus Weber rightly insists that prophetic criticism of the cult is not an unconditional rejection of the sacrificial ritual but a strong devaluation of all ritual which individuals believe can somehow replace right ethical conduct or compensate for the lack of it (284).

As observed earlier, the prophets were all literate and well-informed concerning world events, and they showed no signs of attempting to flee from the world in the Hindu sense. Even the faintest hint of a *unio mystica* is absent from the prophetic literature. The prophets conceived of themselves as neither more nor less than individuals directly inspired by Yahweh, each interpreting the divine message as he understood it in light of the world-historical events transpiring at the time. The form of the inspiration, being always *auditory*, was entirely congruent with the conception of Yahweh as formless and invisible. And the content of the prophetic message, strongly demanding ethically right conduct and social justice, was also entirely congruent with the conception of Yahweh as an Almighty, universal, and *ethical* deity. Universal and Almighty because his Almighty presence had been felt in Egypt, in the Exodus, in the wilderness, in the conquest and settlement in Canaan, in the victories over the Philistines, and in numerous subsequent events in which Yahweh intervened in Israel's behalf.

And now, from the prophetic standpoint, the effects of God's will and presence were unmistakable in determining Israel's destiny in the face of the empires, Assyria and Babylonia. The prophets, in a word, heard the voice of the divine presence, attained clarity of the message's meaning, and communicated with equal clarity what Yahweh had commanded them to proclaim. The Hebrew prophets, then, were not the equivalent of the Indian "holy men," who had attained a holy state. On the contrary, the prophetic charisma was a free gift of Yahweh's grace, a gift to "ordinary" individuals who had felt themselves called by Yahweh and who now faced the task of "self-legitimation."

THE PROPHETIC ETHIC

The Hebrew prophets made no claim that they were conveying Yahweh's message verbatim. They had to interpret Yahweh's intention in the light of foreign and domestic events. What Weber underscores repeatedly is that the "wonders" attributed to the prophets were always effected by the spoken or written word invoking the will of God, but never by any sort of sympathetic or other magical manipulation. The prophets sometimes acted as if they had the ability to influence Yahweh. Abraham and Moses had served as intercessors, and Amos, the first of the eighth-century prophets of social justice, occasionally appears as an intercessor. But no prophet had ever even reckoned with the possibility of influencing Yahweh by means of magic. Nor had any prophet ever claimed the right to be worshiped or even venerated, or to be free of sin. The prophets never judged themselves to be in possession of holiness. They conceived of themselves as nothing more than a means of communicating Yahweh's imperatives. For Weber, this "emissary type" of prophecy had never before been so highly developed.

The Hebrew prophets concerned themselves primarily with ethics, the ethic enjoined upon Israel through the covenant. They were, therefore, proclaiming no new conception of God, no new means of grace, no new commandments. It is presupposed that God and his will are known to all concerned: "He has shown thee, O man, what is good" (Micah 6:8), "to abide," in Weber's words, "by those commandments of God which are known from the *Torah*. Isaiah also called the Torah of God his own prophecy" (30:9) (300). Hence, from the prophetic standpoint, the Torah provided the ethical principles with which to approach the threats to national sovereignty posed by Assur, Babel, and Egypt. Panic, rage, and fear of devastation and enslavement naturally agitated the people and determined the content and urgency of the prophetic messages. There was no doubt, however, in the prophetic mind that the only correct answer to the question of why the misfortune had befallen the nation was that Yahweh had willed it so: "Shall there be evil in a city, and the Lord hath not done it?" (Amos, 3:6).

Opinions differed as to whether the zealous God of the confederacy or the sublime world monarch stood more in the foreground. Yahweh had in the past, Weber observes, "repeatedly visited military disaster on the enemy and rescued Israel; often, however, this was only after having let his people suffer ... [frightful] misfortune for quite a time. Therefore, and for this reason alone, the prophets became politicians" (301). They were "politicians" in that they urgently concerned themselves with the current political crisis facing the nation; but their political approach to the crisis was determined by the belief that the crisis was willed by God as punishment for the nation's sins. This meant, for the prophets, that the nation had failed, above all, to abide by God's *ethical* commandments. That was the view commonly held by Amos, Hosea, Isaiah, Micah, and Jeremiah. The ethical commandments implicit in their criticisms and demands were, in substance, identical with the commandments of the Torah.

It is misleading, Weber demonstrates, to speak of the Hebrew prophets as "prophets of doom." No prophet absolutely opposed the hope of better times returning after a disaster, nor could he have done so and still exert any influence on the audience. The whole point of the prophetic understanding of the covenantal relationship was that it always held out hope if the offenders would change their ways. Jeremiah, for example, "considered a true prophet only one who lashed the sins of the people and—in connection therewith—prophesied disaster. But misfortune must not be absolute and definitive, but conditional through sin" (306).

The inner-worldly or this-worldly orientation of the Hebrew prophets and their world-political concerns, domestic and international, meant that it would never have occurred to them to ask a metaphysical question such as What is the "meaning" of the world and life? Nor did the prophets, out of a need for salvation, seek the perfection of the "soul" as against the imperfect world, as did the "holy men" of India. Indeed, the idea of the "soul" as a spiritual entity that survives the death of the body and lives on to eternity is absent from the Hebrew Bible. The idea of the "soul" first appeared in postbiblical Judaism and early Christianity under Hellenistic and other influences.

The *this-worldliness*, then, of the prophets meant that Yahweh's motives were understandable and justifiable, and world events were rational in character, that is, determined neither by blind chance nor by magical forces. What Yahweh demanded in his ethical commandments every child could understand, and though Yahweh was formless and transcendent, this was never transformed into a philosophical problem by the prophets. Insofar as the prophets engaged in careful reflection, it focused on the human condition. So Ezekiel (chaps. 14 and 18), for example, first posed the question of why the righteous suffered with the wicked; and Jeremiah (31:29) offered hope for a future in which every individual will suffer only for his own misdeeds, and one would no longer say, "The fathers have eaten sour grapes and the children's teeth are set on edge."

In the prophetic view, evil in the human condition resulted from actions carried out in opposition to God's commandments. There was no antigod principle, force, or domain in biblical Judaism, and hence no problems requiring a theodicy. In Weber's words,

> The prophetic horizon remained ... completely this-worldly in contrast [not only to the Far Eastern religions, but also] to the Hellenic mysteries of the Orphic religion which operated throughout with promises of the beyond. ... Yahweh's commandments like his ancient promises were quite concrete and positive and purely this-worldly. ... Conduct according to the commandment of God, not knowledge of the meaning of the world behoved man. (317)

The religion of Israel, as represented by the prophets, required "good works," as is evident from their admonitions and demands. However, the prophets also demanded a certain kind of "faith":

> The faith which the Jewish prophets demanded, was not that internal behavior which Luther and the Reformers intended. In truth it [the faith of the prophets] signified only the unconditional trust in Yahweh's omnipotence and the sincerity of his word and conviction in its fulfillment despite all external probabilities to the contrary. ... Obedience and particularly humility were the ensuing virtues and both

were especially appreciated by Yahweh, especially humility, the strict avoidance not only of *hybris* in the Hellenic sense, but in the last analysis of all trust in one's own abilities and all self-renown. This representation was of great consequence for the development of later Jewish piety. (318)

And although the prophets judged the conduct of the people and, in particular, some of their foolish practices, such as venerating the shapes of wood and stone that they had fashioned with their own hands, it was the conduct of the ruling strata of Israel that was decisive in determining the nation's destiny. For Weber, then, there could be no doubt that it was the tremendous influence of the prophets that reinforced and rendered authoritative the conception of Yahweh as the Almighty ethical God of the universe: "The entire inner construction of the Old Testament is inconceivable without its orientation in terms of the oracles of the prophets. These giants cast their shadows through the millennia into the present, since this holy book of the Jews became a holy book of the Christians too, and since the entire interpretation of the mission of the Nazarene was primarily determined by the old promises to Israel" (334).

THE "PARIAH" COMMUNITY

The prophets and the Torah teachers thus played a central role in the rationalization of biblical Judaism. However, the documentation of the radical "disenchantment" of Judaism was only one of the tasks Weber had set for himself in this extraordinarily meticulous and insightful study. Another important question was how the Jews came to constitute a pariah community. This, Weber shows, must be viewed as the result of both prophecy and the special ritual requirements of Judaism, which the Jews took with them into exile and held to, stubbornly and tenaciously.

With the destruction of the First Temple in 586 B.C.E. and the exile of the Jews, sacrifice, permissible only in Jerusalem, became impossible. The question therefore first arose among the Babylonian exiles of how to preserve the faith based upon the Torah and the prophetic tradition. The answer, as it took shape over time, was to establish a "temporary" house of study and worship, where the Torah texts could be read and pondered, and where the congregants could pray to God and worship him.

It was to be a "temporary" house of worship because, given the general Jewish acceptance of the prophetic eschatology, the Jews of the Diaspora lived in the hope that God would, in due course, restore them to their homeland. It was in this context that the protosynagogue was invented to serve the religious needs of the people until the time of their return and the reconstruction of the Temple. In exile, preserving the faith based on the Torah and the prophets meant not only following the ethical commandments but also remaining ritually pure by guarding against any and all polytheistic influences. Slowly, there emerged a distinctive, religious community organization with new institutions peculiar to the exile.

The destruction of the Temple and the resulting exile were, of course, interpreted by the Jews as God's punishment for offenses against his commandments; and since the prophets had taught that after the chastisement of the nation and its repentance, their commonwealth would be restored, the exilic community became especially zealous in its efforts to insulate itself against the influence of polytheism. So Weber proposes that "toward the outside world Jewry increasingly assumed the type of a ritualistically segregated guest-people (pariah people). And indeed Jewry did this voluntarily and not under pressure of external rejection" (417).

In the earliest period of the diaspora the Jews had ritually segregated themselves out of fear of ritual "pollution" and owing to their antipathy toward the polytheistic beliefs and practices of the "host" peoples. However, the resistance to breaking bread with the host people and intermarrying with them engendered a reciprocal antipathy.

When the Babylonians were defeated by the Persians, the Jews were eventually allowed in the fifth century B.C.E. to return to Judea and to rebuild Jerusalem and the Temple. There the religion based on the Torah and the prophets was rejuvenated and the sacrificial cult was restored. By that time, however, the religious institution that had originated in exile—the synagogue—had become so firmly a part of Jewish cultural life that it was successfully transplanted in Judea and throughout the land. With the expansion of the Roman Empire into the Near East, Judea and Israel, the northern part of the land, became subject to Roman rule. The Jewish revolt against Roman rule that broke out in 66 C.E. was finally put down by the Roman legions under Vespasian and Titus in 70 C.E. The result was the destruction of the Second Temple and Jerusalem, and of much of Judea. And once again a large portion of the Jews was forced into exile. The Romans, vengeful over the protracted Jewish war against their domination, and resolving that the land of Israel-Judea should be erased from memory, gave the land the new name of Palestine, a name derived from the Philistines whom the Israelites under David had conquered many centuries earlier. The Romans also tried, unsuccessfully, to change the name of Jerusalem to Aelia Capitolina.

It was therefore under Roman imperial rule that the Jews now lived in exile. And since they refused to venerate the Roman, pagan deities whose "guest-rights" they enjoyed, and since the Jewish God was invisible, the hosts often regarded the Jews as godless. Owing, then, to the self-segregation of the Jews and to the anti-Jewish feelings of the host-people, the Jews acquired the status of what Weber calls a "pariah people."

This status had definite implications for the economic role the Jews played in the societies of their hosts. Weber rejects the thesis of Werner Sombart, who proposed that the Jews had played a key role in the founding of modern capitalism. Contra Sombart, Weber argues that the form of capitalism in which the Jews engaged was premodern: trade, commerce, and moneylending, but not industrial capitalism based on wage labor. Moreover, because of their pariah status, the rational religious ethic of the Jews never diffused among their hosts. The rational, religious ethic of the Jews did not lead to the "spirit of capitalism" as did Puritanism.

Christian ethics, Weber maintains, had momentous significance for economics in the West not only because it weakened the power of the sib and other kinship ties but also because it produced a uniform ethic. This, as we have seen, reached its high point with the ascetic Protestant sects, whose "religiously-determined economic ethic gave them superiority over the competition of the godless according to the principle 'honesty is the best policy'" (344).

As we look back on Weber's careful and fastidious studies of religions east and west, with his special attention to the economic and social relevance of religious ideas and how they became effective forces in history, we should be able to appreciate the enormity of his contribution to our knowledge.

NOTES

[1]Max Weber, *The Religion of China: Confucianism and Taoism*, translated and edited by H. H. Gerth (Glencoe, IL: Free Press, 1962), p. 28, italics added. Hereafter, all page references to this work will be cited in parentheses immediately following the quoted passage.

[2]Max Weber, *The Religion of India*, translated and edited by Hans H. Gerth and Don Martindale (Glencoe, IL: Free Press, 1958), p. 111. Hereafter, all page references to this work will be cited in parentheses immediately following the quoted passage.

[3]Max Weber, *Ancient Judaism*, translated and edited by Hans H. Gerth and Don Martindale (New York: Free Press, 1952), p. 4. Hereafter, all page references to this work will be cited in parentheses immediately following the quoted passage.

[4]See Edith Hamilton, *Mythology* (New York: Mentor Books, 1940), p. 27.

[5]Max Weber, *Economy and Society*, edited by Guenther Roth and Claus Wittich (New York: Bedminster Press, 1968), vol. 2, p. 431.

[6]Max Weber, *The Sociology of Religion*, translated by Ephraim Fischoff and introduced by Talcott Parsons (Boston: Beacon Press, 1963), p. 36.

[7]Ibid., p. 26.

CHAPTER 8

E. B. TYLOR

The second volume of E. B. Tylor's classic study bearing the title *Religion in Primitive Culture* opens by addressing the question of whether there is evidence of human groups being so "low" in cultural development that they have no religious conceptions whatsoever. Evidently some early theorists of human society had posited a prereligious stage, just as they had posited the existence of human groups without language and without the use of fire. Tylor acknowledges the theoretical possibility that such protohuman groups might have existed but insists rightly that such groups are yet to be found. Indeed, religion, like language, is an integral element of human society no matter how backward it might be technologically. In opposition, therefore, to those ethnographers who had somehow divested "primitive" groups of religious experiences, Tylor proceeds to demonstrate that the ethnographers' own records belie their assertions.

Andrew Lang, for example, had asserted that the Aborigines of Australia "have nothing whatever of the character of religion, or of religious observance, to distinguish them from the beasts that perish."[1] Other writers followed Lang, accepting his assertion uncritically. Tylor observes, however, that Lang and his followers had overlooked details in Lang's own ethnography that demonstrate the very opposite. When, for instance, a disease like smallpox attacks the natives, they ascribe the affliction to the influence of Budyah, an evil spirit that delights in mischief. Hence, when the natives effectively steal honey from a wild bees' hive, they leave a little for Budyah to propitiate him. More extreme efforts at propitiation are evident in the biennial gatherings of the Queensland tribes, during which young girls are slain in sacrifice to pacify an evil deity. Moreover, without recognizing its full significance, Lang cited the experience of a Reverend W. Ridley, who, whenever he had conversed with the Aborigines, "found them to have definite traditions concerning supernatural beings" (3). Other observers of so-called primitive peoples, whether in Africa or Australia, denied in one sentence that they possessed any notion of an individual's immortality but then stated in another sentence that the word for the shades or manes of the dead is *liriti*. Still other observers declare that certain native tribes have no religion, while at the same time mentioning that they bury arms and clothing with their dead, possess notions of some future life, and believe in a Being who rewards good and punishes evil. Tylor, then, was a pioneer in successfully debunking the notion that primitive groups are somehow "godless," a notion that emerged from the prevalent missionary prejudice against pre- or non-Christian, polytheistic (pagan) beliefs.

In Tylor's time and throughout the nineteenth century, the doctrine of social evolutionism had become dominant. The doctrine proposed that the human species has evolved and progressed culturally from the lowest stages of "savagery" and "barbarism" to "civilization." Those were the actual terms employed, as were the correlates of "primitive" peoples and "lower races." Today, in the light of the dark history of the twentieth century and, indeed, the dark beginning of the twenty-first, it is doubtful in the extreme that the so-called civilized peoples are morally superior to the "primitive" societies. In our exposition of Tylor's analysis, however, we will continue, for the sake of clarity and coherence, to employ his vocabulary, since we have not been able to find value-neutral substitutes for them.

Tylor's refutation of the erroneous denial of religious experience to primitive peoples rested on his implicit definition of religion. He recognized, however, that for the systematic study of primitive religions, it would be useful to provide an explicit, minimal definition. He therefore defines "religion" as "the belief in Spiritual Beings" (8). Tylor then proceeds to propose the term *animism* to refer to the "deep-lying doctrine of Spiritual Beings, which embodies the very essence of Spiritualistic as opposed to Materialistic philosophy" (9). The concept of "animism" is essential for an adequate understanding of religion, whether that of the savages or the civilized. Animism consists of two dogmas that form one consistent doctrine. The first concerns the souls of individuals, which continue to exist after the body dies; the second concerns other spiritual forms, from the lowest and weakest to the highest and most powerful deities. Animism, then, refers to the widespread belief that spiritual beings affect or control the material world and human life here and in a hereafter. Moreover, it is believed that such spiritual beings communicate with humans and are either pleased or displeased with human action, from which it follows almost necessarily that humans sooner or later begin to revere and propitiate the spiritual beings. Animistic religion thus implies some kind of active worship of spiritual beings, as well as moral standards by which to judge whether certain actions are good or bad, right or wrong.

How, according to Tylor's theory of animism, did the idea of the soul emerge? To provide a convincing reply to that question, Tylor surmises that the thoughtful primitive was impressed by two groups of biological problems: (1) What makes the difference between a living body and a dead one? What causes "waking, sleep, trance, disease, death?" (2) "What are those human shapes which appear in dreams and visions?" (12). As the savage philosopher contemplated these two groups of problems, he inferred that every individual possesses two things—a life and a phantom. And since both belong to the body, they belong to one another and are "manifestations of one and the same soul" (13). The personal soul or spirit is thus believed to be the cause of life, consciousness, and will in the body of its individual owner. The soul is capable of leaving the body and moving from place to place, and it appears to humans when awake or asleep as a phantom separate from the body and capable of entering into and possessing the bodies of other human individuals, animals, and even things.

The primitive philosopher arrives at all such characteristics of the soul by reflecting rationally on the plain evidence of his senses. As Tylor reviews the words used by primitives, in diverse cultures, to describe the phenomenon of the soul, it becomes clear that the soul is conceived as an insubstantial form like a shadow or reflection, and that the English word *shade* captures something of the primitive conception of the soul. The idea of the soul as the cause of life or the *breath* of life may be traced in the main religions and philosophical currents of the world: in biblical Hebrew the word *nefesh* (breath) implies "life," "soul," "mind," and "animal," while *ruach* and *neshama* imply "breath" and "spirit." The Arabic *nefs* and *ruh* correspond to the Hebrew, and the same transitions of meaning may be discerned in the Sanskrit *âtman* and *prana*, the Greek *psyche* and *pneuma*, and the Latin *animus*, *anima*, and *spiritus*. Tylor discerns what appears to be the common idea underlying all these terms: It is especially when the body is asleep that the soul departs and wanders. If it absents itself beyond a certain time, disease sets into the body, and if the soul leaves permanently, its owner dies.

Tylor goes a step further, suggesting that even in waking life primitive individuals find it not at all easy to distinguish between subjective and objective, between imagination and reality. Thus primitives often come to believe in the objective reality of the specters they see in sickness, exhaustion, or excitement. Throughout the diverse, primitive cultures the soul is conceived to bear some likeness to its flesh-and-blood body. Tylor therefore concludes that it can be nothing other than *dreams* and visions that placed in the minds of individuals the idea that souls are ethereal images of bodies. For it is taken for granted in animistic philosophy that the souls set free from the body are recognized by their likeness to it, whether as ghostly wanderers in this world or as inhabitants of the hereafter.

Souls or ghosts are seen and heard; they have voices. They also share some of the vulnerability of the body. The souls of the dead may be hurt and driven away like any living creature. Souls may also be conceived as substantial bodies, not merely ethereal entities. Thus it is not unusual in certain cultures to make openings in solid materials to enable souls to pass through. Among his numerous examples Tylor cites a saying of German peasants in his own day, who taught that it is wrong to slam a door, for it might injure a soul. He cites, too, the common practice of spreading ashes to reveal the footprints of ghosts or demons, which again shows that they are regarded as substantial bodies. Among primitives, even the original conception of the human soul as ethereal suggested a "vaporous materiality" rather than a metaphysical notion of immateriality.

The idea that souls animate not only humans but animals as well also has its roots in primitive philosophy. Primitives talk as seriously to animals, alive or dead, as they would to humans. They offer animals homage and beg their pardon when it is their painful duty to hunt or kill them. Tylor cites the conduct of North American Indians who reason with their ponies as if they were rational. Some spare the life of a rattlesnake for fear that the spirit of the dead snake would seek vengeance. If an Indian is assaulted by a bear, it is often interpreted as deliberate, perhaps to avenge the injury done to another bear. When a bear is killed, the perpetrators beg his pardon or even prompt him to condone the offense "by smoking the peace pipe with his murderers, who put the pipe in his mouth and blow down it, begging his spirit not to take revenge" (52).

The range of evidence Tylor has considered leads him to suggest that no absolute psychical distinction between man and beast is to be found among primitives; for they discern in an animal the very same characteristics which they attribute to the human soul—life and death, will and judgment, and the phantom image seen in a dream. Hence, the doctrine of metempsychosis, the transmigration of souls, also has its origins in primitive philosophy. Primitives believe not only that an animal possesses a soul but also that this soul may have dwelled in a human being. A creature might therefore be one's own ancestor or once familiar, older clansman or tribesman. It follows logically for the primitive philosopher that animals may be slain so their spirits may continue to serve their human associates appropriately. Tylor provides a few examples of this phenomenon:

> The Pawnee warrior's horse is slain on his grave to be ready for him to mount again, and the Comanchee's best horses are buried with his favorite weapons and his pipe, all alike to be used in the distant happy hunting grounds. Certain Eskimaux...would lay a dog's head in a child's grave, that the soul of the dog, who is everywhere at home, might guide the helpless infant to the land of souls. (56)

In Tonquin, even wild animals have been customarily drowned at funeral ceremonies of princes, to be at the service of the departed in the next world. Among Semitic tribes, an instance of the custom may be found in the Arab sacrifice of a camel on the grave, for the dead man's spirit to ride upon. (57)

The doctrine of the migration of souls applies to the vegetable kingdom as well. Plants, like humans and animals, partake of life and death and health and sickness, and are therefore viewed as possessing souls. In a wide range of diverse cultures, plants are said to possess a living principle, that is, a soul or spirit, whose departure from the body of the plant causes sickness and, ultimately, death. Tylor provides several illustrations of this doctrine and remarks that the idea of spirits of plants lies deep in the cultural history of Southeast Asia but was to a large degree superseded in Buddhism. "The Buddhist books," writes Tylor, "show that in the early days of their religion, it was a matter of controversy whether trees had souls, and therefore whether they might lawfully be injured. Orthodox Buddhism decided against the tree-souls, and consequently against the scruple to harm them, declaring trees to have no mind or sentient principle, though admitting that certain *dewas* or spirits do reside in the body of trees, and speak from within them" (59–60).

Souls inhabit not only humans, animals, and plants but also physical objects. What we call inanimate objects, such as rivers, stones, tools, weapons, and so on, are regarded by the primitive as intelligent beings that can be spoken to, propitiated, and punished for the harm they do. Tylor cites David Hume's "Natural History of Religion" and his remarks on the personifying stage: "There is a universal tendency among mankind to conceive all beings like themselves, and to transfer to every object those qualities with which they are familiarly acquainted, and of which they are intimately conscious . . . . Nor is it long before we ascribe to them thought and reason, and passion, and sometimes even the limbs and figures of men, in order to bring them nearer to a resemblance with ourselves" (61). It was Auguste Comte, Tylor observes, who defined the personifying impulse as a state of "pure fetishism, constantly characterized by the free and direct exercise of our primitive tendency to conceive all external bodies soever, natural or artificial, as animated by a life essentially analogous to our own, with mere differences of intensity" (62).

Tylor raised the question of how the animistic impulse applies to funeral-object sacrifice. The sacrifice of property for the dead is a widespread religious ritual. Does that necessarily mean that those who destroy the deceased person's articles at a funeral ceremony believe that the articles possess spirits, which are transmitted to the deceased? For Tylor the answer is in the negative, since there are peoples who entertain no such theory but who nevertheless deposit offerings with the dead.

Even in primitive cultures there are several other reasons for such rites—an expression of affection, a symbolic act, a horror of death leading the survivors to rid themselves of anything associated with death—and there are other motives besides. And yet, when due allowance is made for all such motives, there are many other peoples who, though they may never have stated the object-soul theory explicitly, nonetheless recognize and practice it. After reflecting on a wide survey of funeral sacrifices throughout the world, Tylor proposes that a prevalent motive is to benefit the deceased, either out of kindness or out of fear of the deceased's displeasure. To explain this phenomenon, Tylor reminds us again that animism implies that every object has its spirit or ghost. Moreover, the animistic imagination is highly potent. True, the individual appears to be dead, but it is still possible to fancy him alive and to hear and speak to him in one's dreams. In Tylor's words: "Granted that the man is dead and his soul gone out of him, then the way to provide that departed soul with food or clothes or weapons is to bury or burn them with the body, for whatever happens to the man may be taken to happen to the objects that lie beside him and share his fate, while the precise way in which the transmission takes place may be left undecided" (69). Although the buried articles rot in the ground, they nevertheless come to be possessed by the dismembered souls for which they are intended. Tylor explains: "Not the material things themselves, but phantasmal shapes corresponding to them, are carried by the souls of the dead on their far journey beyond the grave, or are used in the world of spirits; while sometimes the phantoms of the dead appear to the living, bearing property which they have received by sacrifice, or demanding something that has been withheld" (71). The very fact that the objects rot implies, for these peoples, that the objects possess souls and will become useful to the deceased in the soul form of their existence.

We can see now that the many manifestations of animism, as described by Tylor, correspond to what Weber called the magic and animism that dominated the mentality of the Far Eastern religious cultures. As we have seen, the Far East had remained, for Weber, an enchanted garden, just as for Tylor the primitive cultures he surveyed were also enchanted gardens. If, then, we have another look at some of the world religions, we can see rather clearly how the animistic theory permeates them.

Tylor begins with the example of Buddhism, which recognized the transmigration of souls between deities, human beings, animals, plants, and even things. How the Buddhist authors elaborated the doctrine of metempsychosis may be seen in the numerous legends of Gautama himself undergoing his 550 births, suffering pain and misery through countless eras until he finally gained the power of freeing sentient beings from the suffering inherent in all existences (97). Buddhism, like the

Brahmanism from which it seceded, holds that an individual's life in former existences determines his present form of existence, while at present he is accumulating either merits or demerits that will determine
his fate in future lives. An individual may prosper for a time in this life
owing to the merits he had earned in earlier births, but if he does not
continue to observe the precepts or virtues, his next birth will be a hellish demotion—born again ugly or as a demon or a worm. Tylor, like
Weber, recognizes that the Buddhist doctrine of karma is a truly remarkable form of ethical speculation that strives to solve the "theodicy
problem." If the wicked prosper in this world, it is because they had
earned considerable merit in their previous form of existence; because
they are now wicked, however, they will pay for their wickedness in the
next life. And if the innocent or pure of heart suffer in this life, that is
also the result of unmeritorious conduct in a previous life. But now that
they are virtuous, they will be rewarded in the next life.

Illustrating further the doctrine of the transmigration of souls,
Tylor cites examples from Judaism, Christianity, and Islam. In a late
form of Jewish mysticism, the *kabala*, the "rolling on" of souls was taken
for granted. The soul of Adam passed into David and shall be passed from
him into the Messiah, for those are the initials in the name of Ad(a)m.
Souls migrate into beasts and birds and vermin, for Yahweh is the "Lord
of the spirits of all flesh." And "He who gives a Jew unclean meat to eat,
his soul shall enter into a leaf, blown to and fro by the wind;...and he
who speaks ill words, his soul shall pass into a dumb stone, as did
Nabal's, 'and he became a stone'" (100).

In Christianity, metempsychosis was most pronounced among the
Manicheans who taught that sinners' souls transmigrate into beasts, the
more serious the offense, the viler the beast. He who kills a fowl or rat
will himself become a fowl or rat. Souls can pass into plants and thus acquire sense. The souls of reapers pass into beans and barley, "to be cut
down in their turn, and thus the elect were careful to explain to the
bread when they ate it, that it was not they who reaped the corn it was
made of" (100).

In the twelfth century it was said of the Druses of Mount Hermon, a
Muslim sect, "that the soul of a virtuous man is transferred to the body of
a newborn child, whereas that of the vicious transmigrates into a dog, or
some other animal" (100). And Tylor points out that such ideas were very
much alive in his own day. "Among the Nassairi," he writes, "transmigration is believed in as a penance and purification: We hear of migration of
unbelievers into camels, asses, dogs, or sheep, of disobedient Nassairi into
Jews, Sunnis, or Christians, of the faithful into new bodies of their own
people, a few such changes of 'shirt' (i.e., body), bringing them to enter
paradise or become stars" (101). If one asks what it is in the human psyche that accounts for the doctrine of metempsychosis extending from

humans to animals, to plants, and to objects, Tylor offers the following explanation:

> The beast is the very incarnation of familiar qualities of man; and such names as lion, bear, fox, owl, parrot, viper, worm, when we apply them as epithets to men, condense into a word some leading feature of a human life. Consistently with this, we see in looking over details of savage transmigration that the creatures often have an evident fitness to the character of the human beings whose souls are to pass into them, so that the savage philosopher's fancy of transferred souls offered something like an explanation of the likeness between beast and man. (103–4)

Animism also sheds light on diverse ideas of the resurrection of the body. Though we speak of the soul as "spirit," the primitive conception of the soul is that it consists of a filmy, vaporous, and hence corporeal nature, capable of leading an independent existence as do corporeal creatures. Tylor calls attention to the common practice of preserving relics of the dead, from mere fragments of bone to whole mummified bodies. The famous pictures of Egyptian funeral rituals show the departed soul often revisiting the remains of the body. Tylor acknowledges, however, that the doctrine of the soul's transmigration into bodily remains or a new body does not quite equate with, say, the conception of resurrection in Judaism and Christianity, where the body enjoys new life, where the "bones rise again" thanks to God's grace.

RETRIBUTION THEORY?

What may be universal in primitive religion is the view that one will be rewarded or punished in a future life in accordance with one's conduct in this life. But Tylor as a pioneer anthropologist recognized that in addressing this question one confronts a basic methodological problem: Are the ideas we encounter in a primitive context original, or were they borrowed from one or another of the world religions whose influence had extended into primitive cultures? Tylor's review of the evidence for the North American native peoples suggested that in at least some of the myths having a moral sense attached to them, the moral element was original and indigenous, not borrowed. The dead, for example, face an ordeal separating the good from the wicked. Thus there is the account of the Choctaw souls "journeying far westward, to whom the long slippery barkless pine log, stretching from hill to hill, bridges over the deep and dreadful river; the good pass safely to a beauteous Indian paradise, the wicked fall into the abyss of waters, and go to the dark hungry wretched land where they are henceforth to dwell" (180–81). In Captain John Smith's account of the Massachusetts Indians, they say "at first there was no king but Kiehtan, that dwelleth far westerly above the heavens, whither all good men go when they die, and have plenty of all things. The bad men go thither also and knock at the door, but he bids them go wander in endless want and misery, for they shall not stay there" (181). Similarly, the Salish Indians of Oregon believed "that the good go to a happy hunting-ground of endless game, while the bad go to a place where there is eternal snow, hunger, thirst, and are tantalized by the sight of game they cannot kill, and water they cannot drink" (181). On balance, then, the ethnographic evidence appears to support the proposition that the doctrine of moral retribution is a definite element of primitive "theology."

DEVELOPMENT OR DEGENERATION?

When, in the nineteenth century, Tylor and other outstanding pioneering anthropologists conducted their studies, "degeneration theory" was still influential. This theory held, for example, that primitive ideas about future life and retribution were not fully original and indigenous but were borrowed or modified by the influences of the major world religions. It was in the same period that "development theory," or social evolutionism, became dominant either as a corrective or, ultimately, as a repudiation of "degeneration theory." Tylor acknowledges the difficulty of assessing the influence of the world religions on primitive culture—the difficulty of determining decisively which elements are the products of invention and which have been borrowed through diffusion from "higher" cultures. For Tylor, "development theory" was more fruitful because it "affords a satisfactory explanation of the occurrence in the midst of cultured [world] religions, of intellectually low superstitions, such as that of offerings to the dead, and various others. These, which the development theory treats naturally as survivals from a low stage of education lingering on in a higher, are by no means so readily accounted for by the degeneration theory" (188). For Tylor, then, if one follows the course of animism from its most primitive stages and observes definite survivals in medieval and modern society, this lends force to the development theory of culture.

THE SOUL AS THE SOURCE OF ANIMISM

What Tylor wishes to trace, in particular, is the development of animism *within* primitive contexts. And his aim is to propose that animism has its starting point in the idea of the soul. If, as he has shown, souls and other spiritual beings are conceived as essentially similar, and the concept of "soul" first emerges from an individual's own direct and personal dream experience, then it follows, for Tylor, that the earlier experience is fundamental for an understanding of the later. Thus Tylor proposes that the doctrine of souls, founded on the natural, sensory, and imaginative experiences of individuals in primitive culture, gave rise to the doctrine of spirits. Indeed, it is the souls of certain deceased individuals that are often transformed into spirits and demons. "Nothing," writes Tylor, "can bring more broadly into view the similar nature of souls and other spiritual beings than the existence of a full transitional series of ideas. Souls of dead men are in fact considered as actually forming one of the most important classes of demons and deities. It is quite usual for savage tribes to live in terror of the souls of the dead as harmful spirits" (197).

Although, as we shall see in a later chapter, Émile Durkheim tends to shrug off Tylor's theory in this regard, Tylor provides an abundance of evidence from many diverse cultures to support his thesis—evidence from Australia, New Zealand, from the Caribs, the Sioux Indians, several tribes of central Africa, from the Patagonians, from the Turanian tribes of north Asia, from the Mongols, from China, Indochina, and India. The phenomenon was called "Manes worship" in Tylor's time. Manes worship, Tylor reminds us, "is one of the great branches of the religion of mankind. Its principles," he writes, "are not difficult to understand, for they plainly keep up the social relations of the living world. The dead ancestor, now passed into a deity, simply goes on protecting his own family and receiving suit and service from them as of old; the dead chief still watches over his own tribe, still holds his authority by helping friends and harming enemies, still rewards the right and sharply punishes the wrong" (199).

Most frequently it is the head of each family who receives the worship or veneration of his kin. A Zulu, for example, explains why it is natural and reasonable to do so. The father is above all others who are venerated. He is a great treasure to his kin even when he is dead. The head of each household is venerated by the children of that household, for they know him best through their personal relations with him. Of the ancient, dead fathers they know little or nothing, hardly remembering their names. But their own father, the Zulu informant continues, "whom they knew, is the head by whom they begin and end in their prayer, for they knew him best, and his love for his children; they remember his kindness to them whilst he was living; they compare his treatment of them whilst he was living, support themselves by it, and say, 'He will still treat us in the same way now he is dead. We do not know why he should regard others beside us; he will regard us only' " (202). But if Manes worship appears to be characteristic of "primitive" tribal societies, it appears to be no less characteristic of advanced civilizations such as China. "Nowhere," Tylor remarks, "is the connection between parental authority and conservatism more graphically shown. The worship of ancestors, begun during their life, is not interrupted but intensified when *death makes them deities....* Among the Chinese, Manes worship is no rite of mere affection. The living want the help of the ancestral spirits, who reward virtue and punish vice" (204, italics added). Let us note the italicized passage, "death makes them deities." For Tylor, the evidence tends to support this interpretation of Manes worship. For Durkheim, however, as we shall see, it is not at all clear why death, in and of itself, should raise a human individual to divine status. But the evidence from classic Europe shows that apotheosis is a historical fact, as was the case with Julius Caesar, Augustus, and others. Indeed, Tylor observes:

> The most special representatives of ancestor worship in Europe were perhaps the ancient Romans, whose word "manes" has become the recognized name for ancestral deities in modern civilized language; they embodied them as images, set them up as household patrons, gratified them with offerings and solemn homage, and, counting them as or among the infernal gods, inscribed on tombs D.M., "Diis Manibus." The occurrence of this D.M. in Christian epitaphs is an often noticed case of religious survival. (206)

Tylor observes with regard to "survivals," that although ancestor worship is not practiced in modern Christendom, a "crowd of saints, who were once men and women, now form an order of inferior deities, active in the affairs of men and receiving from them reverence and prayer, thus coming strictly under the definition of manes" (206).

FETISHISM AND IDOLATRY

Fetishism refers to the veneration of objects such as trees, fish, plants, idols, pebbles, claws of beasts, sticks, and so on. In modern society we might add to the list amulets, charms, and, say, the sailor's rabbit's foot, all of which are believed by the individuals carrying them to be magically effective. Auguste Comte, as mentioned earlier, used the term *fetishism* to denote a general theory of primitive religion in which physical objects are regarded as animated by a life analogous to the human's. Tylor prefers the term *animism* for the doctrine of spirits in general, and he views fetishism as a subordinate phenomenon: the doctrine of spirits either "embodied in, attached to, or conveying influence through certain material objects" (230). Fetishism may include the worship of "stocks and stones," and idols. But there is something distinctive about fetishes: They are *not*, for the most part, considered to be the vessels, vehicles, or instruments of spiritual beings. Fetishes are understood by those who employ them as objects possessing magical powers, by an imagined conveyance of their special properties, as an iron ring gives firmness and strength, a bird's foot gives swift flight, or a rabbit's foot somehow provides protection and "good luck." So although fetishism might include the notion of a spirit embodied in the object and acting through it, it also includes the attitude toward a physical object itself, in which it is talked to, worshiped, prayed to, sacrificed to, petted or ill treated, and so on.

At its most primitive level, fetishism expresses itself in the worship of stocks and stones, a worship that soon passes into idolatry. Wood and stone are now carved and sculpted to create definite images. An excellent example of fetishistic idolatry is found in the Hebrew Bible, in Deutero-Isaiah. There we read about a man who has cut a log in two: "He burneth part thereof in the fire; with part thereof he eateth meat; he roasted roast, and is satisfied.... And the residue thereof [the other part of the log] he maketh a god, even his graven image: he falleth down unto it, and worshippeth it, and prayeth unto it, and saith, Deliver me; for thou art my god" (44:16–17). When the Hebrew prophets criticized some of the people for their idolatrous practices, a careful reading shows that they criticized them for worshiping wood and stone. In Hegelian terms, we recall, they criticized them, in effect, for being so alienated from themselves as to fail to recognize themselves in the otherness they have created with their own hands and turned into "other gods." Tylor calls attention to the persistence of idolatry in the world religions. In Vedic religion the Brahmans give no legitimacy to idolatry, and yet idolatry is prevalent. Christianity had never abrogated or repudiated the Jewish law against image worship, yet such worship became and remains widespread and deeply rooted in certain denominations of Christianity.

Tylor now acknowledges an old and formidable difficulty in studying fetishism and idolatry. In effect, he recognizes the need for what Weber called *Verstehensoziologie*, the need to grasp as authentically as possible the *meaning* actors assign to their actions: "The old and greatest difficulty in investigating the general subject is this, that an image may be, even to two votaries kneeling side by side before it, two utterly different things; to one it may be only a symbol, a portrait, a memento; while to the other it is an intelligent and active being, by virtue of a life or spirit dwelling in it or acting through it" (255).

Tylor supposes that the earliest idols need not have been conceived by their makers as living or active beings. It is likely that the primary meaning of the image was simply to serve as a sign or representative of some soul or deity. Tylor supposes further that it was at a later stage that the idol came to be treated as a living, powerful being. A few examples from Asian religions tend to support his supposition:

> What could be more anthropomorphic [writes Tylor] than the rites of modern Hinduism, the dances of the nautch-girls before the idols, the taking out of Jagannath in procession to pay visits, the spinning of tops before Krishna to amuse him? Buddhism is a religion in its principles little favorable to idolatry. Yet, from setting up portrait statues of Gautama and other saints, there developed itself the full worship of

images, and even of images with hidden joints and cavities, which
moved and spoke as in our own middle ages. (256)

So fetishism may refer to a "pure fetish" like a feather, log, stone, amulet,
or whatever, the notion behind it being that the object itself, without any
indwelling spirit, possesses magical powers. But fetishism also refers to
the form of idolatry in which "the worshippers mostly imagine that the
deity dwells in the image or, so to speak, is embodied in it, whereby the
idol becomes a real god capable of giving health and prosperity to man"
(263). So although fetishism in both forms is a prevalent feature of primitive cultures, there are also many conspicuous survivals of both forms in
the "advanced" religious cultures, east and west.

TOTEMISM

Tylor reviews the various forms of water worship, tree worship, and animal worship and then takes up the phenomenon of totemism, which is
important not only in its own right as a religious form but also because it
becomes the focus of both Freud's and Durkheim's analyses of religion.

Totemism is intimately associated with certain forms of kinship organization. A tribe is primarily a political association, while a clan is a
kinship unit. Tribes typically consist of clans, most of which are exogamous: marriage is prohibited within a clan but permitted between clans.
Each clan calls itself by the name of some animal or plant. Thus among
the Ojibwa Indians of America, Bear, Wolf, Tortoise, Deer, and Rabbit
were the clan emblems designating the intermarrying clans into which
the tribe was divided. Clan members were actually spoken of as bears,
wolves, and so on. Each clan, then, had a totemic animal with which it
identified, and a totemic emblem representing the clan. Among the Australian Aborigines, totemism was the dominant form of religion, and
when the origin of totemic names was asked of the natives, they replied
that the names were derived from the animal or vegetable that was very
common to the district, which the clan inhabited. The totemic emblem
was not an attempt at a realistic image of the plant or animal but rather
a symbolic representation, in much the same way that a flag represents a
particular nation-state.

Tylor cites the famous Spencer and Gillen studies of the Aborigines in central Australia, where those ethnographers learned that the
natives believed that the totemic animals or plants were the quasi-
human founder-ancestors of the clans, whose souls are reborn in human
form in successive generations. A clan member may not kill or eat his
totemic animal, nor clothe himself in its skin, but if he must kill a
predatory, menacing animal, he asks pardon of it and purifies himself
from the sacrilege. "The three motives of animal worship which have

been described," Tylor writes, "viz., direct worship of the animal for it-self, indirect worship of it as a fetish acted through by a deity, and veneration for it as a totem or representative of a tribe- [or clan-] ancestor, no doubt account in no small measure for the phenomena of zoolatry among the lower races [*sic*], due allowance being also made for the effects of myth and symbolism, of which we may gain frequent glimpses" (323). More light will be shed on totemism in the upcoming chapters on Frazer, Freud, and Durkheim.

POLYTHEISM

It is in his discussion of polytheism that Tylor anticipates the heart of Durkheim's theory of religion as presented in his *Elementary Forms of Religious Life*. There, as we shall see in chapter 12, Durkheim makes the claim that conceptions of the Divine are collective representations of the power and moral rules of society. For Durkheim, society and God are, in effect, one. For Tylor, similarly, the divine world is the reflex of humanity. He writes:

> Among nation after nation it is still clear how, man being the type of deity, human society and government became the model on which divine society and government were shaped. As chiefs and kings are among men, so are the great gods among the lesser spirits.... Above the disembodied souls and manes, the local genii of rocks and fountains and trees, the host of good and evil demons, and the rest of the spiritual commonality, stand these mightier deities, whose influence is less confined to local or individual interests, and who, as it pleases them, can act directly within their vast domain, or control and operate through the lower beings of their kind, their servants, agents or mediators. (334)

Tylor surveys the diverse deities of polytheism—heaven gods, rain gods, thunder gods, wind gods, earth gods, water gods, sea gods, fire gods, war gods, and more. And he explores once again the influence of the world religions on primitive cultures. There was, for instance, the important question of whether the dualism of good and evil deities was indigenous to North American Indian culture or the product of foreign influence. Tylor's careful review of the evidence suggested that the American Indians have more than once begun the same mythological transition, which in ancient Asia transformed the contrast of light and darkness into the contrast of good and evil. But the evidence also suggested that this rudimentary indigenous dualism tended to amalgamate with similar foreign ideas, to produce the numerous forms of dualism found in the diverse regions of the North American continent.

As noted earlier, Tylor, like many of his contemporary social scientists, subscribed to the "development theory" or what was eventually called "social evolutionism." Therefore, as he prepares to bring his survey to a close and takes into account the varieties of religious experience, he sets forth the following developmental sequence: from animism to polytheism to dualism to monotheism. Tylor thus concludes the task he had set for himself, to portray "in outline the great doctrine of Animism, as found in what I conceive to be its earliest stages among the lower races [*sic*] of mankind, and to show its transmission along the lines of religious thought" (445).

NOTE

[1] E. B. Tylor, *Religion in Primitive Culture*, part II of *Primitive Culture*, with an introduction by Paul Radin (New York: Harper Torchbooks, 1958), p. 2. Hereafter, all page references to this work will be cited in parentheses immediately following the quoted passage.

CHAPTER 9

JAMES GEORGE FRAZER

It was during the latter period of Tylor's extraordinary influence on anthropological thought and analysis that the writings of J. G. Frazer began to attract attention. His little book *Totemism*, published in 1887, was a precursor of the gigantic, four-volume *Totemism and Exogamy* (1910), which was eventually dwarfed by the twelve-volume third edition of *The Golden Bough* (1911–15).

Before he became directly concerned with anthropological questions, Frazer had established himself as an editor of classical texts, the most notable of which was Pausanias's *Description of Greece*. His other writings include such well-known works as *Folklore in the Old Testament* (1918). Both studies dealt with early religious beliefs and practices, thus being dress rehearsals, so to speak, for his monumental *Golden Bough*. So monumental, indeed, that he recognized the need to reduce the twelve volumes, and did so in 1922, producing a one-volume, nine-hundred-page abridgment. That was also the year of the first Frazer Lecture in Social Anthropology and the publication of Bronislaw Malinowski's *Argonauts of the Western Pacific* and Radcliffe-Brown's *Andaman Islanders*.

In his introduction to the one-volume abridgment, George W. Stocking Jr. has discerned an irony in the fact that Malinowski's and Radcliffe-Brown's famous works were published in the year of the Frazer lectureship, since those works "are customarily seen as marking the emergence of a 'social anthropology' fundamentally antithetical to Frazer's."[1] It is true that Frazer wrote primarily for the intelligent general reader, and that some professional anthropologists had leveled criticisms at his major work, suggesting that his contributions, "while not negligible, shrink to moderate proportions."[2] It is worth noting, however, that Malinowski, who must be regarded as one of the greatest anthropologists of all time, acknowledged the enormity of his debt to Frazer not once but again and again. In his essays collected under the title *Magic, Science and Religion,* Malinowski acknowledges several times the profound influence Frazer had exercised upon him. There are rites, Malinowski states, in which the act forecasts its result or,

> to use Sir James Frazer's expression, the rite imitates its end. Thus in the black magic of the Melanesians recorded by myself, a characteristic ritual way of winding-up the spell is for the sorcerer to weaken the voice, utter a death rattle, and fall down in imitation of the rigor of death. It is, however, not necessary to adduce any other examples, for this aspect of magic and the allied one of contagious magic has been brilliantly described and exhaustively documented by Frazer. Sir James Frazer has also shown that there exists a special lore of magical substances based on affinities, relations, on ideas of similarity and contagion, developed with a magical pseudo-science.[3]

In his essay "Myth in Primitive Psychology," Malinowski actually offers a dedication to Frazer:

> If I had the power of evoking the past, I should like to lead you back some twenty years to an old Slavonic University town—I mean the town of Cracow, the ancient capital of Poland and the seat of the oldest university in Eastern Europe. I could then show you a student leaving the medieval college buildings, obviously in some distress of mind, hugging, however, under his arm, as the only solace for his troubles, three green volumes with the well-known golden imprint, a beautiful, conventionalized design of mistletoe—the symbol of *The Golden Bough.* (93)

> Thus both magic and science show certain similarities, and, with Sir James Frazer, we can appropriately call magic a pseudo-science (87).

> Let me discuss in more detail another class of mythical stories, those connected with magic.... The foundations of this study have been laid by Sir James Frazer who has also erected a magnificent edifice thereon in his famous theory of magic. (138)

> Magic is thus akin to science in that it always has a definite aim intimately associated with human instincts, needs and pursuits.... Thus magic and science show a number of similarities, and with Sir James Frazer, we can appropriately call magic a pseudo-science. (140)

> Our discovery of this cultural function of magical myth fully endorses the brilliant theory of the origins of power and kingship developed by Sir James Frazer in the early parts of his *Golden Bough.* According to Sir James, the beginnings of social supremacy are due primarily to magic. (143)

> The claims and merits, however, are not mine, but are due once more to Sir James Frazer. *The Golden Bough* contains the theory of the ritual

and sociological function of myth, to which I have been able to make but a small contribution, in that I could test, prove, and document in my field work. (147)

It is evident, then, that for Malinowski, Frazer's contribution was more than merely moderate. Although Frazer conducted no personal fieldwork among so-called primitive peoples, his comparative studies of the religions, mythologies, and literatures of the world have yielded insights that, for the most part, have stood the test of time.

It is true that understanding *The Golden Bough* presupposes considerable background knowledge of the world's mythologies, and that the complexity and subtlety of Frazer's masterpiece require a patient and careful reading. The term *subtlety* is altogether fitting, since Frazer had designed his work so as not to give away to readers the climactic conclusions of his detailed analysis. It is almost as if Frazer conceived of his work and modeled it on a "whodunit." This seems evident from his reluctance to summarize his work or to provide the essence of it. Explaining his reluctance to describe the book for two literary periodicals, he wrote that he found it "rather difficult to state summarily the gist of the book without disclosing what I may call the plot. . . . I do not wish to announce the result beforehand, and for the same reason I have refrained from giving a full table of contents. . . . it seemed to me like the mistake of a novelist who should prefix a summary of the plot to his novel."[4]

Frazer's deliberate attitude in that regard makes an adequate exposition of *The Golden Bough* exceptionally difficult. As his masterpiece grew from two to three and then to twelve volumes, Frazer wrote a letter to his publisher, George Macmillan, informing him of a soon-to-be-completed "study in the history of primitive religion." In that letter Frazer suggested that "by an application of the comparative method," his study would explain the legend of the priesthood of the grove of Nemi (or Aricia)—Macaulay's "priest who slew the slayer and shall himself be slain." It is therefore fortunate that in Frazer's letter he does provide the gist of his work, which will help us follow my full exposition. "I believe," wrote Frazer,

> that I can make it probable that the priest represented in his person the god of the grove—Virbius—and that his slaughter was regarded as the death of the god. This raised the question of the meaning of the widespread custom of killing men and animals regarded as divine. I have collected many examples of this custom and proposed a new explanation of it. The Golden Bough, I believe I can show, was the mistletoe, and the whole legend can, I think, be brought into connexion, on the one hand, with the Druidical reverence for the mistletoe and the human sacrifices which accompanied

their worship, and on the other, with the Norse legend of the death of Balder. Of the exact way in which I connect the Golden Bough with the priest of Aricia I shall only say that in explaining it I am led to propose a new explanation of the meaning of totemism. This is a bare outline of the book which, whatever may be thought of its theories, will be found to contain a large store of very curious customs, many of which may be new even to professed anthropologists. The resemblance of the savage customs and ideas to the fundamental doctrines of Christianity is striking. But I make no reference to this parallelism, leaving my readers to draw their own conclusions, one way or the other.[5]

In Frazer's own 1922 preface to the abridgment, he sheds more light on the primary aim of his book, which is to explain the remarkable rule regulating the succession of the priesthood of Diana at Aricia. In the abridgment, Frazer added fresh evidence of the widespread custom of putting kings to death either at the end of a fixed term or whenever their health and strength began to fail. A striking example of this is provided by the powerful medieval kingdom of the Khazars in southern Russia, where the kings were put to death either at the end of a term or whenever some disaster, natural or social, appeared to indicate a failure of the king's powers. A similar practice of regicide was found in Africa, a custom formerly observed in Bunyoro of selecting every year from a particular clan a mock king who was supposed to incarnate the late king, and who was allowed to cohabit with the deceased king's widows at his tomb, but after reigning for a week was strangled. This custom is reminiscent of and closely parallels the ancient Babylonian festival of the Sacaea, where, too, a mock king was attired in royal robes, allowed to enjoy the real king's concubines, "and after reigning for five days was stripped, scourged and put to death" (xxxii). In a word, numerous examples of such similar customs suggest that the rule of succession to the priesthood of Diana at Aricia was not unique.

Frazer also cautions us in his preface not to misinterpret his lengthy discussions of the worship of trees. If he dwells at length on such worship, it is not because he has somehow mistakenly exaggerated its importance in the history of religion but because he could not ignore the subject in attempting to explain the significance of a priest who bore the title of King of the Wood, and one of whose titles to office was the plucking of a bough—the Golden Bough—from a tree in the sacred grove" (xxxiii). Indeed, Frazer regards tree worship as entirely subordinate to other factors, "and in particular to the fear of the dead, which, on the whole, I believe to have been probably the most powerful force in the making of primitive religion" (xxxiii). With this background in mind we can undertake a full exposition of Frazer's work.

THE KING OF THE WOOD

We begin with the sacred grove of Diana and a certain tree around which a certain grim figure might be seen to prowl. He carried a drawn sword and peered warily about him as if expecting to be assaulted by an enemy. The wary figure was a priest and a murderer, just as the man whom he feared was soon to murder the murderer and assume the priesthood in his place. Such was the sequential role and pattern of the sanctuary: He who aspired to the priesthood could succeed only by slaying the incumbent, and, having slain him, serve in office until he himself was slain by someone stronger or wilier. Since this strange rule has no parallel in classical antiquity and, therefore, cannot be explained from it, Frazer begins his long inquiry into barbaric customs with the aim of discovering the motive for the rule and its meaning. First, however, he strives to grasp adequately the meaning of the Diana myths.

Diana, like Artemis, was a goddess of fertility in general and of childbirth in particular. As such, she, like her Greek counterpart, needed a male partner, who appears to have been Virbius, the founder of the sacred grove and the first king of Nemi. Virbius is thus the mythical predecessor of the line of priests who served Diana under the title of Kings of the Wood and who, like Virbius, came one after the other to violent ends. The kings stood to the goddess in the same relation in which Virbius had stood to her: each mortal King of the Wood had for his queen the woodland Diana herself. As the sacred tree that the king guarded was assumed to be her special embodiment, her priest-king may not only have worshiped the tree as his goddess but embraced it as his wife. Frazer alerts us to the fact that the custom of physically marrying men and women to trees was still practiced in his time, so why, he asks, should it not have existed in ancient Latium?

Why was Diana the object of worship? Because she was regarded as the goddess of woodlands, of wild creatures and domestic cattle, and of fruits of the earth. She was also believed to bless men and women with offspring and to assist mothers in childbirth. What is also known about the Diana cult that is highly probable is that her holy fire, tended by chaste virgins, burned perpetually in a round temple, and that Diana was assisted by a water nymph, Egeria, in helping women in travail, and that Diana of the Wood had a male companion, Virbius, who was to her as Adonis to Venus and Attis to Cybele. Finally, the mythical Virbius was represented in historical times by a line of priests known as Kings of the Wood who were regularly slain by their successors, whose lives were dependent on a certain tree in the grove, because so long as the tree was uninjured, their lives were safe.

Frazer next reviews the ethnographic evidence showing that kings not only were revered as priests, as intercessors between humans and gods, but also were looked upon as gods themselves. As we listen to Frazer, we hear of phenomena highly similar if not identical to those described by Tylor under the heading of "animism" and described by Weber as elements of the "enchanted garden" of the Far East. Thus Frazer notes the pervasiveness of the belief in spiritual beings, in apotheosis, in black and white magic, the basis of which is a conception of a supradivine, invariable order. For Frazer, the principles of magic may be divided into two types: The first is that "like resembles like," or that an effect resembles its cause. The second is that things that were once in contact with one another continue to affect one another even in the absence of contact. The first principle Frazer calls the Law of Similarity, and the second, the Law of Contact or Contagion. Typically, the magician believes that both laws apply not only to human actions but to the entire universe. Frazer subsumes both types of magic under the general heading of "sympathetic magic."

Sympathetic magic consists of both positive and negative precepts, the positive telling one what to do, the negative informing one of what to leave undone. The positive precepts are *charms* (fetishes), the negative are *taboos*. The magician gains his powers, he believes, by learning the operational secrets of inexorable, impersonal laws and forces that are quite independent of human will. He or she knows that positive magic produces certain unavoidable results, just as negative magic prevents certain undesirable events from occurring.

As the magician advances in status from private practitioner to public functionary, that is an important step for the political as well as religious development of a society. For now the welfare of the entire tribe or clan is dependent on the magician's competent performance of the magical functions, so the magician rises in political influence and may readily acquire the rank and authority of a chief or king.

As a rule, the fundamental conception underlying the belief in magical powers is an idea virtually identical with that underlying modern science. The magician, like the scientist, believes in the uniformity of the laws governing the cosmos. The magical practitioner does not doubt that the same causes will always produce the same effects. The practice of magic must be distinguished from the practice of religion. The magician does not supplicate a higher power or abase himself before a deity. Magical powers are great, but by no means arbitrary, derived as they are from the inexorable laws of an impersonal force higher and more powerful than any deity. The magician must therefore learn the laws governing the workings of the impersonal, supernatural forces. He or she must observe those laws in the smallest particular, or fail and thus expose himself as an incompetent practitioner and suffer the consequences that would follow. It is in that sense that Frazer posits an analogy between magical and scientific thinking. In both magic and science the succession of events is assumed to be perfectly regular and predictable "determined by immutable laws the operation of which can be foreseen and calculated precisely" (59).

Whereas, however, physical scientists concern themselves with the regularities of the physical or natural world, magicians concern themselves with the *super*natural, as it is manifest in their erroneous apprehension of two apparently fundamental laws of thought: the association of ideas by similarity and the association of ideas by contiguity in space or time. Hence, magic is inherently false, but that does not mean, for Frazer or for Malinowski, as we shall see, that it is useless or lacking in beneficial consequences.

Religion, for Frazer, in contrast to magic, does entail the propitiation and conciliation of superhuman powers believed to direct and control the course of nature and of human life. Religion implies not only that we believe in divine beings but that we fear them and wish to please them. The belief must lead to a corresponding practice. Frazer cites Saint James's words: "Faith, if it hath not works, is dead, being alone." In other words, Frazer avers, no individual is religious who does not govern his conduct by the fear or love of God or the gods.

Religion differs from magic in another basic respect. The religious attitude assumes that the course of nature is in some degree elastic or variable, and that humans can implore or persuade the deities to deflect the flow of events from the direction in which they might otherwise head. The religious conception of the elasticity or variability of nature is therefore antithetical to both magic and science, based as they are, respectively, on supernatural and natural laws that are invariable in their operation. For religion, the powers governing the cosmos are conscious and personal; for magic, the powers are unconscious and impersonal. Religion implies propitiation and conciliation; magic implies learning how to control supernatural, impersonal forces, and *coercing*, not conciliating, all beings, superhuman and human. Magic assumes that ultimately all beings, whether human or divine, are subject to an Impersonal Force, which, however, can be controlled and manipulated by means of the appropriate "knowledge" and "skills." Frazer cites well-known examples from ancient Egypt, where "the magicians claimed the power of compelling even the highest gods to do their bidding, and actually threatened them with destruction in case of disobedience" (62). The impersonal, supradivine force is the ultimate source of the powers of the magicians which enable them to coerce the gods. It is also the "inside" knowledge of that force that enables the magician to achieve apotheosis. "Similarly," Frazer writes, "in India at the present day the great Hindu Trinity itself of Brahma, Vishnu, and Siva is subject to the sorcerers, who, by means of their spells, exercise such an ascendancy over the mightiest deities, that these are bound submissively to execute on earth below, or in heaven above, whatever commands their masters the magicians may please to issue" (62).

FROM MAGIC TO RELIGION

The basic distinction Frazer has made between magic and religion, and the assumption that the former is older than the latter, leads him to the question of how and why humans made the transition from one to the other. His tentative answer is that in time humans began to recognize their inability to manipulate forces that they had hitherto believed themselves capable of controlling. Humans lost the illusion that it is they, through their magical powers, who guided the heaven and the earth in their courses. They, in effect, relinquished sovereignty over nature: If the world proceeded on its way without the illusory magical powers, it must be because there are other beings, but far stronger, who though unseen, are the directors of the world's course and of human destiny. Humans now became impressed with their relative helplessness, and the might of the invisible beings to whom they believe themselves to be subject.

Frazer now wants to connect this discussion with the phenomenon of priesthood as kingship. In the earliest forms of primitive society every man and woman is, more or less, his or her own magician. They practice charms and incantations for their own good and for the injury of their enemies. But it is a very significant social change when a special class of professional magicians, who practice magic in public, has been instituted. A stratum of individuals now emerges who are excused from the everyday need of earning their livelihood by manual toil, and who are expected and encouraged to pursue researches into the secret ways of the impersonal, supradivine force that is the source of their magical powers. They are expected to learn those secrets in order to control both natural and supernatural forces for the common good.

We thus catch a glimpse of where Frazer is heading: The institution of public magic and the professional magician helps us understand the nature of early kingship, since in primitive society chiefs and kings often appear to owe their authority, in great measure, to their reputation as magicians. Indeed, this source of authority appears to be equally characteristic of advanced civilizations. Let us recall Weber's analysis of Tao in China, where the emperor was, in effect, the chief magician whose primary political responsibility it was to learn the secrets and workings of the Mandate of Heaven so that he might properly regulate the waters of the empire, both the rain and the canals, dikes, and sluice gates of the riverine, artificial irrigation systems.

Regarding the urgent need for rain, Frazer cites examples from both the Far East and western Europe where prolonged drought evoked both magical and religious responses. He also documents the range of other phenomena, such as sun and wind, which humans strive to control by magical means. What the wide range of evidence suggests is that the practitioners of the magic arts are personages of considerable importance and influence in their respective societies. By virtue of the reputation they enjoy and the awe they inspire, they attain positions of authority and often become chiefs and kings. In Africa, for example, it appears that kingship evolved out of the role of magician, and especially out of the role of the rainmaker. Thus among the Wambugwe, a Bantu people of East Africa, the original form of government was a republic consisting of federated clans, but the immense power of the sorcerers, a status transmitted through inheritance, soon raised them to the rank of lords and chiefs. Of the three chiefs in the area in 1894, two were much feared as magicians, and the great wealth they possessed in cattle they had acquired through gifts bestowed upon them for their services.

However, the power of the magician carries with it a definite responsibility that makes the position precarious; for where the people truly believe that the magician has it in his power to make the rain fall, the sun to shine, and the products of the earth to grow, the people view drought and dearth as due to his incompetence, negligence, or willful obstinacy and punish him accordingly. Frazer cites data from India to Ireland, and historically from ancient Greece and the European Middle Ages to show how widespread was the notion that kings possessed supernatural powers. In Homeric Greece, kings or chiefs were often spoken of as divine, and it was thought that a good king caused the earth to bring forth wheat and barley, the trees to be heavy with fruit, the flocks to multiply, and the sea to yield fish plentifully. For Frazer it is therefore a fair generalization that in many parts of the world the king emerged out of the old magician or medicine man. Once a special class of professional, magical practitioners emerges, and is entrusted with the common welfare of the community, the sorcerers begin gradually to rise to wealth and power until they become sacred or divine kings. In time, however, as Frazer had observed earlier, the fallacy of magic becomes more and more evident to the acuter minds, and is slowly displaced by religion. The magician gives way to the priest who, renouncing the attempt to control the processes of nature directly,

> seeks to attain the same end indirectly by appealing to the gods to do for him what he no longer fancies he can do for himself. Hence, the king, starting as a magician, tends gradually to exchange the practice of magic for the priestly functions of prayer and sacrifice. And while the distinction between the human and the divine is still imperfectly drawn, it is often imagined that men may themselves attain to godhead, not merely after their death, but in their lifetime, through the temporary or permanent possession of their whole nature by a great and powerful spirit. (109)

In recorded history, the prototypical example of the apotheosis of kings is evident in ancient Egypt, where the Pharaoh was divinized in his lifetime for reasons quite similar to those that accounted for the Chinese emperor having been regarded as the chief magician.

THE WORSHIP OF TREES

In order to connect the foregoing analysis with the thesis Frazer aims ultimately to defend concerning the "golden bough," he wants us to grasp how trees and groves become sacralized. Following Tylor's theory of animism, Frazer agrees that to the primitive mind the entire world is animate; all the phenomena of nature, without exception, possess souls as do humans. Frazer reinforces Tylor's theory by showing that a certain attitude toward the vegetable world is characteristic of certain world religions as it is of, say, a religion in East Africa where the Wanika believe that every tree, and especially every coconut tree, has its spirit. There the destruction of a coconut tree is regarded with the same horror as matricide because the tree gives life and nourishment, as does a mother to her child. In Siam (Thailand), similarly, the Buddhist monks believe that souls exist everywhere and that to destroy anything in nature is forcibly to dispossess a soul. The monks would no sooner break a branch of a tree than break the arm of an innocent person. "But," Frazer emphasizes, "Buddhist animism is not a philosophical theory. It is simply a common savage dogma incorporated in the system of a historical religion" (135).

In a later stage in the development of tree worship, the tree is no longer conceived as the body of the tree spirit but simply as the abode of the spirit. For Frazer, this denotes a transition from animism to polytheism. The tree itself is no longer viewed as a living, *conscious* being but as the temporary host to a supernatural being who can pass freely from tree to tree and who therefore enjoys a certain lordship over the trees, thus ceasing to be a mere tree soul and becoming a forest god. Moreover, in the course of this process, the emerging forest god increasingly assumes a human form owing to the general tendency of early thought to drape all abstract spiritual beings in concrete human form. Frazer reminds us that in classical art the sylvan deities are portrayed in human shape. But though the form of the tree spirit has changed, the powers it exercised as a tree soul, it continues to wield, much augmented, as a god of trees.

Massive evidence for such beliefs exists in a wide range of primitive and early cultures, but there are also significant relics of tree worship in modern Europe. Frazer cites the customs of the May tree or Maypole so prevalent in the popular festivals of European peasants. Still in Frazer's day, it was customary in spring or early summer to go into the forest, cut down a tree, bring it into the village, and set it up amid general rejoicing. In a variant of this custom, the people cut branches in the woods and display them on every house. The meaning or intention of such customs is to bestow on the village and on every household the blessings and beneficent qualities that the tree spirit has the power to convey.

When the tree spirit becomes a god of trees or of vegetation in general, and is clothed in a human form, it is often conceived as embodied in living men or women. In widespread spring agricultural festivals, the tree spirit or the spirit of vegetation in general is represented either in vegetable form, as by a tree, bough, or flower together with a puppet or as a living person. Sometimes the vegetable god is depicted by dropping entirely an actual tree, bough, or flower, while only the living person remains, dressed in leaves or flowers. The leaf-clad person is led about and becomes in the minds of the festival's participants the symbolic equivalent of the May tree, May bough, or May doll, which is carried from house to house by children. Both the children and the tree symbols they carry represent the vegetable deity whose beneficent visit to a house is recompensed by a gift of food or money.

In such early European spring or summer festivals, the people eventually personified the spiritual powers of vegetation as male and female, attempting thereby, on the principle of homeopathic or imitative magic, to quicken the growth of trees and plants by representing the marriage of the sylvan deities as the King and Queen of May.

Frazer stresses that far from being mere symbolic or allegorical dramas, such representations were understood to be definite magical charms intended to make all growing things flourish and multiply. From the standpoint of the magical mentality of those concerned, it was natural to suppose that the more closely the mock marriage of the leaf-clad mummers aped the marriage of the woodland sprites, the more effective the magical charm would be. Accordingly, it was believed that the marriage of trees and plants could not be fertile without the real intercourse of the human sexes. Frazer explains that the union of the sexes in such fertility rites ought not be regarded as mere outbursts of unbridled passion; the rites were deliberately and solemnly organized as essential to the fecundity of the earth, the trees, their fruit, and the welfare of the community. Frazer also observes, however, that in some cultures the very opposite means of ensuring fertility is employed, namely, sexual abstinence. The forgoing of immediate gratification is a form of sacrifice: One restrains one's sexual impulses with the aim and in the hope of thus ensuring an adequate supply of life-sustaining provisions.

The sacred marriage as a fertility rite brings us closer to the role of Diana in Frazer's thesis. Diana was a goddess of fertility. And as Frazer had proposed in the opening chapter of *The Golden Bough*, there is good reason to suppose that the priest who bore the title of King of the Wood at Nemi had for his mate the goddess of the grove, Diana herself. On the evidence, therefore, of the prevalence of fertility rites and sacred marriages in many parts of the ancient world, there is nothing inherently improbable in the view that Nemi was the scene of an annual rite of that sort. Diana was more than a goddess of trees. Like the Greek Artemis, with whom she was identified, she became a goddess of nature in general and of fertility in particular. A goddess of fertility, it was taken for granted, must herself be fertile, from which it followed that she must have a male partner, namely, Virbius, who was represented or embodied in the King of the Wood at Nemi. That this is a fair inference is shown, Frazer avers, by the many such ancient rites.

In the temple of Babylon no human being spent the night, except for a single woman whom, the Chaldean priests claimed, the god chose from among all the women of Babylon. According to the priests, the deity himself came into the temple at night and slept in the great bed with the woman, as his consort. In Egypt, similarly, a woman slept in the temple of Ammon as the consort of the god. In Athens, the god of the vine, Dionysus, was married to the queen in an annual ceremony. In the mystery cults at Eleusis, in the month of September, the sky god Zeus was united with the corn goddess Demeter, a ceremony in which the chief priest and the priestess represented, respectively, the god and the goddess. In Diana's sacred grove at Nemi, we recall, Frazer had recounted how each priest-king, as partner of the goddess, acquired his status by killing his predecessor and expecting that he would be killed in turn by his successor. Frazer thus proposes that the legends of the violent ends of the Roman kings suggest that the contest by which they ascended to the throne may have been mortal combat. Hence, there is a definite parallel between Rome and Nemi. In both places "the sacred kings, the living representations of the godhead, would thus be liable to suffer deposition and death at the hand of any resolute man who could prove his divine right to the holy office by the strong arm and the sharp sword" (191).

Frazer calls special attention to the worship of the *oak*, and ties it to his analysis of Diana's sacred grove. If the priest of Nemi played the role not merely of king but of a god of the grove, what deity did he impersonate? Earlier we heard that he represented Virbius, the consort or lover of Diana. But, Frazer acknowledges, that does not help us much, since we know little more than the name. Frazer sees a definite clue to the mystery in the vestal fires that burned in the grove. Such perpetual, holy fires in Europe were commonly kindled and fed with oak wood, and in Rome itself, not far from Nemi, the vestal fire consisted of oaken logs; it was fed and maintained with wood of the sacred oak. It is highly likely that at Nemi, too, the hallowed grove consisted of oaks and, therefore, that the tree which the King of the Wood had to guard at the risk of his life was itself an oak. Indeed, Virgil states that it was from an evergreen oak that Aeneas had plucked the golden bough. We know, in addition, that the oak was the sacred tree of Jupiter, the supreme god of the Latins. It therefore follows, for Frazer, that the King of the Wood, "whose life was bound up in a fashion with an oak, personated no less a deity than Jupiter himself" (197).

Frazer thus arrives at the quite credible hypothesis that Virbius was most likely a local form of Jupiter, in perhaps his original aspect as a god of the green wood. We need one more piece of information in order to follow the rest of Frazer's complex analysis. The title "King of the Wood" clearly indicates the sylvan character of the deity whom he served; and since he could only be assailed—and this is the additional piece of information—by him who plucked the *bough* of a certain tree in the grove, his own life was bound up with that of the sacred tree. However, before we work our way through Frazer's further analysis, to learn the nature of the *bough* and the certain tree, we should consider more of the ethnographic evidence.

Frazer shows that in many early or primitive cultures, a king was killed when his strength failed, especially when he was viewed as a kind of man-god. Frazer provides plentiful evidence to show that primitives believe that their safety and welfare depend on the magicians who have achieved apotheosis and have become human incarnations of the divinity. The people therefore strive to take good care of the god-man, out of regard for their lives and well-being. But no amount of care or precaution prevents a man-god from growing old and feeble. His worshipers have to take account of this necessary process and meet it as best they can. The danger of his dying without a replacement is a formidable one, since the welfare of all is contingent upon the active and indispensable role of the deified individual. Given, then, the prevalent belief in the immortality of the soul, there is only one way of averting the possible disaster that would result from the god-man's death: he must be killed as soon as he shows that his powers are failing, so that his soul may be transferred to a young and vigorous successor. From the standpoint of the primitive's logic, there is a definite advantage in putting the man-god to death instead of waiting until he dies of old age. For if the man-god were to die a natural death, that would mean either that his soul has voluntarily departed or that it has been deliberately extracted by a demon or a sorcerer. By slaying him, therefore, the people believe that they ensure catching the soul and transferring it to a suitable successor.

The same reasoning would apply to the King of the Wood. He, too, had to be killed so that the divine spirit incarnate in him might be transferred in its original integrity to his successor. The rule that any particular king was to hold office until a stronger slayed him served to preserve the king's divine life in full vigor and to transfer the office as soon as his vigor began to decline. As the primitive mind grasps such customs, the divine life or soul incarnate in a material and mortal body is liable to be corrupted or tainted by the frail medium in which it has been temporarily enshrined, and if the soul is to be saved from an increasing enfeeblement that it shares with the aging body, it must be detached from the body as soon as it shows signs of decline and speedily implanted in a vigorous successor. Therefore, the killing of the god, that is, his human incarnation, is seen as a necessary step to his resurrection in a superior form. The divine spirit, far from being thus extinguished, enjoys a purer and stronger rejuvenation. This analysis is applicable to the custom of annually killing the representation of the tree spirit or spirit of vegetation in spring. "For the decay of plant life in winter," writes Frazer,

> is readily interpreted by primitive man as an enfeeblement of the spirit of vegetation; the spirit has, he thinks, grown old and weak and must therefore be renovated by being slain and brought to life in a younger and fresher form. Thus the killing of the representative of the tree-spirit in spring is regarded as a means to promote and quicken the growth of vegetation. For the killing of the tree-spirit is associated always (we must suppose) implicitly and sometimes explicitly also, with a revival or resurrection of him in a more youthful and vigorous form. (362)

Youth and vigor of the king or god-man were essential because one of his primary functions was to cohabit with the goddess of fertility. Frazer's survey of the evidence showed the widespread worshiping of a mother goddess who personified all the reproductive energies of nature. Although she was venerated under a variety of names, the respective myths revealed a common pattern: She mated with a series of lovers, divine yet mortal, their intercourse being deemed essential to the propagation of plants and animals. The mythological union of the divine pair was simulated on earth by the real, but temporary, union of male and female at the sanctuary of the goddess for the sake of the fruitfulness of the products of the earth.

As Frazer traces the practice of killing a god-man among peoples at the hunting, pastoral, and agricultural stages of society, he calls attention to the phenomenon of the "transference of evil": "The accumulated misfortunes and sins of the whole people [he writes] are sometimes laid upon the dying god, who is supposed to beat them away for ever, leaving the people innocent and happy" (646). This is one of Frazer's implicit examples of the rootedness of Christian theology in polytheistic beliefs and practices.

Solving the Mystery

Frazer is now ready to begin to answer the two basic questions he raised at the outset: Why did the priest of Aricia have to kill his predecessor? And why did he have to pluck the golden bough before doing so? The first question Frazer has answered, as we have seen, by reviewing the plentiful ethnographic evidence relating to the widespread custom of slaying the man-god. The priest of Aricia may therefore be viewed as a manifestation of that custom. He was a sacred king or human divinity on whose life the welfare of the society and the course of nature were believed to depend. Parallel to the numerous, similar examples in other cultures, the priest of Aricia, the King of the Wood at Nemi, had to be put to death while he was still in a strong and virile stage of manhood so that his sacred soul might be transmitted in its undiminished force to a successor.

As for the second question: What was the golden bough, and why had each candidate for the Arician priesthood to pluck it before he could slay the incumbent priest? Frazer will now proceed to unfold his complex but cogent reply.

He cites examples from Mexico, Japan, Persia, Thailand, and Africa to illustrate the rules or taboos prohibiting a divine personage from touching the ground with his feet. Holiness or magical virtue is conceived by the primitive mind as a substance or fluid that the sacred individual is charged with

> just as a Leyden jar is charged with electricity; and exactly as the electricity in the jar can be discharged by contact with a good conductor, so the holiness or magical virtue in the man can be discharged and drained away by contact with the earth, which on this theory serves as an excellent conductor for the magical fluid. Hence in order to preserve the charge from running to waste, the sacred or tabooed person must be carefully prevented from touching the ground; in electrical language he must be insulated, if he is not to be emptied of the precious substance or fluid with which he, as a vial, is filled to the brim. (713)

Neither were such personages allowed to see the sun. They were, so to speak, suspended between heaven and earth.

This brings Frazer to the myth of the Norse Balder, the good and beautiful god, the son of the great god Odin. And how interesting and apropos it is that Balder's life was neither in heaven nor on earth but between the two. When Balder dreamed dreams foretelling his death, the gods held council and vowed to make him secure against every danger. The goddess Frigg took oaths from all possible sources of danger—fire, water, iron, and all other metals, stones, trees, diseases, poisons, beasts, birds, and creeping things—that they would not hurt Balder, and he now seemed to be invulnerable. The gods now amused themselves by shooting, hacking, and stoning him, but nothing hurt him, and they were all glad—all except Loki the mischief-maker.

Displeased with Balder's apparent invulnerability, Loki went to Frigg, who explained why none of the weapons of the gods could hurt Balder. Then Loki asked whether all things without exception have sworn to spare Balder, and Frigg, unaware of Loki's intentions, revealed that "east of Walhalla grows a plant called mistletoe; it seemed to me too young to swear." So Loki went and pulled the mistletoe, and as he approached the assembly of gods, he noticed the blind god Hother. Loki asked him why he does not shoot at Balder and received the reply, "Because I do not see where he stands; besides, I have no weapon." Then said Loki, "Do like the rest and show Balder honor, as they all do. I will show you where he stands, and do you shoot at him with this twig." Hother took the mistletoe and threw it at Balder, and the mistletoe pierced him through and through, and he fell down dead. And that was the greatest misfortune that had ever befallen gods and men (729). Balder's body was then placed on a funeral pyre of his ship and burned.

Frazer sees in this myth one of those mimetic, dramatized, magical rituals designed to produce the effects described in the figurative, dramaturgical language. The two main incidents of the Norse myth, the pulling of the mistletoe and the burning of the god, find parallels in the fire festivals of Europe. Although Frazer acknowledges several ways of interpreting such festivals, he regards it as a near certainty that in the minds of the participants they fulfilled a purificatory function. Men and animals were burned to death in those festivals, which Frazer interprets as attempts to break the power of witchcraft by burning witches and warlocks. The mode of execution by fire was selected because burning alive was deemed the surest method of getting rid of noxious and dangerous beings.

Now Balder, as we have seen, was said to have been slain by a branch of mistletoe and burned in a great fire. Mistletoe, Frazer reminds us, has been from time immemorial the object of superstitious veneration in Europe. It was worshiped by the Druids, who believed that a potion prepared from the mistletoe would make barren animals bring forth, and that it is an antidote to all poison. Among the other superstitious notions, it was believed that since mistletoe cannot fall to the ground because it is rooted in a branch of a tall tree, an epileptic person cannot fall down in a fit so long as he carries a bit of mistletoe on his person. Frazer has thus shown that the main incidents of the Balder myth have their counterparts in the fire festivals of European peasantry. This strongly suggests that the Balder myth was originally the text for a mimetic, dramatic ceremony that was acted out each year "as a magical rite to cause the sun to shine, trees to grow, crops to thrive, and to guard man and beast from the baleful arts of fairies and trolls, of witches and warlocks. The tale belonged, in short, to that class of nature myths which are meant to be supplemented by ritual; here, as so often, myth stood to magic in the relation of theory to practice" (797).

In approaching the conclusion of his analysis, Frazer calls attention to the role of oak wood in the European festivals. The kindling of sacred fires was done in the most primitive manner, by rubbing two sticks together. And the kind of wood prescribed, whether among Celts, Germans, or Slavs, was generally the oak. Sacred fires were kindled with sacred oak wood. So Frazer maintains that

> the last link between the mid-summer customs of gathering the mistletoe and lighting the bonfires is supplied by the Balder myth, which can hardly be disjoined from the customs in question. The myth suggests that a vital connexion may once have been believed to subsist between the mistletoe and the human representative of the oak who was burned in the fire. According to the myth, Balder could be killed by nothing in heaven or earth except the mistletoe; and so long as the mistletoe remained on the oak, he was not only immortal but invulnerable. Now, if we suppose that Balder was the oak, the origin of the myth becomes intelligible. The mistletoe was viewed as the seat of life of the oak, and so long as it was uninjured, nothing could kill or even wound the oak.... Hence, when the god had to be killed—when the sacred tree had to be burnt—it was necessary to begin by breaking off the mistletoe. For as long as the mistletoe remained intact, the oak (so people might think) was invulnerable. (799–800)

So now Frazer is ready to reveal the full nature of the golden bough. It was the mistletoe, which in popular superstition blazed out into a supernatural golden glory. In tying everything together, Frazer shows the grounds for supposing that the priest of the Arician grove—the King of the Wood—personified the tree on which grew the golden bough. "Hence," writes Frazer, "if that tree was the oak, the King of the Wood must have been a personification of the oak-spirit. It is, therefore, easy to understand why before he could be slain, it was necessary to break the Golden Bough. As an oak-spirit, his life or death was in the mistletoe on the oak, and so long as the mistletoe remained on the oak, he, like Balder, could not die" (844).

If we now ask why the mistletoe was called the Golden Bough, Frazer sees the plausible answer in the fact that mistletoe was gathered at the solstices and viewed as an emanation of the sun's fire. As the ceremonial fires were generally kindled by the friction of oak wood, it appeared to the primitive mind that the sun was periodically rejuvenated from the fire that resided in the sacred oak. The oak was conceived as the original storehouse of the fire that was drawn out, from time to time, to feed the sun. But since the life or soul of the oak was conceived to be in the mistletoe, it must have contained the seed or germ, which emerged by friction from the wood of the oak. "Thus," Frazer concludes, "instead of saying that the mistletoe was an emanation of the sun's fire, it might be more correct to say that the sun's fire was regarded as an emanation of the mistletoe. No wonder, then, that the mistletoe shone with a golden splendor and was called the Golden Bough" (846).

NOTES

[1]James Frazer, *The Golden Bough*, abridged edition (New York: Penguin Books, 1996), p. xv. Hereafter, all page references to this work will be cited in parentheses immediately following the quoted passage.

[2]Robert H. Lowie, *The History of Ethnological Theory* (New York: Rinehart and Company, 1937), p. 104.

[3]Bronislaw Malinowski, *Magic, Science and Religion*, with an introduction by Robert Redfield (Prospect Heights, Ill.: Waveland Press, 1992), p. 72. Hereafter, all page references to this work will be cited in parentheses immediately following the quoted passage.

[4]Stocking in Frazer, *The Golden Bough*, p. xvii.

[5]Ibid.

CHAPTER 10

BRONISLAW MALINOWSKI

A s we reflect on the major contributions of Tylor and Frazer to our understanding of animism and magic, we can, perhaps, see that in their emphasis on the pervasiveness of the magical mentality, they neglected the rational-empirical side of so-called primitive cultures. No society known to us, however primitive it might be technologically, is lacking in knowledge accumulated over many generations and derived from observing natural and social processes carefully. There is, then, a definite sense in which we may speak of primitives as possessing *science* and a scientific legacy, which is, of course, essential to social life.

It is one of Malinowski's chief contributions to have documented the fact that no primitive society is lacking in either science or what may be justifiably called "the scientific attitude." Malinowski was an innovator not only in his explicit documentation of the scientific attitude but also in his ethnographic method. Describing Malinowski's methodological innovation, Edmund Leach writes that

> in 1914, ethnographers ... still viewed their subject matter with considerable contempt. ... The standard methods of ethnographic research were such that the social superiority of the investigator was being constantly emphasized. ... Exotic customs were recorded by questioning "good informants," [while] the ordinary day-to-day lives of primitive peoples were presumed to be quite uninteresting and were largely ignored. ... But Malinowski's Trobriand fieldwork changed all this. The most crucial innovation was that he actually pitched his tent in the middle of the village, learned the language in its colloquial form, and observed at firsthand just how his Trobriand neighbors behaved throughout the 24 hours of an ordinary working day. No European had ever done this before and the kind of ethnography that resulted was completely new. Where his predecessors had spent their time describing the manners and customs and artifacts of a primitive

tribe, Malinowski found himself describing a way of life; ethnography became social anthropology.[1]

On the ground, then, of his own fieldwork and a careful perusal of the accounts of other ethnographers, Malinowski avers that in every society one can discern two clearly distinguishable domains, the sacred and the profane, a domain of magic and religion, on the one hand, and of science, on the other. The sacred domain consists of acts carried out with reverence and awe, and which are always associated with the belief in supernatural forces, especially those of magic, or with ideas about spirits, ghosts, deceased ancestors, or deities. In the profane domain of everyday life, however, it is quite evident that in the primitive society's arts and crafts, its organized forms of hunting, fishing, tilling, or searching for food—that all such activities are informed by careful observation of natural processes and a recognition of their regularity.

Malinowski therefore sees the need to introduce a corrective where Tylor's ethnography is concerned. Tylor's view of primitive social life was too narrow from Malinowski's standpoint, for his fieldwork had demonstrated that the primitives were more interested in their essential economic activities such as fishing and gardening than they were in contemplating their dreams and visions. Malinowski turns therefore to Frazer, whom he credits with having set forth the three main problem areas of anthropology: magic and its relation to science; totemism and the sociological aspects of early religion; and the significance of fertility and vegetarian cults. Describing Frazer's *Golden Bough* as the "great codex" of the primitive outlook, Malinowski reminds us of what Frazer had shown—namely, that primitive society seeks above all to control nature for practical ends and strives to do so both by scientific means and by rite and spell. Only later, as primitives recognize the limitations of their magic, do they turn to religion and appeal to higher beings in supplication. Religion, as a confession of human impotence in certain matters, raises the human being above the level of magic and maintains its autonomy alongside science.

Malinowski proceeds to clarify the nature of magic, and in doing so he reexamines some of the fundamental elements of polytheism that we have already encountered in Weber's analyses. Magic, Malinowski reminds us, springs from the belief in a mystic, impersonal force, called *mana* by some Melanesians, *arungquiltha* by certain Australian tribes, *wakan, orenda*, and *manitu* by various American Indians. Virtually universal wherever magic flourishes is a "belief in a supernatural, impersonal force, moving all those agencies which are relevant to the savage and causing all the really important events in the domain of the sacred. Thus *mana*, not animism, is the essence of 'pre-animistic religion,' and it is also the essence of magic, which is thus radically different from science."[2]

In order to make his point and to establish that science is an essential element of the primitive's mind and social life, Malinowski had to deal with certain influential theories of the time that portrayed primitives as if they were hopelessly and totally immersed in a mystical state of mind. Lévy-Bruhl, for example, had asserted that primitives are incapable of dispassionate observation, that they lack the ability to reason, that they do not learn from experience, and that they are unable rationally to comprehend the laws of nature. In a word, they are, for Lévy-Bruhl, "pre-logical." Malinowski therefore proceeds to refute this widely shared view and to show that every primitive community possesses a substantial body of knowledge based on experience and reasoning. Malinowski draws upon his own fieldwork among the Melanesians and Papuo-Melanesian tribes of eastern New Guinea and the surrounding archipelagoes. And since the Melanesians were regarded as especially steeped in magic, Malinowski employs them as a test case of whether primitives possess empirical and rational knowledge.

The natives of the Trobriand archipelago whom Malinowski had studied were expert fishermen and industrious manufacturers and traders who relied primarily on gardening for their subsistence. Although their tools were quite rudimentary—a pointed digging stick and a small axe—they were able to raise crops sufficient for the sustenance of a dense population, and even to produce a surplus. Their agricultural success rested on their extensive knowledge of the varieties of soil, the diversity of cultivated plants, the interdependence of these two factors, and, of course, their knowledge of the necessity of hard work applied intelligently: selecting the soil and the appropriate seedlings; fixing the time for the clearing and burning of the scrub; planting and weeding; training the vines of the yam plants. In addition, these people had to be guided by a knowledge of seasons, weather, and harmful pests. The primitives were fully aware that if all their tasks were not carried out accurately, their crops would fail, and all concerned would suffer the consequences.

And yet all these activities are accompanied by magic, by a series of rites performed every year in rigorous sequence. Indeed, leadership of the garden work is in the hands of the magician, and ritual and practical work are so intimately connected that the superficial observer might suppose that the natives fail to distinguish the difference between magic and scientific analysis. But Malinowski shows that it would be a big mistake to entertain such a view. It is true that the natives regard the magical rites as absolutely indispensable. Why? Because they have learned from long experience that their gardens are menaced by numerous potential disasters—blight, drought, excessive rain, bush pigs, and locusts. They therefore *always* accompany their practical work with magic. Does that mean, however, that the natives believe disasters are prevented by magic alone? "Certainly not," Malinowski replies:

> If you were to suggest to a native that he should make his garden mainly by magic and scamp his work, he would simply smile on your simplicity. He knows as well as you do that there are natural conditions and causes, and by his observations he knows also that he is able to control those natural forces by mental and physical effort. His knowledge is limited, no doubt, but as far as it goes it is sound and proof against mysticism. If the fences are broken down, if the seed is destroyed or has been dried or washed away, he will have recourse not to magic, but to work, guided by knowledge and reason. (28)

Then why does he resort to magic?

> His experience has taught him also, on the other hand, that in spite of all his forethought and beyond all his efforts there are agencies and forces which one year bestow unwonted and unearned benefits of fertility, making everything run smooth and well, rain and sun appear at the right moment, noxious insects remain in abeyance, the harvest yields a superabundant crop; and another year again the same agencies bring ill luck and bad chance, pursue him from beginning till end and thwart all his most strenuous efforts and his best-founded knowledge. To control these influences and these only, he employs magic. (28–29)

There is, then, a clear-cut division in the social context of gardening between practical work and ritual. The two functions are kept strictly apart. Although in his lay character the magician directs the practical work, his two roles never overlap or interfere with one another. Every native knows when the individual in question acts in his role as magician or as leader in the gardening work.

The same is true of the other urgent economic activities of the Trobrianders, like building outrigger canoes, which requires definite empirical knowledge of materials, technology, and principles of stability and hydrodynamics. The natives understand perfectly well, for example, that the wider the span of the outrigger, the greater the stability; but they also know that the wider the span, the smaller the resistance against strain. They can therefore explain why the span must be a certain width in relation to the length of the dugout. They can also explain how they must conduct themselves in a sudden gale, and why the outrigger must always be on the weather side. They have, in a word, a whole set of principles of sailing, which they recognize as rationally and empirically valid.

But the Trobrianders nevertheless supplement their science with magic. To explain why they do so in this case, Malinowski calls attention to the uncontrollable and unpredictable hazards fishermen face in the deep sea: powerful and incalculable tides, sudden gales during the monsoon season, and hidden reefs. Malinowski remarks in this connection that if modern seamen, with their advanced, scientific navigational principles and their steel-built ships, entertain superstitious notions, why should anyone be surprised that the comparatively primitive Trobrianders reach out for the comfort of magic?

When, then, do the Trobrianders tend to call upon magic? They do so when they face conditions that are dangerous and life-threatening, but that appear to be uncontrollable. The two types of fishing the Trobrianders engaged in provided Malinowski with a rigorously logical test of his proposition and a convincing proof of it. The two types were inner, lagoon fishing and deep-sea fishing. Lagoon fishing yielded plentiful results by the method of drugging the fish, and without either uncertainty or danger; fishing in the open sea, in contrast, was inherently dangerous, and the yields varied. It was most significant, therefore, "that in the lagoon-fishing, where man can rely completely upon his knowledge and skill, magic does not exist, while in the open-sea fishing, full of danger and uncertainty, there is extensive magical ritual to secure safety and good results" (31). Malinowski furnishes additional examples substantiating his thesis further.

Malinowski occasionally employed the term *functionalism* to refer to his method of interpreting primitive beliefs and practices. Accordingly, he would maintain that magic fulfills a definite function in the primitive social context. To explain what he means, let us suppose that in response to his thesis, the modern, rational Western reader might ask: But if magic is fundamentally false and erroneous and fails in actuality to accomplish the aims which the natives imagine it accomplishes, is that not a sign of their irrationality or nonrationality? And why do they persist in their nonrational beliefs? Malinowski replies to such questions by pointing out that the magical beliefs and practices of the natives do in fact fulfill a definite function—reducing their anxiety sufficiently to enable them to go about their business coolly and calmly instead of being paralyzed by fear. One can see clearly why among the Trobrianders magical rites accompany canoe construction and open-sea fishing but not lagoon fishing. The Trobrianders practice magic for much the same reason that the modern seaman might carry a rabbit's foot.

DEATH AND THE FUNCTIONS OF RELIGION

Another example of Malinowski's "functional analysis" is found in his discussion of death and mortuary proceedings, which show a remarkable similarity throughout the world. As death approaches, the nearest relatives and sometimes the entire community gather by the dying individual. Thus dying, the most personal and private act an individual can perform, is transformed into a public event. As soon as death has occurred, the body is washed, anointed, and adorned, and there is always a more or less conventionalized and dramatized show of grief and sorrow, accompanied among the natives by bodily lacerations and the tearing of hair. The mourning ceremony takes place around the corpse, that is usually the center of pious attention and subject to ritual forms of fondling and signs of reverence. But there is ambivalence among the performers of these acts. After a time the body must be disposed of, which brings Malinowski to what he calls a twofold, contradictory tendency: to preserve the body or to annihilate it. Mummification and burning are the extreme manifestations of the twofold, contradictory tendency, which expresses the ambivalence of the surviving relatives, friends, or lovers: There is longing for what remains of the dead person but also revulsion and fear of the dreadful change death has wrought. One example of this two-sided attitude is sacro-cannibalism, a custom of piously partaking of the dead person's flesh. Typically it is carried out with extreme repugnance and followed by a violent vomiting fit. The mortuary ritual is designed, however, to enable the community of survivors to conquer their dread and fears and to console themselves with the belief in a future life in the form of a soul or spirit.

Accepting Tylor's animistic theory in its essentials, Malinowski extends and elaborates it: The savage, like most human beings, has an intense fear of death, which he refuses to believe amounts to total annihilation. Hence, the idea of spiritual existence and immortality is grasped in the way Tylor had analyzed the phenomenon: Individuals attain the comforting belief in spiritual continuity and life after death. Thus religion, for Malinowski, fulfills the vital function of providing a comforting view, a socially and individually valuable belief in immortality. In its various forms, then, religion "saves man from a surrender to death and destruction, and in doing so it merely makes use of the observations of dreams, shadows and visions. The real nucleus of animism lies in the deepest emotional fact of human nature, the desire for life" (51). Especially in a demographically small community, the death of a known and respected member is a serious matter, for the small body politic has been mutilated to that extent. Such an event shocks the community, interrupts its normal course of life, and threatens its moral cohesion. If members of the community were to give in to fear and horror, abandon the corpse, and run away in distress, such conduct would ultimately destroy the material foundations of a primitive culture. Religion, Malinowski avers, thus "counteracts the centrifugal forces of fear, dismay, demoralization, and provides the most powerful means of reintegration of the group's shaken solidarity and of the re-establishment of its morale" (53).

In his discussion of death and the reintegrative function of religion, Malinowski develops several criticisms of Durkheim's theory as set forth in his *Elementary Forms of Religious Life*. I shall present those criticisms in the chapter on Durkheim. To prepare, however, for the critical discussion of Durkheim's theory in which he effectively equates society with the divine or supradivine, it will suffice for the present to call attention to what Malinowski regards as Durkheim's major errors: an exaggeration of the collective, social origins of the religious experience and a corresponding neglect of the role of the individual; the notion that it is out of a great, collective effervescence that the religious ideal is born; and the notion that society is the ultimate source of the idea of God or Divinity, which Malinowski will challenge on the following grounds. Durkheim had maintained that every society distinguishes within itself two domains, the sacred and the profane, the phenomenon of religion being strictly in the sacred domain. Malinowski therefore asks how society can be the prototype and basis of the Divine when so much of society consists of the activities of everyday life—the domain of the profane.

MALINOWSKI'S THEORY OF MAGICAL LANGUAGE

Malinowski begins by observing that the Trobriand magician, like other magicians, often employs in his formulae words of the *abracadabra, sesame, hocus pocus* kind, words that have no meaning in the ordinary sense but are presumed to possess and exercise magical influence. Linguistically, such words are untranslatable. The magical formula is neither a part of conversation, nor a prayer, nor a statement intended to communicate a specific idea. Moreover, no audience of listeners is considered to be necessary for the effectiveness of the spell. The magician's words carry no communicable meaning; they are literally meaningless.

When, for instance, the magician, while striking the soil of the garden, states: "I am striking thee, O soil," to what or to whom is the utterance directed? Is it the land, the stick in his hand, the people who happen to be present, spirits? Malinowski answers these questions on the basis of his field experience. The scene of action or context is believed to be permeated by *mana*. Each rite is believed to "produce" or "generate" a force and to convey it directly or indirectly to a given object, which is then affected by the force. In the Trobriands there was no specific term for this concept, but Malinowski regards it as appropriate to employ the Melanesian term *mana* to describe this impersonal force, which is so evident as a reality in the beliefs and conduct of the natives.

Malinowski illustrates the reality of beliefs with the principal spell employed in Omara-Kana garden magic, which begins with the word *vatuvi*. After certain preparations, and while carefully observing the rules and taboos, the magician collects herbs and makes of them a magical mixture. He then utters an incantation, offers some fish to the ancestral spirits, and recites the main spell, *vatuvi*, over the magical mixture. Having prepared a large receptacle for his voice, a voice trap of sorts, he lays the mixture on a mat and covers it with another mat so that the voice may be caught and imprisoned between them. While reciting, he holds his head close to the aperture and carefully ensures that no portion of the herbs shall remain unaffected by the breath of his voice. He moves his mouth from one end of the aperture to the other, repeating the words of his spell again and again. Malinowski relates that as one watches the magician at work and the fastidiousness with which he applies the verbal action to the substance, and then afterward how meticulously he encloses the charmed herbs in ritual wrappings, one cannot fail to recognize "how serious is the belief that the magic is in the breath and that the breath is the magic."[3] "There is no need," says Malinowski, "to multiply examples. In every act the magician's breath is regarded as the medium by which the magical force is carried" (216). It is not the breath alone, of course, but the breath and the voice uttering the words of an absolutely authentic spell that "generate" the magical force, which acts either directly on the soil, the tuber, or the growing plant or indirectly by impregnating a substance, usually herbs, which is then applied to the earth or the plant.

For the Trobriander, the magician's spell is a rather mysterious sequence of words that from time immemorial has been handed down from accredited magicians to their accredited successors. Although the myths are not perfectly clear on the question, it appears that the first or original wielder of magic is believed to have obtained it by learning the secrets of the workings of the impersonal force, for which Malinowski uses the Melanesian term *mana*. This impersonal force is at work in all magic; but some magicians, grasping the force's secrets better than others, employ it more effectively. Hence, the strong belief prevails that the better the magical system, the greater the fertility. "Luck," a manifestation of the impersonal force, is always accounted for by magic.

Malinowski states again the function of magic in the garden context. Fertility and the adequate production of yams are essential for the material well-being of the community. But since the adequacy cannot be ensured by rational, human efforts alone, magic has always been regarded as a necessary element of the production process. As a general proposition, then, whenever an essential human activity is either dangerous or subject to chance and not completely mastered by technical means, "there is always for the Trobriander a magical system, a body of rites and spells, to compensate for the uncertainty of chance and to forearm against bad luck" (217).

The words employed in a magical spell, as noted earlier, are weird, strange, and unusual. Most often they are chanted in a singsong fashion. According to the Trobriand "theology" of magic, the words of a spell are of primeval origin, and they produce their effects by being breathed into the spiritual or physical substance that is to be influenced. The essence of the magic resides in the spell, properly chanted and applied by an accredited practitioner. The words act and have effect because they are primeval and have been correctly learned by the new magician from his predecessor, and because the rules and taboos have been observed. Magic is thought to be prehuman and to have existed underground long before it emerged with the first ancestors. The natives therefore expect the words of a spell to be different from the words of everyday discourse. Since it is believed that the words of a spell are effective because they have had a different origin, history, and role, the natives deem it natural that spell words and phrases should not resemble the patterns of ordinary speech.

This prompts Malinowski to propose a general theory of magical language. He suggests that language in its origins is both magical and pragmatic. In the context of everyday life, the pragmatic element comes to the fore, and the words employed are for the most part intelligible. The pragmatic-intelligible element is most salient in economic enterprise, in the technical terminology of the arts and crafts as handed down from generation to generation. However, even when the same words of everyday discourse are employed in the emotional attitudes belonging to magic and religion, such words and phrases are loaded with meaning that has no roots in practical, empirical experience. The meaning of words now becomes mystical and unusual, since the words are no longer employed for normal communication.

Malinowski is thus emphasizing the role of context in determining meaning. In the profane context of everyday life, intelligibility is of paramount importance; in the sacred context of magic and religion, words, though intelligible, might nevertheless give rise to a profound mystical-emotional experience.

Explaining his theory further, Malinowski avers that *all* language in its earliest function in the context of infantile helplessness is both protomagical and pragmatic. It is pragmatic in that it enables the child to appeal for help, to gain attention, and to obtain certain objects. Language at that stage is, however, also protomagical in that it manifests to the child the power of words through sound. As a child develops, he or she experiences the *power of words and sounds* when they are heavily laden with emotion and also when they function in conventional communication.

Malinowski is thus proposing as a fruitful hypothesis that the development of speech in the human species must, in its basic principles, have followed the same pattern as the development of speech in the life history of the individual. Based on his prolonged study of the Trobriand language of magic, in which words take on a mysterious and esoteric form, Malinowski holds that

> in Trobriand magic we find hardly a single word, the working of which, that is, the meaning of which, could not be explained on the basis of

associations, mythological data or some other aspect of Frazer's principle of sympathy. This, I think, is but part of the universal, essentially human, attitude of all humans to all words. From the very use of speech humans develop the conviction that the knowledge of a name, the correct use of a verb, the right application of a particle, have a mystical power which transcends the merely utilitarian convenience of such words in communication from man to man. (232–33)

Malinowski again illustrates his point with the experience of a child who "actually exercises a quasi-magical influence over its surroundings. He utters a word, and what he needs is done for him by his adult entourage" (233).

With the growth and maturity of the individual, the technical and social ability to cope with reality grows hand in hand with the knowledge of how to use words. Throughout human society, the familiarity with the name of a thing is closely related to familiarity with how to use the particular thing. Applying a basic principle of pragmatist philosophy, Malinowski states that "the right word for an action, for a trick of trade, for an ability, acquires *meaning* in the measure in which the individual becomes capable of carrying out the action. The belief that to know the name of a thing is to get a hold on it is thus empirically true" (233). Words, terms, and names are, of course, also essential elements in a child's sociological education in a primitive community. He or she learns gradually the complexities of kinship, of taboos, of duties and privileges of fellow clan members, and of the respective social ranks. Here, too, the gradual mastery of proper social conduct in relation to others runs parallel to social terminology.

The "mystical-magical" and pragmatic aspects of words may be further illustrated with the phenomenon of law, where the value of the word, the binding force of a vow, promise, or formula, is at the very foundation of social order and reliability in human relations. Marriage vows, for example, possessing in most human societies the twofold character of sacrament and legal contract, illustrate the power of words in establishing stable human relations. The sacredness of words and their socially sanctioned inviolability are absolutely indispensable for social order. In any stable community most of its members must internalize the belief in the sanctity of legal and sacral words and their creative power. The stronger this belief—which has been systematically inculcated—the greater is the basic honesty of its citizens. For Malinowski, the ethnographic evidence tends to support the proposition that there is a very real experiential basis for the "human belief in the mystic and binding power of words" (235). The knowledge of the right and appropriate words and phrases imparts to humans a power over and above their limited fields of personal action. Ultimately, this power rests on the "conviction that a spoken word is sacred. The fact also that words add to the power of man over and above their strictly pragmatic effectiveness must be correlated with the belief that words have a mystical influence" (235).

The belief in the magical power of words rests on the mental attitude that by affirming health, welfare, and happiness, one actually produces them. Malinowski provides two examples from the Trobriand culture:

> It passes, it passes,
> The breaking pain in thy bones passes,
> The ulceration of thy skin passes,
> The big black evil of thy abdomen passes,
> It passes, it passes.

Or to take a formula of garden magic:

> I sweep away, I sweep away, I sweep away.
> The grubs I sweep, I sweep away;
> The blight I sweep, I sweep away;
> Insects I sweep, I sweep away....
> I blow, I blow, I blow away.
> The grubs I blow, I blow away;
> The blights I blow, I blow away;
> Insects I blow, I blow away. (236–37)

At the very basis of verbal magic there lies what Malinowski calls "the creative metaphor of magic," by which he means that the repetition of certain words is believed to produce the wished-for reality stated in the words. In this regard he cites Freud, who defined magic as the belief in the "omnipotence of thought," the roots of which can be found in the human tendency to dream and daydream, the function of which is to fulfill or strive to fulfill wishes in one's fantasies. For Malinowski, however, Freud's view requires a serious correction, "for man never runs on the side-track of magical verbiage or of magical activities in that idle daydreaming which stultifies action" (239). Organized magic, Malinowski reiterates, always emerges where humans have learned from experience their practical powerlessness in specific situations. In the primitive context, then, the utterances of the magician are essential in helping the members of the community assuage their anxiety in the face of challenges and dangers they can do nothing about by strictly rational-empirical means.

The magical practitioner, by declaring his magical powers and boldly uttering his affirmations and exorcisms, imparts to community members a greater confidence that they and their gardens and their risky fishing expeditions are no longer totally at the mercy of fate and bad luck. Magic in its psychological essence is an expression of hope and a confidence-enhancing means by which the community braces itself to overcome adversity. Insofar, however, as humanity develops really effective means and techniques by which to control one realm of activity after another, magic is replaced by science and technology sometimes for good, but too often for destructive, antihuman purposes. In the Trobriand context, however, Malinowski had demonstrated that the magician functions as a leader and organizer of the community's essential economic activities, and as the representative of its beliefs, hopes, and strivings.

NOTES

[1]See Bronislaw Malinowski, *Coral Gardens and Their Magic*, 2 vols., introduction by Edmund Leach (Bloomington: Indiana University Press, 1965), vol. 1, p. viii.

[2]Bronislaw Malinowski, *Magic, Science and Religion and Other Essays*, with an introduction by Robert Redfield (Prospect Heights, Ill.: Waveland Press, 1992), p. 20. This collection was originally published in 1948. Hereafter, all page references to this book will be cited in parentheses immediately following the quoted passage.

[3]Malinowski, *Coral Gardens and Their Magic*, vol. 2, p. 216. Hereafter, all page references to this volume will be cited in parentheses immediately following the quoted passage.

CHAPTER 11

SIGMUND FREUD

Freud became thoroughly familiar with the anthropological literature of his time and cited it in his *Totem and Taboo*. There one finds numerous references to Frazer's *Totemism and Exogamy* and *The Golden Bough*, to Spencer and Gillen's *Native Tribes of Central Australia*, and to the writings of E. B. Tylor, Andrew Lang, Wilhelm Wundt, Émile Durkheim, Marcel Mauss, and others. Freud found the ethnographic studies of primitive cultures not only extraordinarily interesting in their own right but also relevant to his psychoanalytic theories. He therefore scrutinized the phenomenon of totemism from a psychoanalytic standpoint with the aim of illuminating the origins of religion.

In his *Totem and Taboo* Freud notes that the oldest and most salient taboos are the two basic laws of totemism, prohibiting the killing of the totem animal and prohibiting sexual intercourse with clan members of the opposite sex. Citing Frazer's analysis of totemism as a religious system, Freud observes that clan members take the name of their totem and, as a rule, believe they are descended from it. The totemic animal is regarded as the common ancestor of the clan's members and is venerated as such. For Freud, it was a significant surmise that there was one notable exception to the prohibition of killing the totemic animal. He accepted Robertson Smith's speculation that the sacramental killing or sacrifice of the otherwise forbidden totem animal, and its consumption in common, was, at least once a year, a definite feature of totemic religion. Although Freud was aware of the objections to Smith's theory, of the sacrificial feast, which had been raised by Marcel Mauss and others, he nevertheless accepted Smith's explanation as not having been discredited by criticisms.

Freud therefore decided to propose what he regarded as a plausible reenactment of such a sacrificial feast, embellishing it further with a few probable features. On a solemn occasion, clan members, disguising themselves as the totemic animal and mimicking its actions, kill the animal and together consume it raw. They know that on this occasion they are engaging in an action that is otherwise forbidden to individuals and can be justified only through the participation of all, so that no one can exclude himself from the killing and the feast. After the act, however, the murdered animal is bewailed and lamented, the expression of sorrow being compulsory and enforced by the fear of retribution. It is as if through lamentation one exculpates oneself from responsibility for the slaying. Following the mourning, however, clan members engage in loud festival gaiety accompanied by the unleashing and gratification of every impulse. The occasion is a holiday for them, a time when excess and the violation of prohibitions are permitted or even prescribed. The holiday mood is brought about by allowing what is otherwise forbidden. But, Freud asks, if the men are joyous over the killing of the totem, why do they mourn it? Freud proposes that clan members become holy through the consumption of the totem and thus strengthen their identification with it and with one another. From a psychoanalytic standpoint, the fact that they have absorbed the holy life or spirit of the totem helps to explain both the sorrow of the occasion and the joyous holiday mood. As Freud writes:

> Psychoanalysis has revealed to us that the totem animal is really a substitute for the father, and this really explains the contradiction that it is usually forbidden to kill the totem animal, that the killing of it results in a holiday and that the animal is killed and yet mourned. The ambivalent emotional attitude which today still marks the father complex in our children and so often continues into adult life also extended to the father substitute of the totem animal.[1]

How did the totemic animal become a "father substitute"? In Freud's reply to that question he postulated a pretotemic social condition, which, following a suggestion by Darwin, he called a "primeval horde." In part 2 of *Descent of Man*, where he discusses sexual selection and the "Law of Battle," Darwin writes:

> We may indeed conclude from what we know of the jealousy of all male quadrupeds, armed as many of them are, with special weapons for battling with their rivals, that promiscuous intercourse in a state of nature is extremely improbable....
>
> Therefore, if we look far enough back in the stream of time, it is extremely improbable that primeval men and women lived promiscuously together. Judging from the social habits of man as he now exists, and from most savages being polygamists, *the most probable view is that primeval man aboriginally lived in small communities, each with as many wives as he could support and obtain, whom he would have jealously guarded against all other men.*[2]

It is the italicized portion on which Freud built his hypothetical reconstruction of the "history" of the "primeval horde," in which the strongest male, a violent, jealous father, monopolized for himself all the females and drove away the maturing sons. The fate of the sons, Freud writes, "was a hard one; if they excited the father's jealousy, they were killed or castrated or driven out. They were forced to live in small groups and to . . . provide themselves with wives by stealing them from others."[3] Thus excluded from the supreme pleasure with females of their choice, the sons were also compelled to shoulder the burden of whatever labor had to be done. The social order of the horde survived the death of the primeval father, as one or another of the mature sons succeeded in attaining a position similar to that of the father in the original horde.

The primal, patriarchal despotism prevailed for a while. In time, however, the hatred and resentment it generated were too strong for it to withstand, and it was destroyed. The expelled brothers joined forces, killed and ate the father, and put an end to his domination once and for all. The brothers who had so envied and feared the violent, primeval father, identified with him by devouring him and acquiring a portion of his power. Though they hated the father who had thwarted their sexual desires, they also loved and admired him. With his removal and their hate satisfied, the tender impulses began to assert themselves. Remorse and guilt set in. The prohibitions that the father had physically enforced were now psychically commemorated with a symbolic father substitute in the totemic feast. Thus the brothers "created two fundamental taboos of totemism out of the *sense of guilt of the son*, and for this very reason these had to correspond with the two repressed wishes of the Oedipus complex" (917).

Totemism repressed everything hateful in the father and brought out everything the sons had wished for: protection, care, and forbearance. In return the sons pledged to honor his life, "that is to say, not to repeat against the totem the act through which the real father had perished. Totemism also contained an attempt at justification: 'If the father had treated us like the totem, we should never have been tempted to kill him.' Thus totemism helped to gloss over the real state of affairs and to make one forget the event to which it owed its origin" (918).

The first totemic feasts were therefore the beginning of fraternal social organization, moral restrictions, and religion. The new brotherly solidarity of the clan meant that no one was to treat the other as the primeval father had treated them—nor as they, in the end, had treated him. The father totem was transformed into a wholly benevolent being, and his perfection of power was placed out of reach. It is out of that process, Freud hypothesized, that the idea of "god" emerged. Defending this conjecture on the basis of his clinical experience, Freud explains:

> Psychoanalytic investigation of the individual teaches with special emphasis that god is in every case modeled after the father and that

our personal relation to god is dependent upon our relation to our physical father, fluctuating and changing with him, and that god at bottom is nothing but an exalted father. Here also, as in the case of totemism, psychoanalysis advises us to believe the faithful, who call god father just as they called the totem their ancestor. (919–20)

For Freud, mythologies, properly analyzed, often reveal the repressed wish fantasies of a culture. Myths stand in the same relation to a culture as do dreams to an individual. In the earliest introduction of agriculture, Freud noted, there are clear expressions of father-son tension. In numerous myths, the son's incestuous desires find symbolic expression in laboring over mother earth. There appear youthful male divinities like Attis, Adonis, and Tammuz who enjoy the favors of the maternal deities and who commit incest with them in defiance of the father. The youths, however, do not go unpunished. They suffer either short life or castration at the hands of the father-god appearing in animal form. Adonis was killed by a boar, the sacred animal of Aphrodite; and Attis, the lover of Cybele, died of castration. In that way, Freud suggests, the terrible sense of guilt following upon incest is allayed.

Echoes of the primordial tension may also be heard in the myths of Christianity. Frazer, in his analysis of the festive "eating of the god" in primitive cultures, had remarked that "the Christian communion has absorbed within itself a sacrament which is doubtless far older than Christianity." Building on Frazer's remark, Freud observes, however, that in the Eucharist the son allayed the sense of guilt by sacrificing his own life, thereby redeeming all his brothers from the primal sin. In the Christian myth, man's original sin was an offense against God the Father. Freud therefore assumes that if the redemption of humankind required the sacrifice of the son, the sin must have been "murder" in some sense. Yet in the very self-sacrifice of the son (interpreted in the light of psychoanalysis), which was to achieve reconciliation with the father,

> the son also attains the goal of his wishes against the father. He becomes a god himself beside or rather in place of his father. The religion of the son succeeds the religion of the father. As a sign of this substitution the old totem feast is revived ... in the form of communion in which the band of brothers now eats the flesh and blood of the son and no longer that of the father, the sons thereby identifying themselves with him and becoming holy themselves. ... At bottom, however, the Christian communion is a new setting aside of the father. (925)

Freud thus attempted to posit a definite theoretical connection between totemism and the Oedipus complex: Religion and the idea of god may be traced to the complex. Freud readily acknowledged that in the absence of direct evidence, the primordial act of patricide cannot be proved. However, even if such an act never had occurred, "the mere impulses of hostility toward the father and the existence of the wish fantasy to kill and devour him may have sufficed to bring about the moral reaction which has created totemism and taboo" (929).

RELIGION AS ILLUSION

Freud published *Totem and Taboo* in 1912 and came back to the subject of religion some fifteen years later in *The Future of an Illusion*, published in 1927.

The concept of "civilization" for Freud, includes (1) the knowledge and capacity that humans have acquired to control the forces of nature and to extract from it wealth and resources for human needs, and (2) the rules necessary to regulate human relations, and especially the distribution of wealth. Freud recognized that the creations of civilization are easily destroyed, and that science and technology can be employed for destructive purposes. And yet, in his critique of religion as an illusion, as we shall see, he appears to believe that science can somehow supplant religion as it seems to decline. We shall return to the question of whether science can ever fulfill the human needs ostensibly fulfilled by the varieties of religious experience.

Freud sees an irremediable tension between the individual's nature and the requirements of civilization. Every civilization, Freud avers, must rest on coercion and a suppression of instinctual needs and impulses. Owing, then, to the fact that social organization necessitates the renunciation of instinctual needs, there are present in all humans certain antisocial tendencies, which in a significant number of people are strong enough to express themselves destructively. A degree of coercion is therefore unavoidable in any society because humans are not spontaneously fond of most forms of labor and because they resent the socially instituted frustrations of their natural passions. Hostility to civilization is born afresh, Freud believed, with every child whose instinctual impulses and wishes are thwarted. And in his psychoanalytic experience Freud observed that the repressed instinctual wishes of neurotics are often those of incest and a lust for killing.

In the course of historical development, the external forms of social coercion are gradually internalized. A special mental agency that Freud called the "superego" takes over, and the child becomes more and more of a moral and social being. The growth and strengthening of the superego is a most precious cultural asset because those in whom the superego or moral conscience is strong are converted from opponents to proponents of civilization. The greater the number of such individuals, the more secure is the society, and the more it can dispense with external means of coercion.

Freud recognized that although civilization implies general restrictions to which everyone in a given society is subject, there are also restrictions that apply only to certain classes. The underprivileged classes naturally envy the wealthy and powerful and do everything they can to rid themselves of their own "surplus of privation."[4] And when their efforts fail them, massive discontent prevails within the society and occasionally erupts in violent revolts. In addition, therefore, to the general tension between the individual and society, which produces antisocial behavior, there are class tensions between the haves and the have-nots. It is therefore no cause for surprise, Freud writes,

> that the suppressed people should develop an intense hostility towards a culture whose existence they make possible by their work, but in whose wealth they have too small a share. In such conditions an internalization of the cultural prohibitions among the suppressed people is not to be expected. On the contrary, they are not prepared to acknowledge the prohibitions, they are intent on destroying the culture itself, and possibly even on doing away with the postulates on which it is based.... It goes without saying that a civilization which leaves so large a number of its participants unsatisfied and drives them into revolt neither has nor deserves the prospect of a lasting existence. (191–92)

That is not all, for in addition to the frustrations of repressed individuals and oppressed classes, still another source of frustration often leads to violent and mutually destructive conflict. One not only identifies with one's own culture and its ideals but also tends narcissistically to look down on the cultures of others. Diverse cultural ideals thus become a source of discord and enmity, which is so evident among nations. Nationalism thus also serves to diminish interclass hostility within national units. The narcissistic sense of cultural superiority over others is enjoyed not only by the dominant classes, who derive the most benefit from the social system, but also by the suppressed classes,

> since the right to despise the people outside it compensates them for the wrongs they suffer within their own unit.... This identification of the suppressed classes with the class who rules and exploits them is, however, only part of a larger whole. For ... the suppressed classes can be emotionally attached to their masters; in spite of their hostility to them, they may see in them their ideals; unless such relations of a fundamentally satisfying kind subsisted, it would be impossible to understand how a number of civilizations have survived so long in spite of the justifiable hostility of large human masses. (193)

In his psychical inventory of the elements of civilization Freud now arrives at the role of religious ideas. In his assessment of the value of religious ideas, he begins with a Hobbesian scenario. Freud reminds us of his central thesis, that the hostility to civilization is produced by the renunciation of instinctual needs that civilization demands. So now Freud asks us to entertain a counterfactual thought experiment in which all of society's prohibitions are lifted, thus taking us into a Hobbesian state of nature in which one may take any individual of the opposite sex, one may kill any sexual rival or anyone else who stands in one's way, one may carry off anyone else's property, and so forth. How splendid a life, Freud sardonically remarks, such a string of gratifications would be! But, of course, he reminds us that there is one big problem with this scenario, namely, that "everyone else has exactly the same wishes that I have and will treat me with no more consideration than I treat them" (194). In other words, we would be thrown into a Hobbesian state of nature and war of each against all—a war of every individual against every other individual. So despite the repressiveness of civilization, the imaginary abolition of it would throw us into a far worse condition. But that does not mean, as we have seen, that civilization is an unmixed blessing, or that civilized life can defend us against all adversity.

There are, first of all, the many dangers with which nature threatens us—the earth that quakes and tears itself apart, burying human life and its works, water that drowns everything in its path, storms that devastate, terrible diseases and finally, death—all of which dramatically bring home to us our weakness and helplessness. But in addition to the hazards with which nature threatens humanity, there are the pains endemic to society. For individuals, life is often hard to bear because of the restrictions society imposes upon them, and because of the privations they suffer due to the inequalities of class. Then add to all this what we call fate or bad luck, and we can readily see the many ways in which human beings feel themselves seriously menaced and in need, therefore, of consolation and comfort.

Freud follows Frazer in considering religion as an advance over magic. With the belief in divine beings, humans are still vulnerable in countless ways, but they can now appeal to the deities, adjure, appease, and bribe them, thus finding comfort and hope. This experience for adult humans is not new, since it is a continuation of an infantile, prototypical situation, in which we were in a definite state of helplessness. Freud now once again invokes his Oedipal thesis. As children, individuals not only were dependent on parents but also had reason to fear them, especially one's father. Yet one was sure of his protection against dangers. Thus it was natural for early or primitive individuals to assimilate the childhood experience of helplessness with that of the adult. In both cases, Freud maintains, drawing upon his theory of dreams, *wishing* played its part as it does in dream life. Dream work knows how to transform a dreaded event into a favorable wish fulfillment.

The adult individual makes the forces of nature into persons, but not persons with whom he can associate on an equal footing. That would fail to do justice to the overpowering impression that nature, society, and fate make upon the individual. When he personifies a power that can help and protect him, he therefore gives it the character of a father, thus following an infantile prototype. Humans thus turn forces into gods, but because their helplessness remains, they long for the help the gods may offer them in their threefold task: "They must exorcise the terrors of nature, they must reconcile men to the cruelty of Fate, particularly as it is shown in death, and they must compensate them for the sufferings and privations which a civilized life in common has imposed on them" (197).

A store of religious ideas is thus built up from the memories of childhood helplessness and from the childhood helplessness of the human species—ideas striving for wish fulfillment and expressing the hope of gaining protection from the dangers of nature and fate, on the one hand, and from the injuries and injustices that are endemic to life in society. Religious ideas include a benevolent Providence that watches over us, a conception of death as the beginning of a new kind of existence, and a view that a divine Providence rules the entire universe in accordance with transcendent principles of morality and justice.

Turning his attention to the monotheistic religions, Freud observes that God having become a person, human relations to him could regain the intimacy and intensity of a child's relation to his father. But here Freud reminds us that from his psychoanalytic standpoint, a child's attitude toward his father is colored by a peculiar ambivalence, which continues to characterize religious conceptions of God. When the maturing individual learns that he is destined to remain a child forever, and that he will always need protection, he creates for himself a supreme power with the features belonging to the image of his father. The father-god in whom the individual entrusts his protection remains an object of ambivalence, both loved and feared.

FREUD'S REPUDIATION OF RELIGIOUS BELIEFS

In *The Future of an Illusion*, after stating his claim that the religious experience is rooted in both childhood helplessness and the general vulnerability of human beings, Freud is intent upon exposing what he regards as the total irrationality of religious beliefs. As we grow up and ask questions about arithmetic, science, geography, and history, we expect answers based on logic and evidence. Although we take on trust some of what we learn in school about those subjects, we expect that the teacher, if challenged, would produce good grounds for his or her claims. When it comes to religion, however, Freud observes that our questions are met with answers of a very different kind, as, for example, that the religious doctrine in question deserves to be believed because it was believed by our ancestors, and, besides, it is forbidden to ask such questions. Without much difficulty, then, Freud makes the point that religious beliefs are the least well authenticated of any, and that religious doctrines are definitely outside the realm of reason. Given the significant role religion plays in social life, it is bizarre, says Freud, that people do not demand reasonable answers to their questions concerning religious doctrine. Freud cites the attitude of one of his children who when listening to a fairy tale would ask whether it was a true story, and when told it was not, would turn away with a look of disdain. And Freud remarks, "We may expect that people will soon behave in the same way towards the fairy tales of religion" (211).

Freud fully realizes that his critique of religion is far from original. His real aim in *The Future of an Illusion* is not merely to criticize religion but to illuminate the psychic origins of religious ideas. The teachings of religion, he argues, are not the product of experience or rigorous thinking. They are, instead, "illusions, fulfillment of the oldest, strongest and most urgent wishes of mankind. The secret of their strength [i.e., of religious ideas] lies in the strength of those wishes" (212).

What is characteristic of illusions, for Freud, is that they are produced by wishes and thus come close to psychiatric delusions. A belief is an illusion when it is motivated primarily by the desire for wish fulfillment and when its relation to reality is ignored. Religious doctrines are illusions in that sense; they can be neither proved nor refuted.

At this point, Freud's imaginary interlocutor challenges him with this question: Why not believe in the assertions of religion, "since they have so much on their side—tradition, the agreement of mankind, and all the consolations they offer?" (214). Freud's rationalistic response unfolds in something like the following manner. He acknowledges that religion, historically, has performed great services for civilization, primarily by taming the asocial instincts. But religion has had thousands of years in which to prove itself in making the majority of human beings happy and in comforting them. And if religion had succeeded in that respect, no one, and least of all Freud himself, would have dreamed of impugning the religious state of mind. But what do we see instead? Massive discontent with civilization!

As Freud proceeds, his central concern appears to be the decline and loss of religion, especially among the uneducated, and the destructive consequences that might follow from the resulting moral vacuum. In effect, Freud feared that the great mass of oppressed are bound to learn one day either that "God is dead!" in Nietzsche's sense or that there is no God. "Is there not a danger here," Freud asks, that the hostility of these masses to civilization will throw itself against the weak spot that they have found in their task mistress? If the sole reason why you must not kill your neighbor is because God has forbidden it and will severely punish you for it in this or the next life—then, when you learn that there is no God and that you need not fear His punishment, you will certainly kill your neighbor without hesitation, and you can only be prevented from doing so by mundane force. (222)

What is Freud's so-called solution to the danger of a moral vacuum? Science must fill the vacuum!? It needs, therefore, to be said that Freud's notion of reason and science somehow supplanting religion strikes one as not only naive in the extreme but also failing to deal effectively with the realities he discerned so well. For while he fears the moral vacuum that increasing secularization might create, he at the same time counsels us to admit the purely human origin of civilization's laws and precepts. "Along with their pretended sanctity," he writes, "these commandments and laws would lose their rigidity and unchangeableness as well. People could understand that they are made, not so much to rule them as, on the contrary, to serve their interests; and they would adopt a more friendly attitude to them, and instead of aiming at their abolition, would aim only at their improvement" (224–25). But if we were to admit the "purely human origin" of our commandments, laws, and precepts, would not that tend to accelerate the very tendency toward moral relativism and nihilism that Freud ostensibly feared? Moreover, Freud speaks in the quoted passage of serving interests. He himself had earlier noted the salience of class inequalities in modern society. So when he speaks of serving interests, we need to ask, "Whose interests?" Also, "Why wouldn't the admission of the purely human origin of our laws and principles heighten the danger of civilization's degeneration into a Hobbesian 'war of each against all,' a condition which could only be brought to an end by the tyrannical imposition of *arbitrary* laws?" We need to remind ourselves that Thomas Hobbes himself would never have approved of such methods of imposing order; for what was presupposed and emphasized in his insistence on the necessity of a common power, or Leviathan, as the precondition of order, is that it had to rest on the moral virtues which were at the same time the divine laws. For Hobbes, those virtues and laws included, at the very least, justice, equity, and mercy.

Freud nevertheless urges upon us an experiment in irreligious education. He calls it an "education to reality" and confesses that the sole aim of this book of his is to argue the necessity of this "forward step." There is a definite Nietzschean ring to Freud's discussion here. Freud says, "You are afraid, probably, that you will not stand up to the hard test" (233). But whereas Nietzsche and his protagonist, Zarathustra, aimed to replace the "slave morality" of Western culture with a "master morality" of "higher-type," human specimens, Freud somehow sees "science" as the savior. "We believe," he writes, "that it is possible for scientific work to gain some knowledge about the reality of the world, by means of which we can increase our power and in accordance with which we can arrange our life" (239). And Freud concludes: "No, our science is no illusion. But an illusion it would be to suppose that what science cannot give us we can get elsewhere" (241).

In thus singing the praise of science, Freud appears to be more of a nineteenth-century heir of the Enlightenment than a twentieth-century thinker. Indeed, he died in 1939, before he could witness the full horrors of the genocidal, totalitarian regimes. But even with regard to his own era, Freud's unstinting praise of science effectively ignores the insight he himself had stated in the opening pages of *The Future of an Illusion*, namely, that "human creations are easily destroyed, and science and technology, which have built them up, can also be used for their annihilation" (185).

Furthermore, Freud's view of science and reason also fails to recognize a fundamental insight of Max Weber's—that science and reason can provide us with a measure of clarity concerning the consequences of employing a certain *means* to attain a given end, but science cannot tell us what ends to choose, or even what means to choose in the face of the probable consequences of employing one means over another. It is the acting, willing individual, in accordance with his or her own conscience, who must weigh the values to be gained against the values to be lost.

In other words, science can provide some clarity concerning the probable results of, say, pursuing an end with violent or nonviolent means; but science *cannot* tell us whether the means chosen is *morally justifiable*. Weber understood that when one enters the realm of questions concerning morality and justice, one leaves the realm of science. Indeed, Freud should have understood what David Hume had demonstrated centuries earlier, that one cannot derive an "ought" from an "is." So Freud should have known that by means of science or reason alone we cannot inform ourselves how we ought to live, how we ought to relate to others, and how we ought to organize our social lives.

NOTES

[1]See Sigmund Freud, *Totem and Taboo*, in *The Basic Writings of Sigmund Freud*, translated and edited with an introduction by A. A. Brill (New York: Modern Library, 1938), p. 915. Hereafter, all page references to this work will be cited in parentheses immediately following the quoted passage.

[2]Charles Darwin, *The Descent of Man*, introduction by John Tyler Bonner and Robert M. May (Princeton, N.J.: Princeton University Press, 1981), vol. 2, p. 362, italics added.

[3]Sigmund Freud, *Moses and Monotheism* (New York: Vintage Books, 1939), p. 102.

[4]See Sigmund Freud, *The Future of an Illusion* in *Civilization, Society and Religion*, The Penguin Freud Library, vol. 12, translated by James Strachey, edited by Albert Dickson, (London: Penguin, 1985), p. 191. Hereafter, all page references to this work will be cited in parentheses immediately following the quoted passage.

CHAPTER 12

ÉMILE DURKHEIM

É mile Durkheim's primary aim in his *Elementary Forms of Religious Life* was to analyze the most primitive and simple religion known to ethnographers, that of the Australian Aborigines. A religious system, he proposed, may be regarded as the most primitive when it fulfills two conditions: (1) when it is found in a society whose organization is surpassed by no others in simplicity; and (2) when it is possible to explain the workings of its religious system without employing elements borrowed from a previous religion. Durkheim's study was therefore a reexamination, but under new conditions, of the old question of the origin of religion. What he had hoped to accomplish was to lay bare the ever-present conditions upon which the most essential forms of religious thought and practice depend.

The first task was to define the subject matter. What do we mean by religion? The definitions prevalent during Durkheim's time all stressed a belief in supernatural and spiritual beings. That, as we have seen, was the view of the British anthropologist E. B. Tylor, who suggested that the best minimal definition of religion is "the belief in spiritual beings." Durkheim found that definition inadequate, however, because it failed to include those religions in which the idea of spirits is absent. Buddhism is a case in point. In none of its original principles does it concern itself with the notion of spirits or deities.

After reviewing several other definitions and finding them deficient, Durkheim offers his own. All known societies, he avers, divide the social world into two domains: the *sacred* and the *profane*. For Durkheim, it is the totality of beliefs and practices concerned with the sacred that constitutes what we call "religion." When members of a society think and act in the same way with respect to the sacred, they share a common religion. They are members of a common "church"—a moral community formed by all the believers in a single faith. Thus a "religion," writes Durkheim, "is a unified system of beliefs and practices relative to sacred things, that is to say, things set apart and forbidden—beliefs and practices which unite into one single moral community called a Church, all those who adhere to them."[1]

Armed with that definition, Durkheim proceeds to confront the leading theories of his day, which could be divided into two schools. The first was the theory of *animism*, of which E. B. Tylor was a chief representative. Tylor, as we have seen, held that primitive religion is a form of animism, a belief in souls, spirits, and a future state. Where did the primitive philosopher acquire the idea of a soul or spirit? He acquired it, wrote Tylor, by reflecting on two questions: "What is it that makes the difference between a living body and a dead one...? [And] what are those human shapes which appear in dreams and visions?" Tylor continues:

> Looking at these two groups of phenomena, the ancient savage philosophers probably made their first step by the obvious inference that early man has two things belonging to him, namely, a life and a phantom.... As both belong to the body, why should they not also belong to one another, and be manifestations of one and the same soul? Let them then be considered as united, and the result is that well-known conception which may be described as an apparition—soul, a ghost-soul.[2]

For Tylor, then, the idea of the soul originated in the experience of dreams and fantasies.

For Durkheim, however, that theory was quite unsatisfactory, for even if one admits the plausibility of the dream origin of the soul idea, the theory had one crucial defect. It failed to explain why a phantom—a simple image of an individual—should have been elevated to the rank of a *sacred* being. Animistic theory, Durkheim argues, fails to provide a convincing answer to this all-important question: "If, while it [the phantom-soul] lived, it was only a profane thing, a walking life-principle, how would it suddenly become a sacred thing and the object of religious feelings?" (57). Durkheim tends to dismiss Tylor's theory too easily. He ignores the significance of ancestor cults, the widespread veneration of deceased ancestors for which the evidence is plentiful. Tylor and Frazer had provided it for primitive cultures as had Weber for the religions of China.

The other school with which Durkheim quarrels he calls *naturism*. Naturistic theories held that the first objects of religious sentiment were external, natural phenomena. The things and forces of nature were the first to be deified. Nature purportedly presents to the primitive individual numerous awesome spectacles that suffice to inspire religious ideas in him. He personifies and spiritualizes such spectacles by means of metaphors and images.

For Durkheim, however, naturism suffers from the same defect that he attributed to animism. Natural forces, he argues, are, after all, merely natural forces, however intense and spectacular they might be. Missing from the theory, therefore, is an explanation of how they acquired a sacred character. It is doubtful, says Durkheim, that the sense of sacredness can be derived directly from natural phenomena. In thus rejecting the propositions of both schools, Durkheim has prepared the way for his own distinctive sociological theory.

TOTEMISM: AN ELEMENTARY RELIGION

Durkheim was fully familiar with the anthropological literature on totemism. He observed that the word *totem* appeared in 1791 in a book by J. Long, an Indian interpreter, and that for almost fifty years totemism was regarded as an exclusively North American institution. It was George Grey who in 1841 called attention to similar practices in Australia. The anthropological students of North American Indian cultures had recognized that totemism was connected with a definite form of social organization and that tribal society was divided into clans. Lewis Henry Morgan had documented the connection of totemism with the clan structure of tribal societies among the Indian tribes of North and Central America, and soon afterward many additional studies were carried out under the auspices of the Bureau of American Ethnology. Then Frazer summarized the evidence in a small book titled *Totemism*.

And yet, a fully functioning totemic system had not been studied directly until Baldwin Spencer and Francis James Gillen discovered in the interior of the Australian continent a large number of tribes whose religious system was based on totemic beliefs. The writings on the subject by Spencer and Gillen had great influence because their reports were based on firsthand experience. So Durkheim centers attention on the small, aboriginal clan communities of Australia, which offered the best opportunity for the study of totemic beliefs. Such beliefs, anthropologists widely agreed, formed an elementary religion, the most elementary known to scholars. Evidence of totemic beliefs was also available for ancient Egypt, Arabia, ancient Greece, and the southern Slavs. But in none of those societies did totemism appear in as pure a form as it did among the Australian peoples.

Typically, Australian tribes were divided into clans, or exogamous kinship units. Members of each clan presumed themselves to be descended from a common ancestor. Each clan was symbolically represented by an animal or plant species, but most often by an animal species, which was called a *totem*. The clan's totem was also that of each individual member, who was then known as, say, kangaroo or crow. A group of clans united by fraternal bonds was called a *phratry*, and phratries also had their totems. Typically, an Australian tribe was divided into two phratries, and in almost all cases the phratry totem was that of an animal species.

The term *totem* refers to the species representing the clan and its individual members, but it also refers to the *symbolic* representation of the species and clan. A totem in that sense is an emblem, "a true coat of arms," says Durkheim, "and its resemblance to the heraldic coat of arms has often been commented upon" (111). Just as the nobles of the European feudal era engraved and displayed their coats of arms on their castle walls, their weapons and all kinds of objects belonging to them, so did the peoples of Australia with their totems. Totemic images were placed on the walls of huts, on the sides of canoes, and on the bodies of men. One of the principal initiation rites by which a young man entered into the religious life of the clan consisted of painting the totemic sign on his body.

The fact that the totemic image is prominently displayed on diverse objects and also tattooed on the initiated male's body suggested that the image is more than just a name and emblem. The totemic images are employed in religious ceremonies and are part of the liturgy. Indeed, says Durkheim, things are classified as sacred or profane by reference to the totem: "It is the very archetype of sacred things" (118). That is evident from the role of the *churinga*, a ritual instrument that anthropologists have dubbed a "bull-roarer." Oblong pieces of wood or polished stone, suspended by a string, are rapidly whirled in the air so as to produce a loud humming sound. The *churinga* is employed in all important rituals, but ritually profane persons, such as women and boys yet to be initiated into religious life, are prohibited from touching the instrument. While *churinga* is a noun, it is also an adjective, meaning "sacred." The *churinga* is also believed to possess extraordinary magical properties. By contact, it heals wounds and illnesses; it imparts to clan members strength and courage, and it ensures an adequate reproduction of the totemic species.

The *churinga* is distinguished not only by its use in a ritual context but also by the totemic mark engraved upon it. Typically such instruments are either zealously guarded from profane contact by being placed in a "holy ark" or constructed each time anew and then, once the rite is over, stripped of the sign, dismantled, and scattered. It is the totemic emblem that imparts a religious character to such instruments.

The next step in Durkheim's inquiry was to examine the clan's attitude toward the totemic species. As an animal or plant, its profane use would have been to serve as food. But its sacredness was demonstrated by the fact that all clan members were forbidden to eat it. And yet, surprisingly, although the *churinga* and all other objects bearing the clan emblem were never to be touched by ritually profane persons, such persons were allowed to come into contact with the totemic animal or plant. If, therefore, the degree of sacredness of an object may be measured by the pains taken to isolate it from the profane, "we arrive at the remarkable result that *the images of the totemic being are more sacred than the totemic being itself*" (133). Durkheim has thus distinguished three categories of things that totemism recognizes as sacred in varying degrees: the totemic emblem, the totemic species, and the clan members.

For Durkheim, it was a highly significant fact that the totemic sign is more sacred than the totemic species; for that suggested that the sign is most sacred not because it represents a species but because it represents something else. Furthermore, since the totemic species and the clan members are also regarded as sacred, that must mean that the sign, the species, *and* the clan all share some common "principle." It is the common partaking of that principle that makes them all sacred. What is that principle? It is an *anonymous impersonal force*, independent of all subjects in which it incarnates itself; it precedes and survives them. In Durkheim's words, "Taking the word 'god' in a very broad sense, one could say that it [the impersonal force] is the god that each totemic cult worships. But it is an impersonal god, without name, without history, immanent in the world, diffused in a numberless multitude of things" (191).

The divine principle is a "force" in both the physical and the moral sense. An individual failing to take proper ritual precautions receives a shock comparable to the effect of an electric charge. However, an individual observes the rites not merely out of fear of such physical effects but because his ancestors have always done so and because he feels a strong moral obligation to conduct himself likewise. Thus the totemic cult, though it may appear to be addressed to plants, animals, or other objects, is actually addressed to the "force" that permeates them. If a species of plant or animal or even the sun, moon, or stars are adored, it is due not to their intrinsic nature but to the fact that they partake of the sacred force.

The clan members themselves have only a vague notion of the force. But the belief in its existence is quite evident in other polytheistic cultures. The ancient Greeks, for example, called it *moira*, or fate and conceived of it as *supra*divine, because the most powerful gods were powerless before it. Yet the gods partake of that force when they produce rain, wind, or crops. Zeus, Poseidon, Hades, and the other Greek gods all retain marks of their original impersonality. The impersonal force or principle is inherent in and permeates all the objects of the environment—rocks, streams, plants, trees, animals, winds, storms, thunder, lightning, and so on. In those terms, it is the same "principle" or "force" we have encountered in Weber's "enchanted garden" of the East, in Frazer's conception of the supradivine, impersonal force that makes magic possible, and in Malinowski's adoption of the Melanesian concept of *mana* as the ultimate source of magical powers among the Trobrianders. Durkheim, too, employs the concept of *mana* to explain the forces that the Australian magician has at his disposal (199).

The impersonal force lying above the later personified gods is the chief cause of all the movements occurring in the cosmos. Hence, what we find in Australian religion is the first form of the idea of "force" as it was later conceived in Western philosophy and science. Students of ancient Greek culture have shown that Greek philosophical ideas such as necessity,

cause, substance, nature, matter, and so on are all rooted in the much more ancient religious conceptions of a sacred, all-powerful, impersonal, cosmic force.

But the most important question remains: What is the ultimate
source of the idea of a supradivine, impersonal force? We have said that the
totemic emblem is so highly sacred because it is a symbol of something
else. If we can discover what that "something else" actually is, reasoned
Durkheim, then we will have found the real basis for the idea of the Divine
or Supradivine. If we have followed Durkheim's analysis thus far, we can
see that the totem symbolized two things: (1) the impersonal divine force,
or "god," and (2) a specific society, namely, the clan. The totem is the clan's
"flag," the sign by which one clan distinguishes itself from another. "Thus,"
writes Durkheim,

> if the totem is the symbol of both the god and the society, is this not
> because the god and the society are one and the same? How could the
> emblem of the group have taken the form of that quasi-divinity if the
> group and the divinity were two distinct realities? Thus the god of
> the clan, the totemic principle, can be none other than the clan itself,
> but the clan transfigured and imagined in the physical form of the
> plant or animal that serves as totem. (208)

Upon reflection, argues Durkheim, it seems quite evident that society has all the attributes necessary to inspire a sense of the divine. Society
is, after all, experienced as a superior force on which everyone depends.
Members submit to its authority even when it is felt to be repressive. They
yield to its rules not only because it is strong enough to overcome them but
also because it is an object of respect. The social pressure brought to bear
on individuals by "society" is largely of a spiritual kind. Ultimately, it is
social reality that gives humans the idea that there exists a superhuman
principle, all-powerful and moral, on which they all depend. It is the experience of society, therefore, that gives rise to what Durkheim calls a "collective representation"—a collective intuiting of the Divine.

But it is not the profane, everyday experiences that produce that
effect. It is, rather, those special, sacred ritual occasions in which people
find themselves dominated and carried away by an external power.
Often lasting days on end, such ceremonial occasions transport the
participants from the gray world of everyday life into the extraordinary
and effervescent world of the sacred. "The effervescence," writes
Durkheim,

> often becomes so intense that it leads to outlandish behavior; the pas-
> sions unleashed are so torrential that nothing can hold them. People
> are so far outside the ordinary conditions of life, and so conscious of the
> fact, that they feel a certain need to set themselves above and beyond
> ordinary morality. The sexes come together in violation of the rules
> governing sexual relations. Men exchange wives. Indeed, sometimes

incestuous unions, in normal times judged loathsome and harshly condemned, are contracted in the open with impunity. If it is added that the ceremonies are generally held at night, in the midst of shadows pierced here and there by firelight, we can easily imagine the effect that scenes like these are bound to have on the minds of all those who take part. They bring about such an intense hyper-excitement of physical and mental life as a whole that they cannot be borne for very long. The celebrant who takes the leading role eventually falls exhausted to the ground. (218)

So for Durkheim, "It is in these effervescent social milieux, and indeed from that very effervescence, that the religious idea seems to have been born. That such is indeed the origin tends to be confirmed by the fact that what is properly called religious activity in Australia is almost entirely contained within the periods when these gatherings are held" (220). Since religious force is nothing other than the collective and anonymous power of the clan, and since this can be represented in the mind only in the form of the totem, the totemic emblem is like the visible body of the Divine. Hence, when humans believe in a moral power on which they depend, that is no illusion, for that power exists: It is society!

Sacred assemblies serve the apparent function of strengthening the individual's bonds with the Divine, but at the same time they serve the real function of strengthening an individual's bonds to the society of which he is a member, for "god" is only a symbolic expression of society. "Religious force," Durkheim proposes, "is none other than the feeling that the collectivity inspires in its members, but projected outside the minds that experience them, and objectified" (230).

Durkheim maintains that just as there is no known society that is devoid of religion as he has defined it, there is no known religion, however elementary, that lacks a doctrine of the "soul." It follows from Durkheim's analysis, however, that contrary to Tylor's view, the soul is no mere phantom, dream image, or mental reproduction of the individual. Souls, for Durkheim, consist of the same substance as the totemic principle. The soul is the experience each clan member has of the totemic principle incarnate in him. The soul is what society implants in every individual. The individual soul is a particle of the great collective soul of the group.

ASCETIC RITES

For Durkheim, the ethnographic literature seemed to confirm that sacred beings are systematically kept separate from profane beings. Whole series of rites are designed to prevent contact between them. One finds even in the elementary forms of religious life definite prohibitions in the form of *taboos*, a Polynesian term signifying that certain things are withdrawn from use in everyday life. Such religious prohibitions are derived from the notion of a sacred domain, which they are intended to preserve.

Not only are sacred beings separated from profane beings, but a great effort is made to prevent the concerns of profane life from penetrating the sacred realm.

Among the Australian tribes, accordingly, all worldly occupations are suspended when the great religious ceremonies take place. As Spencer and Gillen had observed, the Australian's life consists of two distinct realms: One is devoted to hunting, fishing, and war; the other is dedicated to the cult. Durkheim refers to the latter as a "negative cult" because it consists of prohibitions and taboos rather than positive injunctions or obligations. The negative cult includes abstinences. The barrier between the sacred and the profane means that individuals may enter into intimate relations with the sacred only if they empty themselves of everyday concerns and interests. The negative cult therefore implies *asceticism*.

As an example, Durkheim cites the Australian initiation rites in which the novice is subjected to various forms of extreme self-denial. Obliged to withdraw from all human relations, the novice is not only forbidden to see women and uninitiated men; he goes far into the bush under the supervision of a few old men serving as "godfathers." Such initiation rites might last for months, during which time the novice is subjected to every sort of abstinence. He is forbidden to partake of a wide variety of foods and is allowed only enough food as is necessary to sustain life. He also endures long and rigorous fasting, or is made to eat disgusting food, and so on. Before initiation he was excluded from the cult, but after the ordeal of the rite he is admitted to the company of men and to participation in the cult, for he has acquired the quality of sacredness. The metamorphosis is so complete that it is often interpreted by the people concerned as a second birth—the profane, preinitiated youth has died and has been replaced by a new individual properly qualified for admission to the privileges of the cult.

For Durkheim, such rites of passage help us to understand asceticism and its role in religious life. The ascetic individual raises himself to new heights by acquiring a special sanctity through fasts, vigils, retreats, silence, and other forms of self-denial. Asceticism, then, far from being an exceptional, rare, and abnormal phenomenon in religious life, is an essential element of it. "Every religion," writes Durkheim, "has at least the seeds of asceticism, for there is none without a system of prohibitions" (316). Evidence of the "negative cult" among the Australians, Durkheim avers, thus supports the proposition he enunciated in the beginning of his *Elementary Forms*: that all the essential elements of religious thought and life are found, at least embryonically, in the most primitive religions.

Moreover, Durkheim wishes to employ the phenomenon of asceticism to reinforce his central thesis, that society is the real basis of the collective representation of the Divine (or supradivine, impersonal force), and that religious interests are only social and moral interests in symbolic form. In restating his general theory in the light of asceticism, Durkheim presents an analysis similar to that of Freud in his *Future of an Illusion* and *Civilization and Its Discontents*. "The ideal beings to which cults are addressed," Durkheim writes,

> are not alone in demanding of their servants a certain contempt for pain; society, too, is possible only at that price. Even when exalting the powers of man, it is often brutal toward individuals. Of necessity, it requires perpetual sacrifices of them. Precisely because society lifts us above ourselves, it does constant violence to our natural appetites. So that we can fulfill our duties toward it, our conditioning must ready us to overcome our instincts at times—when necessary to go up the down staircase of nature. There is an inherent asceticism in all social life that is destined to outlive all mythologies and all dogmas. (321)

In sum, Durkheim has sought to advance the proposition that society is the ultimate source of the feeling or notion of a superhuman, divine, or supradivine reality, and that the sacred is nothing other than society hypostatized and transfigured. All notions of the Divine, whatever their form, originate in the reality of social life. That is even true of the idea of immortality: Though individuals die, the clan lives on. There must therefore be some principle or force that enables the clan-society to possess eternal life. Finally, the idea of good and evil spirits and deities, far from being aroused by either dreams or awesome natural spectacles, is also rooted in the realities of social life. Religion, accordingly, reflects both the good and evil sides of social life, its just ideas and practices as well as its moral ugliness. As Durkheim explains:

> There have been gods of theft and trickery, lust and war, sickness and death. As uplifted as its idea of divinity is, Christianity itself was obliged to make a place in its mythology for the spirit of evil. Satan is an essential component of the Christian system; yet, even if he is an impure being, he is not a profane being. The anti-god is a god—lower and subordinate, it is true, yet invested with broad powers; he is even the object of rites, at the very least negative ones. Far from ignoring and disregarding the real society, religion is its image, reflecting all its features, even the most vulgar and repellant. (423)

CRITICISMS OF DURKHEIM'S THEORY

We see, then, that for Durkheim and his followers society and God are one. Society, unconsciously divinized, is the stuff of which all religions are made. Since Durkheim rested his theory on evidence from primitive cultures, it will be instructive to return briefly to Bronislaw Malinowski, to hear his critical comments.

Malinowski acknowledges that his own research supports the view that religion is a tribal affair and that primitive religion appears to be a concern of the community rather than of the individual. And yet, Malinowski observes, even in so-called primitive religion some of the most meaningful and profound religious moments come in solitude. Referring to some of the same rites cited by Durkheim, Malinowski notes that the novice is often secluded at initiation and subjected to a personal ideal, including a communion with spirits and deities. It is therefore hard to see, says Malinowski, the social basis of those sacred powers in such lonely and isolated spots. It is especially difficult to see how the belief in immortality can be explained without considering the state of mind of the *individual* facing his inevitable death in fear and sorrow. Moreover, Durkheim's theory virtually ignores the role of the individual, though evidence is plentiful that in primitive religion prophets, seers, interpreters, and other practitioners play a prominent role. Such facts strongly indicate that the stuff of religion cannot be regarded as purely social.

Or take the essence of morals—as opposed to "laws"—that are enforced by *conscience*, and not by an external agency. The primitive individual observes the taboos not out of fear of public punishment; he abstains from breaking rules partly because he fears *divine* punishment and mainly because his sense of personal responsibility and his conscience forbid him from doing it. "The forbidden totem animal," Malinowski writes,

> incestuous or forbidden intercourse, the tabooed action or food, are directly abhorrent to him. I have seen and felt savages shrink from an illicit action with the same horror and disgust that the religious Christian will shrink from the committing of what he considers sin. Now this mental attitude is undoubtedly due in part to the influence of society, in so far as the particular prohibition is branded as horrible and disgusting by tradition. But it works in the individual and through forces of the individual mind. It is, therefore, neither exclusively social nor individual, but a mixture of both.[3]

Also questionable is Durkheim's argument that the idea of the Divine is somehow derived from primitive ceremonies and festivities. The religious idea, he maintains, "is born out of their effervescence." Durkheim thus tends to place the entire weight of his analysis on the emotional excitement one feels while participating in such gatherings. To this Malinowski replies that just a little

> reflection is sufficient to show that even in primitive societies the heightening of emotions and the lifting of the individual outside of himself are by no means restricted to gatherings and to crowd phenomena. The lover near his sweetheart, the daring adventurer conquering his fears in the face of real danger, the hunter at grips with a wild animal,

the craftsman achieving a masterpiece, whether he be savage or civilized, will under such conditions feel altered, uplifted, endowed with higher forces. And there can be no doubt that from many of these solitary experiences where man feels the forebodings of death, the pangs of anxiety, the exaltation of bliss, there flows a great deal of religious inspiration. Though most ceremonies are carried out in public, *much of religious revelation takes place in solitude.* (57–58, italics added)

As for the presumed connection between the religious idea and collective *effervescent* activities, that, too, seems dubious. There are numerous exciting and effervescent occasions of a collective sort in primitive societies, which are nevertheless lacking in the faintest religious coloring. Malinowski cites the collective work in the gardens of Melanesia, "when men become carried away with emulation and zest for work, singing rhythmic songs, uttering shouts of joy and slogans of competitive challenge, [and which] is full of this 'collective effervescence.' But it is entirely profane, and society which 'reveals itself' in this as in any other public performance assumes no divine grandeur or godlike appearance" (58).

Collective effervescence is also evident in battle, in sailing expeditions, in tribal gatherings for trading purposes, and in numerous other occasions, all of which generate no religious experience. Malinowski's decades of fieldwork therefore suggested that an adequate grasp of religion must take account of the solitary experiences of the individual, and that social effervescence may have no religious meaning at all. Finally, Malinowski asks this telling question: How can society be the prototype of the Divine when so large a portion of what we inherit socially—traditions, knowledge, customs, norms, skills, and so on—is profane, not sacred? Society as the keeper of both the sacred and the profane traditions cannot be the basis of divinity, for it is in the sacred domain only.

So for Malinowski, it is going too far to say, as does Durkheim, that at bottom the concepts of society and divinity are different aspects of the same notion. In thus expanding the role of the group to an extreme, as Durkheim does, he effectively eliminates the role of the individual. As Malinowski rightly insists, "without the analysis of the individual mind, we cannot take one step in the understanding of religion" (69). It is noteworthy that where the role of the individual in religion is concerned, William James agreed that personal religion is

more fundamental than either theology or ecclesiasticism. Churches, when once established, live at secondhand upon tradition; but the *founders* of every church owed their power originally to the fact of their direct personal communion with the divine. Not only the superhuman founders, the Christ, the Buddha, Mahomet, but all the originators of Christian sects have been in this case;—so personal religion should still seem the primordial thing, even to those who continue to esteem it incomplete.[4]

For Durkheim, society and God are one because what people call "God" is actually the symbolic manifestation of the powers of society. Individuals are right, says Durkheim, in believing that there exists a power greater than themselves, for that is the moral power on which they depend and from which they receive all that is best in themselves: "That power exists, and it is society" (226–27). It is one thing to say that our moral education is derived from our participation, growth, and development in society; but it is quite another thing to say that "God" is nothing other than a collective representation of the powers of society. For in the latter assertion Durkheim reduces the divine and the sacred to the social. In these terms, Durkheim's method in the *Elementary Forms* not only is reductionist but also ignores the extraordinary importance of what Max Weber meant by *Verstehensoziologie*—grasping the subjective meanings and motives of human actors and striving to understand them as they understand themselves, others, and the world around them. Durkheim acknowledges at one point that in interpreting totemism as he has, "I am not in a position to state positively that he [the primitive individual] imagines these forces with the relative clarity that I have had to give them in my analysis" (193). And late in his *Elementary Forms*, implying that there is no essential difference between one religion and another, and between religious and national assemblies, Durkheim asks: "What basic difference is there between Christians celebrating the principal dates of Christ's life, Jews celebrating the exodus from Egypt or the promulgation of the Decalogue, and a citizens' meeting commemorating the advent of a new moral charter or some other great event of national life?" (429). The answer, of course, is that there exists a world of difference in the minds of the respective participants.

The result of Durkheim's method is that it ignores the *subjective meaning* that religious beliefs and acts have for the actors concerned. But one cannot grasp the authentic meaning of religious acts without recognizing that they are directed to the divine, not to "society." To grasp religious acts authentically, they must be understood in their own right, and not reduced to the social. If one accepts this methodological principle, one can see clearly that Durkheim's approach was quite antithetical to that of Weber, for whom the meaning and motives of actions were of paramount importance.

NOTES

[1]Émile Durkheim, *The Elementary Forms of Religious Life*, translated with an introduction by Karen E. Fields (New York: Free Press, 1995), p. 44. Hereafter, all page references to this work will be cited in parentheses immediately following the quoted passage.

[2]E. B. Tylor, *Religion in Primitive Culture*, part 2 of *Primitive Culture* (New York: Harper Torchbooks, 1958), pp. 12–13.

[3]Bronislaw Malinowski, *Magic, Science and Religion* (Prospect Heights, Ill.: Waveland Press, 1992), p. 57. Hereafter, all page references to this work will be cited in parentheses immediately following the quoted passage.

[4]William James, *The Varieties of Religious Experience* (New York: Collier Books, 1961), p. 42.

EPILOGUE

The subject matter of this book is *the varieties of religious experience* as analyzed by thoughtful individuals whose analyses have become notable. The italicized words echo the title of William James's classic study of religious experience from a psychological standpoint. And as we have seen, most of the thinkers discussed in this book would have agreed that an adequate grasp of the psychological makeup of the individual is in fact a precondition for an adequate sociological grasp of religion. Let us have a look at what James had to say about that makeup.

For James, the roots of an individual's religious experiences may be traced to the unique human capacity for creating symbols, concepts, and abstractions. That capacity means that abstract concepts often have a greater influence on one's beliefs than sensory experience. We can acquire a sense of reality other than that given by the special senses. James coined the phrase "the reality of the unseen" to describe the unique human ability to posit hypothetical "somethings" that not only exist but are greater than humans. In certain circumstances, humans hold these "somethings" in awe; they love them, fear them, bless them, and hate them, just as if they were concrete beings.

In the various layers of human consciousness, hypothetical beings are experienced as real, objective presences. What we have here is a product of the mind, a feeling of reality lying deeper than both the cognitive faculties and the senses. Such is the nature of human mental processes that they can grasp and create unpicturable beings whose existence is more real to those who hold them than any direct sensory experience. When those beings evoke in an individual a solemn attitude, whether glad or sad, we may say that he or she partakes of what might be called a religious experience.

James documented the diversity and complexity of religious experience. Religion, he recognized, involves joy and fear, gladness and sadness, moods of expansion and contraction. In the "religion of healthy-mindedness," joy and happiness produce in an individual a sort of solemn feeling of gratitude. Most individuals partake at least occasionally of the religion of the healthy-minded type. They see more good than bad in all things and are thankful for it. But there are also individuals with a "radically opposite view, a way of maximizing evil ... based on the persuasion that the evil aspects of our life are of its very essence, and that the world's meaning most comes home to us when we lay them most to heart."[1] In that attitude, says James, it is the religion of the "sick soul" that emerges. Evil is so radical and general that no rearrangement of the environment or of the inner self can eliminate it. What is required is a *supernatural* remedy.

What is it that gives rise to the belief in the supernatural? In all societies and in all epochs, most human beings have valued for themselves, and for their loved ones, life over death, health over sickness, happiness and joy over pain and suffering, freedom over slavery, and the ready availability of life-enhancing goods over want and privation. But life, health, and happiness are so often bound up with their negations. Indeed, the negations are essential facts of existence. "The fact that we *can* die," wrote James, "that we *can* be ill at all, is what perplexes us; the fact that we now for a moment live and are well is irrelevant to that perplexity. We need a life not correlated with death, a health not liable to illness, a kind of good that will not perish, a good in fact that flies beyond the goods of nature" (123).

This, James wisely observed, is the essence of the religious problem: "Help! Help!" (139). The crying need for help is met by the belief in immortality and by the belief in benevolent spirits and deities who can overcome the evils besetting human existence. In their awareness of their limited, corporeal, earthly existence, humans are unique in the animal kingdom. By means of religious beliefs, humans gain a sense of safety and peace. In their religious attitude, humans see the visible world as part of a greater spiritual universe, the real source of life's meaning, and their hope for salvation. And we have seen in the analyses reviewed in this book how central the hope for salvation is in virtually all religions.

The classic theories reviewed in this book are themselves a manifestation of the scientific-rational spirit: an attempt to understand religion by subjecting it to rational analysis. It was the eighteenth-century Enlightenment thinkers who first began to apply rational methods in the study of religion; and it was they who proposed that the application of the scientific-rational spirit to ever more social spheres would result in the gradual decline and ultimate disappearance of religious myths, rites, beliefs, and practices. As a consequence, modern culture was destined to become more and more pragmatic-minded and worldly—in a word, secular.

That a marked degree of secularization has in fact taken place in Western societies, and in others as well, cannot be denied. But there are definite psychological limits to secularization, as William James maintained. For James, some form of religious experience is endemic to the human species because all humans feel on occasion that they are passing through the valley of the shadow and longing to come out in sunlight again. All humans experience an uneasiness, "a sense of something wrong about us," and long to be "saved from the wrongness by making proper connection with the higher powers" (393). There are, after all, forms of "wrongness"—sorrow, pain, and illness—for which social reconstruction and science can provide only a partial remedy; and another wrongness—death—for which they can find no remedy at all. In these terms, James would see definite limits to secular-mindedness. Some form of religious experience will never disappear because the human need for comfort and solace cannot be met by alternative agencies.

If we now turn to the theorist who claimed, in effect, that society and the Divine are one, it seems clear that Durkheim would have agreed with James that the disappearance of religion is quite unlikely. But while James traced the reasons for the perpetuation of religion to the nature of the human individual, Durkheim traced them to the nature of society. There "is something *eternal in religion*," wrote Durkheim,

> which is destined to survive all the particular symbols in which religious thought has successively enveloped itself. There can be no society which does not feel the need of upholding and reaffirming at regular intervals the collective sentiments and . . . ideas which make its unity and personality. Now this moral remaking cannot be achieved except by the means of reunions, assemblies and meetings where the individuals, being closely united to one another, reaffirm in common their common sentiments; hence come ceremonies which do not differ from regular religious ceremonies, either in their object, the results which they produce, or the processes employed to attain these results.[2]

What Durkheim proposes here is that however rational and scientific societies might become, they would never be able to dispense with religious ceremony. For it is in the very nature of society that it reconstitutes and revitalizes itself by "religious" means—rites, assemblies, and doctrines designed to *bind* members together. Traditional religions may decline, but they will inevitably be replaced by new national or civil religions. The experience of the totalitarian regimes of the twentieth century tends to support Durkheim's proposition; for although those regimes were officially and militantly atheistic, they turned their ideologies into religions replete with "sacred" texts, doctrines, rites, massive assemblies, and the deification of leaders in personality cults.

Max Weber, as is known, saw all major spheres of modern Western social life succumbing to formal, technical rationality—to secularization. He recognized, however, that rationality has its limits and that fundamental moral values cannot be derived from science. For Weber, indeed, there exists an unbridgeable gulf between reason and moral values. With respect to the moral conscience, Weber wrote, "Here we reach the frontiers of human reason, and we enter a totally new world, where quite a different part of our mind pronounces judgments about things, and everyone knows that its judgments, though not based on reason, are as certain and clear as any logical conclusion at which reason may arrive."[3] In the same context he wrote that "the idea of the Good and the contemplation of the Beautiful rest on laws which are basic for human nature." Such statements suggest that for Weber the realm of ultimate values possesses a validity that one can never test by scientific-rational means. Human beings derive their sense of life's ultimate meaning and purpose from that realm. Secularization can therefore never entirely eliminate fundamental, religious-moral experiences.

William James, like so many of his predecessors considered in this book, calls attention to the extent to which the religious experience is a cry for help; and a moment of reflection will show just how salient the hope for salvation and redemption is in the major world religions and in the religions of the so-called primitive cultures. The salvation element implies that owing to the manifold vulnerabilities of humans, there is a degree of self-interest in the individual's relation to the Divine. By "self-interest" I mean a primary concern for oneself and for one's loved ones. This is not to deny that some individuals might possess an exquisite love of the Divine. But even the most exquisite such love, as was the case with Job, carries with it a concern for oneself and one's loved ones, and a trust that the Deity will reciprocate for the offerings made to him. We are told in the Book of Job that when Job learned that his sons had invited their sisters to a feast, he "sanctified them and rose up early in the morning, and offered burnt offerings according to the number of them all; for Job said: 'It may be that my sons have sinned, and blasphemed God in their hearts.' Thus did Job continually," (1:5). This suggests that in making his offering, Job expected a reciprocal consideration from the Deity.

Indeed, Henri Hubert and Marcel Mauss, in their study of sacrifice,[4] took for their central theme a Vedic principle that sacrifice is a gift that compels the Deity to make a return: I give so that you may give. It is likely that this earlier work by Hubert and Mauss inspired Mauss's later classic study *The Gift*, in which he documents his thesis of a morally sanctioned gift cycle upholding the cycle of social life. The gift cycle in social life, with its obligatory reciprocity, became the model for the conception of the human being's relation to the Divine. Although Mauss studied this phenomenon in primitive societies, his work suggested that the hope or expectation of reciprocity from the Deity is a more general phenomenon. And we have seen that such hopes and expectations for reciprocity from the Divine are evident in both the world religions and the religions of primitive cultures.

NOTES

[1]William James, *The Varieties of Religious Experience* (New York: Collier Books, 1961), p. 116. Hereafter, all page references to this work will be cited in parentheses immediately following the quoted passage.

[2]Émile Durkheim, *The Elementary Forms of Religious Life*, translated from the French by Joseph Ward Swain (London: George Allen and Unwim 1915), p. 427.

[3]In a letter to Emmy Baumgarten, cited in J. J. Mayer, *Max Weber and German Politics* (London: Faber and Faber, 1956), p. 35.

[4]See Henri Hubert and Marcel Mauss, *Sacrifice: Its Nature and Function*, translated by W. D. Halls, foreword by E. E. Evans-Pritchard (Chicago: University of Chicago Press, 1964).

INDEX